TE KOROWAI O TE RANGIMĀRIE

Edited by Don Moffat with K.D. Taylor

St John's Theological College

Just sitting and being before the altar. A feeling I really miss these days, just being before the Lord clothed in my korowai, sitting in the posture I was taught in Kapa Haka (women sit with legs sideways).

Cover image, courtesy of Koriniti Mckillop (Rongowhakaata, Te Aitanga a Māhaki, Whakatōhea, Ngati Kahu, NgaiTakoto, Ngapuhi)

Published by
St John's Theological College
Auckland, Aotearoa New Zealand
July 2022

Softcover POD ISBN 978-0-473-64337-9

eBook ISBN 978-0-473-64338-6

Kindle ISBN 978-0-473-64339-3

E rere e ngā Karere a Te Karaiti,
Kawea te kupu ki te tini ki te mano.
Ruia i runga i te whakaaro nui,
Ruia i runga i te whakaaro pono.
Waiho ko te aroha o te Atua
Matua, Tama, Wairua Tapu
Hei kākahu kiwi mōu
Āianei, ā, āke tonu atu. **Āmine.**

From HE KARAKIA ATA
A SERVICE FOR MORNING PRAYER

Take wing O messengers of Christ
Carry the Word to the multitudes
Sow it in wisdom
Sow it in truth
And may the Love of God
Creator, Redeemer and Giver of Life
Be the feathered cloak that surrounds you
Now and always. **Amen.**

From HE KARAKIA ATA
A SERVICE FOR MORNING PRAYER

Contents

Contributors vi

Introduction xi

R. Aldred, Bicultural Relationships 1

R. Nicholson, "Walking into the future facing history:" An Introduction to Bicultural Treaty Partnership in a Three Tikanga Anglican Church 27

L. Drake, Episcopal Fragmentation in Te Pouhere 57

D. Moffat, Treaty, Partnership and Covenant Theology 73

D. Tovey, A Commonwealth of Koinōnia: A New Testament Concept with which to Weave Te Korowai o te Rangimārie 91

K. Taylor, Partnership as Validating Voices: Reading Relational Faithfulness in Matthew's Judgment Parables 111

A. Ellithorpe, Friendship, Aotearoa, and the Anglican Church 135

E. Mateiviti-Tulavu, Theologising *Solesolevaki* as a Form of Social Capital for Partnership in a Three Tikanga Church 167

J. Bright, C. Eramiha, Te Puna Atuatanga/ The John Kinder Theological Library, a Journey in Partnership 191

Glossary of Māori Terms 207

References 212

Contributors

Rev Dr Ray Aldred is a husband, father, and grandfather. He was first ordained with the Christian and Missionary Alliance in Canada and is now ordained with the Anglican Church of Canada. He is Cree from Treaty 8. Born in Northern Alberta, he now resides with his wife in Richmond, British Columbia, Canada. Ray is the director of the Indigenous Studies Program at the Vancouver School of Theology whose mission is to partner with the Indigenous Church around theological education.

Judith Bright has been Librarian of the John Kinder Theological Library, Anglican Church in Aotearoa New Zealand and Polynesia: Te Hāhi Mihinare ki Niu Tireni, ki Ngā Moutere o Te Moana Nui a Kiwa since 1976. She has overseen the growth of the Library and Provincial Archives as a national resource for the Church, which welcomes and supports research by and for all Tikanga. She has developed the Church's archival resources into a significant research collection and has worked to ensure that the resources of all Tikanga, wherever held, are safe, identified and accessible.

The Ven Dr Lyndon Drake (Ngāi Tahu) serves as Archdeacon of Tāmaki Makaurau in the Māori Anglican bishopric of Te Tai Tokerau. He is married to Miriam with three children. Until 2010, Lyndon was a Vice President at Barclays Capital, trading government bonds and interest-rate derivatives. Since then, he has served as a pastor in a city centre church in New Zealand, as well as teaching theology and serving in a range of Christian leadership roles. Lyndon has degrees in science and commerce (Auckland), a PhD in computer science (York), two degrees in theology (Oxford), and a number of peer-reviewed academic publications in science and theology. He is working on a Theology DPhil at Oxford on theology and economic capital in the Hebrew Bible/Old Testament. He sits on a number of boards, including as chair of Te Hui Amorangi ki Te Tai Tokerau Trust Board, Te Kaunihera (Governors) of St John's College, the Venn Foundation, and Te Whare Ruruhau o Meri Trust Board. Lyndon has written *Capital Markets for the Common Good: A Christian Perspective* (Oxford: 2017, Oxford Centre for Enterprise, Markets, and Ethics).

Colenso Eramiha is the Kaiwhakamana at the John Kinder Theological Library. His iwi affiliations are Ngapuhi and Ngati Hine.

Dr Anne-Marie Ellithorpe is Research Associate at Vancouver School of Theology. A practical theologian, her research focuses on themes of community and friendship — personal, ecclesial, and civic. Anne-Marie was born in Tāmaki-makau-rau (Auckland). She worked as a teacher and educational consultant in Te Upoko o Te Ika a Maui (the Wellington region) before embarking on theological studies. She has subsequently lived internationally, including on Turtle Island (US and Canada) and in Singapore. Anne-Marie completed a PhD in theology through the University of Queensland in Brisbane, Australia. She is co-chair of the Religious Reflections on Friendship seminar unit of the American Academy of Religion, co-convenor of the Pacific Section of the Society for Christian Ethics, co-editor of *Visions of the End Times: Revelations of Hope and Challenge* (Pickwick Publications, 2022), and author of *Towards Friendship-Shaped Communities: A Practical Theology of Friendship* (Wiley Blackwell, 2022).

Rev'd Dr Eseta Mateiviti-Tulavu taught for 12 years in various religious Secondary Schools around Fiji. She has tutored at the University of the South Pacific through DFL, mentored and tutored students at the University of Auckland. Graduated with MA(Hons) and PhD from the University of Auckland. Her subject of interest is Identity, Leadership, Indigenous theology and Discipleship. She was appointed in 2013 as Tokoni for Tikanga Polynesia and currently lectures at St Johns the Evangelist, Auckland and St Johns the Baptist, Suva, Fiji. Her current area of research is Women and ordination in the Diocese of Polynesia

Dr Don Moffat is the Sir Paul Reeves Lecturer in Biblical Studies at St Johns College. His role encompasses teaching undergraduates and supporting the postgraduate community at St Johns. He is also a regular visiting lecturer for in the University of Otago Theology programme. Don has a background in teaching and management at Laidlaw College and has been a visiting lecturer at several institutions including the University of Auckland. He has a particular interest in the way sociological theory can enhance our understanding of the Bible. He is author of *Ezra's Social Drama* (Bloomsbury, 2013) and editor of *Te Awa Rerenga Maha; Braided River* (Anglican Church of Aotearoa, New Zealand and Polynesia, 2018). His current research interests include a focus on Māori and Pasefika world views as windows that aid the interpretation of the Old Testament.

Rev'd Dr Rangi Nicholson, **Ngāti Raukawa, Ngāti Toa Rangatira, Ngāi Tahu, Ngāti Kahungunu,** is related to chiefs who signed Te Tiriti o Waitangi, the Treaty of Waitangi, in 1840. He is also the great, great, grandson of an English missionary who signed the Treaty. He began studying Aotearoa New Zealand history, including the Treaty, in 1970 at the University of Canterbury. His qualifications include a doctorate in contextual theology, a master's degree in I language revitalisation and two bachelor's degrees majoring in Māori language and linguistics and Māori language and theology. His doctoral thesis is entitled "Ko te mea nui, ko te aroha. The greatest thing is love:" Theological Perspectives on Māori Language and Cultural Regenesis Policy and Practice of the Anglican Church (2009). Syntheses of Anglican Church regenesis policy and practice are viewed through bicultural Treaty of Waitangi partnership and contemporary Māori theological lenses. He has taught Aotearoa New Zealand history at several institutions including the University of Canterbury, Massey University and St John's Theological College. In addition, he was a past Tikanga Māori representative of the Anglican General Synod's Tiriti/Treaty, Church and Nation Commission and the Commission on Treaty and Partnership Issues. A paper entitled "Treaty of Waitangi, Anglican Church and Aotearoa New Zealand: Creating Space for Hope" was delivered at the 2021 International Symposium of NAIITS (the North American Institute of Indigenous Theological Studies). Finally, he wishes to acknowledge his late wife, Ellen, for her incessant support with his studies, research and teaching.

Karen Taylor is a doctoral candidate in practical theology with St Johns Nottingham and the University of Chester. She practiced law in South Auckland for a few years before shifting to corporate training. With Methodist roots and now in Tikanga Pākehā she has served in lay leadership roles in protestant and pentecostal churches over the past few decades.

Rev'd Dr Derek Tovey was a lecturer in New Testament at the College of St. John the Evangelist, and honorary lecturer at the University of Auckland, from 1995–2015. Prior to that, he did his doctoral studies on the Gospel of John at the University of Durham, in the United Kingdom. He is an ordained Anglican priest, having trained at St. John's College in the late 1970s, and served in parish ministry for ten years in the Diocese of Christchurch. He is married to Lea and, now in retirement, they live in Glen Eden, Auckland. Publications include three books, five chapters in edited books, several journal article (refereed and non-refereed), and several dozen book reviews.

Introduction

The church in Aotearoa New Zealand, and in a number of other countries, is faced with a significant task as it works out how to act justly on a post-colonial era. In our context, the British Empire and its colonising activity is gone, but the structures and attitudes of colonisation remain deeply embedded. Aotearoa New Zealand is in the unique position of having a treaty agreed by representatives of the British crown and a substantial portion of the indigenous Māori leadership in 1840. That document, Te Tiriti o Waitangi/ the Treaty of Waitangi now plays a significant role in the decolonising process.

The Anglican Church of Aotearoa, New Zealand and Polynesia has made Te Tiriti o Waitangi and bicultural partnership key foundations of its constitution. The papers in this book are the outcome of a conference held in 2019 on the theological foundations of bicultural partnership focusing particularly on the Anglican church of this province. It continued a process of theological reflection on this Anglican Church that commenced in 2017 with a conference titled "Three Tikanga Church: Reflecting Theologically." The papers from that conference were published in D. Moffat, ed. *Te Awa Rerenga Maha: Braided River*, Auckland: Anglican Church of Aotearoa, New Zealand and Polynesia, 2018.

The title of this book *Te Korowai o te Rangimārie* repeats the title of the 2019 conference which translates as The Cloak of Peace. The title reflects a practice where the placing of a cloak on a condemned person signalled mercy. The sub-title of the conference was "cultivating bonds of affection through theologies for partnership and bicultural development." It is hoped that these papers will indeed encourage bonds of affection. They contain rich reflections that draw on theology, history and biblical studies to point the Church to a fuller expression of partnership that is based on the reconciling work of God, accomplished by Jesus Christ, and guided and empowered by the Spirit.

Introduction

The opening chapter in this volume is by Ray Aldred and is titled, "Bicultural Relations." Under that simple title Aldred explores the complex challenge that is bicultural relations in a context that has a colonial past and a multi-cultural present. Drawing on his Canadian context he identifies and explores three issues that need to be addressed for true partnership between Indigenous peoples, governance structures and the layers of migrants. Those issues are: adopting an Indigenous understanding of Treaty, repentance as a path to establishing a true treaty relationship and articulating a truly indigenous theology. Aldred's approach lays a foundation for the following papers. The second paper, "Walking into the Future Facing History" by Rangi Nicholson is a complement to Ray Aldred's paper. It also lays ground work that supports the papers that follow. Nicholson helpfully reviews the public debates about treaty and partnership in New Zealand. He briefly discusses biculturalism and multiculturalism and then focuses on the partnership principle as established by the Crown. Nicholson then discusses the issues he has raised in the context of the Anglican Church and its three Tikanga structure.

Lyndon Drake's "Episcopal Fragmentation in Te Pouhere" questions the current episcopal structure in the Anglican Church of Aotearoa, New Zealand and Polynesia in the light of historical practice. He argues that the current overlapping episcopal boundaries create practical problems and ignore the theological reasons for having a single Bishop in each geographical area. Drake reviews the history of episcopacy, argues for a deeper theological reflection on the current structure and suggests an alternative structure based on Canada's episcopal arrangements.

The next two chapters are biblically focused. Don Moffat's "Treaty, Partnership and Covenant Theology" addresses the claim that Te Tiriti o Waitangi is a covenant. He describes the way the treaty was explained to Māori that equated it with Old Testament covenants. Then he examines current covenant theology and notes its implications for responding to treaty matters in ways that value partnership. Derek Tovey draws on the New Testament idea of koinonia in his chapter titled, "A Commonwealth of Koinōnia: A New

Testament Concept with which to Weave Te Korowai of Te Rangimārie." Tovey explores the breadth of partnerships expressed by koinonia and its cognates in the New Testament. He draws out the richness of the ideas of partnership and communion it expresses and points to where these ideas can guide partnership in the Church.

The next three chapters all focus on applied theology approaches. Karen Taylor's "Partnership as Validating Voices: Reading Relational Faithfulness in Matthew's Judgment Parables" uses pastoral theology to read the parables in a relational way. Taylor draws on Matthew's judgment parables as the basis for structured conversation she calls WisdomCafe. She does so on the basis that issues of relationality and accountability are fundamental to the parables. She argues WisdomCafe style conversations are a practical way of building relationships across Tikanga. Anne-Marie Ellithorpe's "Friendship, Aotearoa and the Anglican Church" applies a practical theology of friendship to the Anglican three Tikanga church. Anne-Marie argues that ideas of friendship and partnership can co-exist. Also, that friendship is not limited to personal relationships but is also important in civic relationships. She points to the example of a befriending God at the heart of the biblical message as inspiration for a practice that embraces "friendship, mutuality, right-relatedness and reconciliation."[1] Chapter 8 is Eseta Mateiviti-Tulavu's "Theologising *Solesolevaki* as a form of Social Capital for Partnership in a Three Tikanga Church." Mateiviti-Tulavu draws on her Fijian culture and its communal mindset in presenting *solesolevaki* as a pattern for the three Tikanga church. She argues that *solesolevaki*, while focused on achieving things together in a spirit of partnership, when applied to the church can also contribute to building relationships and to the process of decolonisation.

The final chapter is a case study of enacting partnership within the Anglican church. "Te Puna Atuatanga/The John Kinder Theological Library, a Journey of Partnership" was presented by

---

[1] Annie-Marie Ellithorpe, "Friendship, Aotearoa and the Anglican Church", 171.

Introduction

Judith Bright with a contribution from Colenso Eramiha. The chapter traces the development of the library with a particular focus on the efforts since 2004 to move to a model that is more inclusive of Māori and Pasefika values.

One paper that is not in this volume is Moeawa Callaghan's "Biculturalism and Democratic Decision-Making" which will appear in *Thresholds of Theology in Aotearoa New Zealand*. Eds. Jione Havea, Emily Colgan and Nasili Vaka'uta. Lexington Books, forthcoming. We commend that paper to those interested in these issues.

This book is the product of the efforts of a dedicated team of people. I want to thank first of all the contributors to *Te Korowai* conference and the authors of the papers that comprise this volume. A special thanks to Rev Dr Ray Aldred who came as our international voice and provided very good foundation for the conference. That first paper is also an appropriate introduction to the topics covered in this volume. Particular thanks to Karen Tayor who, alongside her doctoral studies, did a great deal of the copy editing for this volume. In addition, she also took on part of my workload, including following up editing matters with contributors. This work along with her eye for detail and style has been a significant contribution to the production of this volume. I am also thankful to Rev'd Dr Paul Reynolds, director of Te Piri Poho Research Network here at St Johns College, who took over the management of the last stages of publication while I was on research leave. His organisation and pastoral approach kept the project on track. Richard Cook proposed the publication process and I am thankful for his production assistance.

I also want to acknowledge the support of the past Manukura/Principal of St Johns College Rev'd Canon Tony Gerritsen and his successor Rev'd Katene Eruera who both actively supported the *Te Korowai* conference and the publication of these papers. Thanks also to members of the college's governing board, Te Kaunihera. In particular thanks is due to, Te Kaunihera's chairperson Ven. Dr Lyndon Drake and to Rev'd Dr Rangi Nicholson who also contributed papers. Rangi originally suggested the theme and has been a constant background supporter of the conferences.

Theological reflection on the nature of the Anglican Church in Aotearoa, New Zealand and Polynesia needs to continue in the Church. There is much yet that can be improved for all. It is the hope of all the contributors that these papers will fuel words and actions that lead to reconciliation and justice.

Don Moffat
St Johns College, June 2022

1

Bicultural Relationships

REV DR RAY ALDRED

BICULTURAL RELATIONS

Introduction[2]

THE CHALLENGE OF bicultural relations is not new to most of you. In Canada, of course, we do have multi-culturalism, although, for the Quebecois and the Anglophones, theirs is more of two great solitudes.[3] For the First Nations of Canada (specifically the treaty First Nations) the relationship of our treaties is Nations to Nation. With regard to these relationships or identities, there seems to be a greater willingness (at least recently) to try and hold these different identities in tension. My input into this conference is really a summary of the same challenge that is faced by the people who call Canada home. This might have some insight for the task you face in New Zealand.

For Indigenous treaty people in Canada, our ancestors made treaty with the newcomers. In making treaty they were attempting to hold the identity of the other in tension with their own in the hope that the treaty would be a space for collaboration. They did not, and current elders in our communities do not give me permission to break treaty during difficulties but put forward reconciliation as the way ahead. This reconciliation involves turning back to the treaty in order to find the basis for proper relatedness. It is about sharing the land or territory and living out the harmony of a good creation.

To live in a land that holds different peoples together I want to highlight three things. First, there is a need to find a shared narrative in order to keep moving ahead, this is the historic treaty process

---

[2] This paper is a compilation of excerpts from two published papers used with permission and my thesis. These represent three areas I have spent the last few years engaging in theological reflection about how Indigenous people seek to hold together their different Indigenous nations and the Nation State of Canada.

[3] Two Solitudes, referring to Anglophone and Fracophone people and their lack of communiction, was popularized in Canada by Hugh MacLennan's novel, *Two Solitudes* (Montreal: McGill-Queens University Press, 2018).

understood as covenant.[4] Second, there is a need for a reinterpretation of repentance so that we can continue to turn toward life in our effort to deal with the trauma of colonial and neo-colonial relationships. Finally, there is a theological exigency to see how these challenges are taken up in the person of Jesus Christ who is the teleological goal for our identity as human beings and present with us in the sacraments.

COMMUNAL IDENTITY REQUIRES A SHARED STORY

Reclaiming a group identity or proper relatedness in our modern era is the challenge for bicultural or nation to nation relationships. Since Descartes and the Enlightenment, the autonomous individual has held sway. The thinking individual soul as a basis for identity seemed to usher in a firmer foundation for identity. However, modernity has lapsed into scepticism and Western theologies have produced alienation rather than intimacy and solidarity. In my doctoral thesis I suggested that this approach to identity has not been productive in the First Nations in Canada, of which, the Cree are part.[5] They hold the group and individual agency in balance so that theirs is a communal identity. They concept of communal identity is not limited to people, however, but includes the land, or creation. A familial relationship with land means that the identity of the people on the land are inseparable. To maintain this relationship, with the coming of European people to turtle island, or Canada, the Indigenous people sought a group to group identity.

To understand the relationship of Indigenous people in Canada, to the land, would require an entire paper in itself. This paper will limit its remarks to how narrative works to maintain the

---

[4] Excerpts for this idea in this essay are taken from a previous essay. See Ray Aldred, "A Shared Narrative," in *Strangers in This World*, eds., Allen G. Jorgenson, Hussam S. Timani, and Alexander Y. Hwang (Minneapolis: Fortress Press, 2015).

[5] The Cree, although having a decentralized approach to societal makeup, place the relationships or relatedness as primary. See Richard J. Preston, *Cree Narrative: Expressing the Personal Meanings of Events*, 2nd ed., Carleton Library Series, (Montreal: McGill-Queen's Univ. Press, 2002), 78.

group identity to the *aski* or land. Land takes in the entire creation but is not a generic creation but the land of the Indigenous group. Cree narrative memory maintains the relationship to land.[6] The land is in all our stories and is our soul or spirit.[7] As Cree Anglican Priest Andrew Wesley points out, at the heart of Indigenous life or spirituality is understanding our creation story,[8] the story that connects us to the land. The land teaches us her stories and our language, and we honor the land and creator by living in harmony with all creatures who inhabit the land. The land holds us together and to understand the connection one must understand their creation story.

The category of group to group within Canada is symbolized in the historic treaties of Canada. They continue to provide the basis for our relationship with the newcomers. Treaty affirms four values.[9] First, it affirms the privilege of a peaceful existence. The idea of treaty was used to make relatives of one's former enemies.[10] It was a way to take in the "other" which assumed a change in identity for the First Nations. Indigenous identity is not static but seeks to maintain harmony in all relationships. Group to group being a category for Cree language and understanding. Cree language is always trying to account for the life of the land that flows all around us.

As well as affirming the privilege of a peaceful existence for all, there is also affirmation of access to the land. For the First Nations this was meant to preserve the familial relationship with land. The

---

[6] Neal McLeod, *Cree Narrative Memory: From Treaties to Contemporary Times* (Saskatoon, Sask.: Purich Pub., 2007).
[7] Doug Cuthand, *Askiwina: A Cree World* (Regina: Coteau Books, 2007), 1.
[8] Andrew Wesley, "Traditional Aboriginal Spirituality" (paper presented at the Consultation on First Nations Theological Education, Thornloe University, Sudbury, Ontario, May 21 2009).
[9] Chief Stan Beardy, personal conversation with author, circa April 24, 2015.
[10] Black Elk and Joseph Epes Brown, *The Gift of the Sacred Pipe: Based on Black Elk's Account of the Seven Rites of the Oglala Sioux* (Norman: University of Oklahoma Press, 1982), 70-83.

First Nations desired to live on the land. This in turn led to another privilege. It is our privilege to live by being fed by the bounty of mother earth. Some groups, such as the Mohawk, say we eat from one bowl with one spoon. This is the nature of creation. When negotiating the numbered treaties in Canada, the crown's representative stated that God had made creation for all human beings and Indigenous people did not debate this reality.[11] The final aspect of treaty was to create space for people to be who creator made them to be. This was a way to hold the "other" without vilifying them. This is captured in the two row Wampum treaty of the Iroquois and the Dutch. Represented by a beaded belt of white beads with two rows of purple. The purple beads run parallel the length of belt representing the newcomers and Iroquois each in their own canoe but in one river.[12]

These treaty relationships pre-dated the coming of the Europeans to Canada.[13] For example, the presence of the five nations[14] referred to as the Iroquois is an example of how Indigenous people of Canada were already thinking of political alliances between different groups of people. As one Mohawk stated:

> We Six Nations of Indians feel we have potentially a superior social system to that of the United States. If only we were left alone, we could redevelop our society

---

[11] J. R. Miller, "Compact, Contract, Covenant: The Evolution of Indian Treaty-Making," in *New Histories for Old: Changing Perspectives on Canada's Native Pasts*, eds., Theodore Binnema and Susan Neylan (Vancouver, B.C.: UBC Press, 2007), 84.
[12] "Treaties Recorded on Wampum Belts," 2000, accessed May 21, 2008, 2008, http://www.degiyagoh.net/treaties.htm#treaty_belts.
[13] The discussion of treaty from pages 3 through 8 is reproduced from my doctroal thesis. See Raymond Clifford Aldred, "An Alternative Starting Place for an Indigenous Theology" (ThD University of Toronto, 2020), 93-102.
[14] Later known as the Six Nations because the Tuscarora were welcomed during colonial expansion.

... which was old in democracy when Europe knew only monarchs.[15]

Treaties were part of the First Nations' way of relating around military associations and diplomacy.[16] Treaty was a way of forming agreements between family clans and also between large tribal confederacies. The treaty was the way to forge relationships for trade while also maintaining the distinctiveness of particular peoples. This way of relating to other people flows out of a First Nations understanding of how the Creator was in relationship with people. Thus, treaties had spiritual implications.[17]

This Indigenous understanding of treaty formed the basis for the relationships between Indigenous people, particularly First Nations and Inuit, and the newly emerging British-then-Canadian governments. The Canadian government, however, did not always share this understanding of treaty, and in the minds of First Nations people ideas and practices around treaty-making were continuing to develop. What treaty means to Indigenous people, according to James R. Miller, has evolved in its meaning and use, but treaties have always represented a desire for a harmonious relationship, and that goes beyond mere co-existence. Treaty is an attempt to cultivate a shared identity. A quick historical overview of the process would help to explain the nature and importance of treaty for Indigenous people in Canada and Indigenous communal identity.

HISTORICAL DEVELOPMENT OF TREATY

The treaty process evolved from friendship pacts (as in the Treaty for Peace and Friendship, 1752) to land-related compacts or simple contracts to a form of covenant.[18] Treaty-making would become more complex as contact between the Indigenous people and

---

[15] Sierra Adare, *Mohawk* (New York, N.Y.: Gareth Stevens, 2003), 21.
[16] Miller, "Indian Treaty-Making," 66–68.
[17] R. Laliberte et al., *Expressions in Canadian Native Studies* (Saskatoon, Saskatchewan: University of Saskatchewan Extension Press, 2013), 232–264.
[18] Miller, "Indian Treaty-Making," 66.

Europeans lengthened. Two significant and early alliances or treaties were the "Two Row Wampum" and the "Great Peace of Montreal." The Dutch and the Iroquois entered the "Two Row Wampum" treaty in the seventeenth century. When the British took control of the territory in 1664, the Iroquois assumed that the British had inherited the treaty, which was a partnership between sovereign nations of people, respecting one another's differences and promising not to interfere with one another. In 1701 the "Great Peace of Montreal" secured peace between the French, and their allies, and the Iroquois. Both are examples of peace and friendship treaties.[19]

As the fur trade was losing its economic significance, a growing desire by Europeans to own land had the potential to lead to violence and unscrupulous land dealings. As a result, the Crown issued the Royal Proclamation in 1763 forbidding private citizens from buying or taking land from Indigenous people. Land could be surrendered only through negotiations with the Crown. The Royal Proclamation was made not because the Crown recognized Indigenous land title, but because it recognized Indigenous people as in need of protection. The government of the dominion of Canada, however, did not see treaty as a way to ensure the survival of First Nations; rather, treaty was a way for them to extinguish Indigenous title to land in order to make it available for settlers and agricultural development.[20] Concurrently, Indigenous people began to see the need for treaty for the survival of their people and a way of life connected with land.

First Nations people understood the Royal Proclamation as a treaty. Protocol by the First Nations would assign treaty status to the Royal Proclamation itself, when

> in 1764 William Johnson, Britain's superintendent of the northern Indians, called together some two thousand *First* Nations representatives from districts

---

[19] Miller, "Indian Treaty-Making," 74
[20] Arthur J. Ray, *The Canadian Fur Trade in the Industrial Age* (Toronto: University of Toronto Press, 1990), 30.

from Nova Scotia to the Mississippi, explained the contents of the Proclamation, and procured their agreement to them.[21]

Although it might not have been in William Johnson's mind that he was setting the stage for treaty development, the Royal Proclamation "became a treaty protected by Section 35 of Canada's 1982 Constitution Act."[22]

After the Royal Proclamation, treaties became associated primarily with land transfer. At first, these were simple, and it is at this time they were closest to simple contracts. However, a more thoroughgoing change occurred in 1818, when the government, wanting to save money by not paying lump sums for the surrender of land, decided to pay annuities to First Nations people for the use of land.[23] In the minds of First Nations people, these yearly annuities were a return to the earlier friendship and peace agreements; thus, simple land-exchange was made more complex. The land was at the forefront of the concerns of the Canadian government: land for its new settlers and citizens. Relationship was still important for the First Nations, and as the settlers moved west, relationships not only with the newcomers but also with the land necessitated even more treaties.[24] It was at this time that the numbered treaties of Western Canada came to be considered covenants by the First Nations people.

According to Miller, the "numbered treaties concluded in the West between 1871 and 1877 introduced a third category of treaty: the covenant."[25] The government of Canada did not see it this way, and would argue right through the twentieth century that the treaties were only contracts between two human parties; by contrast, the Western First Nations considered the treaties as three-way

---

[21] Miller, "Indian Treaty-Making," 74.
[22] Miller, "Indian Treaty-Making," 78.
[23] Miller, "Indian Treaty-Making," 80-81.
[24] Miller, "Indian Treaty-Making," 80.
[25] Miller, "Indian Treaty-Making," 83.

agreements between the First Nations, the Crown, and Deity, who "participates and provides oversight." [26] Thus, for First Nations, treaty was not like a contract but like a covenant that binds the parties together and makes the partnership or relationship more important than the terms of any contract. Again, relationship is what was important for First Nations, and these treaties meant that the Crown had entered a family relationship with the First Nations.

Again, the protocol and ceremony surrounding the treaty were evidence that the treaty was a covenant—at least for the First Nations. The other participants in treaty-making gave every indication that the treaty was a covenant kind of relationship. For example, the treaty commissioners took part in the pipe ceremony along with the First Nations people and the Creator or Great Spirit, and in so doing bound the participants in "a sacred relationship.[27] The presence of priests and missionaries as interpreters, who insisted that the negotiations adhere to keeping the Lord's Day, also left the impression with the First Nations that the newcomers believed that the same sacred meaning was attached to the treaty.

Finally, the commissioners themselves used the Great Spirit or Creator in their arguments as to why the First Nations should allow settlers on the land. They pointed out that the Creator was the real owner of the land. Thus, it can be expected that the First Nations believed they were entering a sacred long-term relationship with the newcomers to this country.[28] In his use of the term "covenant," Alexander Morris described the treaty as something that would last forever.[29] Not only were the settlers now co-inhabitants, but the

---

[26] Miller, "Indian Treaty-Making," 83
[27] Morris writes, for example, that he accepted the pipe from the Cree: Alexander Morris, *The Treaties of Canada with the Indians of Manitoba and the North-West Territories: Including the Negotiations on Which They Were Based, and Other Information Relating Thereto* (Toronto: Belfords, Clarke, 1880; repr., 2014); Miller, "Indian Treaty-Making," 84.
[28] Miller, "Indian Treaty-Making," 84.
[29] Morris, *The Treaties of Canada*.

Queen, *kihci-miyikowisyahk* (which can be rendered "an older woman who is rich in relatives"), and all her subjects were understood to be part of the First Nations family through the covenant of treaty.[30]

If the historic treaty process is seen as a covenant, again, it provides a way toward a shared narrative. Treaty was Canada's creation story. Canada, however, did not want to embrace the treaty as a covenant between First Nations, themselves, and the creator. Instead, they chose to see it as a contract, something that they wanted to do away with. As a result, they attempted to annihilate Indigenous relationship with land, extended family, and spirituality. As a result, there is a need to talk about the role of repentance in reconciliation and partnership. There is no way to move forward without working through the pain of the past.

REPENTANCE: EMBRACING OUR INDIGENOUS IDENTITY: RETURNING TO THE COVENANT

In another paper, I explored the idea of an Indigenous reinterpretation of repentance as taking responsibility to begin to work toward the repair and healing of Indigenous relationships.[31] Group to group relationships could not be healed or reconciled without working through the difficulties. Relationships that were in need of healing included relationship with the Creator; relationship with others, both individual to individual but also group to group; relationship to land or creation; and the relationship with self.

An Indigenous reinterpretation of repentance is necessary because Canada was guilty of cultural genocide against Indigenous people. Conversion and repentance were defined as repenting from being Indigenous and converting to being European. I was seeking to give theological support for the idea that Christian theology could

---

[30] McLeod, *Cree Narrative Memory*, 47.
[31] Ray Aldred, "An Indigenous Reinterpretation of Repentance," in *Race and Racism: North Park Symposium on Theological Interpretation of Scipture, 2015*, ed. Klyne Snodgrass (Eugene, Oregon Pickwick Publications, an imprint of Wipf and Stock Publishers, 2016).

conceive of repentance as taking responsibility for the abuse committed against Indigenous people by the Church and Canadian society. While at the same time, wanting to see if repentance was still a useful concept in working through the latter violence that was in our Indigenous communities.

Repentance seen as turning to embracing Indigenous identity also includes taking responsibility for healing the wounds of abuse that have separated family members and communities. It is a healing from colonialism, but colonial multi-generational trauma is more complicated than just removing colonial or neo-colonial policy.

> If colonialism brought our nations to this point, then undoing colonialism must be the answer...[but] It is not just colonial relations that must be undone but all of the consequences (addictions, loss of language, loss of parenting skills, loss of self-respect, abuse and violence and so on). Colonialism is no longer linear, vertical relationships - colonizer does to colonized - it is horizontal and entangled relationships (like a spider web).[32]

Repentance must involve trying to work through the wounding by revisiting the "dark stories," which can serve as sources for healing.[33] It is reimagining the individual story by embracing the good things from our past history but also remembering the difficulties. The act of embracing one's story by continuing to share one's story recasts pain and difficulty as a source of hope by showing that Indigenous identity remains despite facing traumatic events. Telling and listening to our stories ensures we do not forget our relatives who have passed on. It also ensures that we are not

---

[32] Patricia A. Monture, *Journeying Forward: Dreaming First Nations' Independence* (Halifax, N.S.: Fernwood, 1999), 11.
[33] Ila Bussidor and Üstün Bilgen-Reinart, *Night Spirits: The Story of the Relocation of the Sayisi Dene*, Manitoba Studies in Native History, (Winnipeg: University of Manitoba Press, 1997), xix.

romanticizing about some lost ideal trying to engage in a kind of "primitivism" as a form of escapism to some pre-modern period.[34] Rather, it is trying to embrace identity, as it exists, by trying to build upon roots of strength that are within Indigenous culture. This is accomplished by retelling difficult stories in a way that advances healing.[35] The importance of story for healing will also figure into repentance for newcomers.

It is not only relationships between individuals that need to be healed but there is also a responsibility to attempt to return to or heal the treaty relationships between Indigenous people and the newcomers. This idea is part of what it means to be Indigenous or connected with land. Right relationship requires a location, it must be grounded upon the earth.[36] As covenant, Treaty has a spiritual and locative dimension. Particularly as the practice of treaty making in Canada developed. As mentioned above J.L. Miller points out that treaties developed in Canada from friendship compacts eventually to covenants between newcomers, aboriginal people, and the creator.[37] The newcomers, including Church officials engaged in the Indigenous ceremonies that made us like relatives or family.[38] Thus, in the healing of relationships, treaty relationships must be healed but the treaty also serves as a source of healing. As a shared narrative it legitimates or creates shared space. The treaty will hold the individuals and groups those individuals represent together because as covenant the relationship is more important than the exact particulars.[39]

---

[34] Robert J. Schreiter, *The New Catholicity: Theology between the Global and the Local*, Faith and Cultures Series, (Maryknoll, N.Y.: Orbis Books, 1997), 25.
[35] Sophie McCall, *First Person Plural: Aboriginal Storytelling and the Ethics of Collaborative Authorship* (University of British Columbia Press, 2012), 120.
[36] Monture, *Journeying Forward*, 36, 60.
[37] Miller, "Indian Treaty-Making," 84.
[38] Jennifer S.H. Brown, "Rupert's Land, Nituskeenan, Our Land," in *New Histories for Old.*, 34-35.
[39] Miller, "Indian Treaty-Making," 83.

Of course, the healing of all relationships is premised on returning to an Indigenous identity that affirms the goodness of the created world. The starting point for Indigenous Spirituality is the appreciation of a beautiful world. Doug Cuthand writes:

> Our people believe that the earth and all the creatures that live on it are a gift from the Creator. This beautiful land of lakes, forests, rivers, plains, and mountains is a gift from the Almighty and it must be respected and treated properly.[40]

Indigenous Spirituality shows this appreciation for a beautiful world is thanksgiving. The circle of harmony as lived is seen in the Indigenous teaching; if you receive something, you give something back; in this way we live in harmony with all things.[41] Repentance is seeking to live in right relationships or in balance with creator and creation. This is the vision and ideal that Indigenous Spirituality is seeking. However, it will take time to heal. Ila Busidor, who saw her community relocated in the 1950s by the Canadian government, reminds us "healing doesn't happen just once. We have to be healed again and again."[42] In seeking the healing of significant relationships with creation, family, clan, community and all others, Indigenous people return or reinvigorate their relationship with *kise-manitow* (Creator).

A reinterpreted understanding of repentance as a turning to embrace an identity given by the Creator is therefore in keeping with traditional understandings of what it means to be Indigenous. Interestingly the basic meaning of repentance as a contrite sorrow for sin and a turning to a new way of living has not needed to be altered. However, the context has meant repentance has been

---

[40] Cuthand, *Askiwina*, 1.
[41] Clara Sue Kidwell, Homer Noley, and George E. Tinker, *A Native American Theology* (Maryknoll, N.Y.: Orbis Books, 2001), 33.
[42] Bussidor and Bilgen-Reinart, *Night Spirits: The Story of the Relocation of the Sayisi Dene*, 132.

reconfigured as hope through taking responsibility. Therefore, it is possible to conceive of Christian repentance and salvation as being a large enough concept to conceive of turning to Christ as being a return or embracing of a Creator given Indigenous identity. Thus, it is possible to conceive of conversion or salvation in Christ as fulfillment instead of being a replacement for Indigenous spirituality.[43]

REPENTANCE FOR CANADA

What does repentance look like for a Canada that has violated the treaty relationship and is complicit in the abuse of Indigenous people? Would repentance as turning to embrace a God given identity as a human being be sufficient to begin to work through the difficulties from a non-Indigenous side of the relationship? The answer of course is positive, particularly if the treaty relationship is seen as shared narrative. The historic treaty relationship is a large enough concept to include a narrative of troubled relationships but also coming back together or of healing. Some of the principles from restorative justice will be put to use in this description.[44] Restorative justice is an attempt to heal the damage. In this process the affected parties must tell the truth; they must listen; they must come up with a shared plan to repair the damage. All of these come together as an attempt at reconciliation between Indigenous peoples and the Newcomers. It presupposes that Indigenous and Newcomers will both through repentance embrace their identity as created human beings.

---

[43] In proposing fulfilment I am not precluding the relationship between Indigenous spirituality and Christianity could be complementary. Fulfilment might be viewed by some as placing Indigenous spirituality in a lower or lesser role. It is beyond the scope of this paper to address this question but it worth noting. George Lindbeck offers a brief taxonomy of possible interfaith relationships. See George A. Lindbeck, *The Nature of Doctrine: Religion and Theology in a Post-Liberal Age* (Philadelphia: Westminster Press, 1984), 52-53.

[44] Pierre Allard, "Restorative Justice: Lost Treasure," (Regina, Saskatchewan: Canadian Theological Seminary, March, 11, 1999), Lecture.

By embracing the treaty as a shared Narrative, Canada is embracing, as Doug Cuthand points out, their creation story and spirituality or being. They are in relationship to the land through their relationship with the Indigenous people. Repentance as turning to a new way of life for newcomers could mean a return for all to the treaty relationship where they are also treaty people. As treaty people Canadians themselves are healed from being strangers in the land. The idea of treaty is the idea of making relations. Through the treaty newcomers and Indigenous people were to live like family. This secures a place for the First Nations, and it secures a place for Newcomers. The following quote from the office of the treaty commissioner in Saskatchewan emphasizes this point.

> Treaties are beneficial to all people in Saskatchewan. They are considered mutually beneficial arrangements that guarantee a co-existence between the treaty parties. Newcomers and their descendants benefit from the wealth generated from the land and the foundational rights provided in the treaties. They built their society in this new land where some were looking for political and religious freedoms. Today, there are misconceptions that only First Nations peoples are part of the treaties, but in reality, both parties are part of treaty. All people in Saskatchewan are treaty people.[45]

Repentance for Canada could mean to turn and own the mistakes of the past and embrace identity as a human being under covenant that for those in Canada includes the treaty.

Indigenous identity is large enough to include newcomers. By entering into the shared narrative of the Treaties as equals, the possibility exists for a shared identity that does not necessitate the eradication of identity. Instead, it is an opportunity to embrace the

---

[45] Office of the Treaty Commissioner, *Treaty Essential Learnings: We Are All Treaty People* (Saskatoon, Saskatchewan, 2008), https://www.horizonsd.ca/Services/SafeandCaring/Documents/TELS.pdf.

past and be open to a future of walking together in the Creator's land in a good way. Treaty functioning as a shared narrative allows for a re-envisioning of history and becomes a tool for healing. By emphasizing the concept of responsibility, it allows for a more thorough repentance for all parties, the abused and abuser. Repentance as responsibility makes room for the positive aspects of the influence of Christian faith in an Indigenous context interpreted as fulfillment without overwhelming Indigenous identity. Repentance as responsibility equally captures the idea of repentance as a gift to human beings as well as an action of human beings. Repentance is not merely contrition but is also a hope for a new way forward. We must take responsibility for what happened and work towards a new future. As one survivor of the residential schools, Archie Little expressed in 2012,

> [For] me reconciliation is righting a wrong. And how do we do that? All these people in this room, a lot of non-Aboriginals, a lot of Aboriginals that probably didn't go to residential school; we need to work together.... My mother had a high standing in our cultural ways. We lost that. It was taken away.... And I think it's time for you non-Aboriginals ... to go to your politicians and tell them that we have to take responsibility for what happened. We have to work together.[46]

CHRIST REALLY PRESENT IN THE LAND[47]

I am turning to Christology in part because the head of the council of elders for the Nisga'a told me that his elders had long sought for and desired teaching about Indigenous Christology, how Christ fits within traditional Nisga'a law. By showing how Christ

---

[46] Truth and Reconciliation Commission of Canada., Honouring the Truth, Reconciling for the Future Summary of the Final Report of the Truth and Reconciliation Commission of Canada. 9.

[47] This section of the paper is reproduced with permission from an earlier paper I wrote called "The Land is Sacred" soon to be published by the NAIITS journal.

could fit within the treaty relationship, an Indigenous Christology could provide a way forward for the Church in shared space. Christ is present within the sacraments of baptism and communion and is affirming in ways that affirm and fit within an Indigenous treaty spirituality. The sacraments themselves are real symbols that contain the mystery of Christ, who is fully human and fully divine. As such, the sacraments reveal a Christ recognized by Indigenous people, holding together all things visible and invisible: creator and creation.

The Indigenous treaty spirituality was able to hold together Christian faith and Indigenous identity. In the negotiations of treaty 6, Alexander Morris recorded both Indigenous and Christian Ceremony. Morris records that the Indigenous people approached the negotiations singing traditional songs and performed the "pipe stem" dance. There was the exchange of the pipe, but the Indigenous people also asked for a minister to lead them in a Christian service.[48] The Indigenous leaders assumed that Great Spirit looked down upon both newcomers and Indigenous as one. Part of the treaty 6 negotiations included some First Nations asking for missionaries and teachers.[49] The treaty spirituality was attempting to hold faith and identity together so that they could move forward in a friendly harmonious way.

Communal Indigenous identity expressed in a treaty spirituality affirms land and provides an Indigenizing influence upon Christian faith. Land based spirituality can be found within the Christian tradition. Irenaeus points this out. When thinking about the gospel, in an answer to why there were only four gospels, Irenaeus points out that there were four winds and four directions, so there were four gospels.[50] For Irenaeus, creation has shaped the word of God. The invisible word of God had become visible in the Incarnation,

---

[48] Morris, *The Treaties of Canada*, 183.
[49] Morris, The Treaties of Canada, 194.
[50] R. M. Grant, *Irenaeus of Lyons, against the Heresies*, The Early Church Fathers, (New York, N.Y.: Routledge, 1997), 3.11.18.

and this has affirmed the value of creation. Christ taking a human body through a second act of creation then takes in all creation or land. As the back translation of John 3:16 in the Cree bible makes plain: "God so loved the land (*aski*) he gave his son." Creation was the context for salvation, not some ethereal existence on some invisible plain in the mind or in some other dimension or worlds, rather creation was the place and means where salvation is revealed and enacted, where the invisible God become visible via creation.[51]

Salvation occurring within the context of creation rules out the idea that the gospel was merely a metaphor for some metaphysical transaction or some inward feeling of dependence upon a transcendent being. At the same time Irenaeus does not preclude spirituality that includes the invisible. Christ has come in the flesh. The particularity of the incarnation of Jesus Christ being embraced by a people who understood the gospel as having been present in their own culture, before the coming of the Europeans. Father Schmemann points out that for the Eastern Church, creation itself has been the place where communion with God has taken place, it is therefore sacramental.[52] Indigenous treaty spirituality agreed and was specific that this incarnation had impact, not in creation in general, but had occurred here, in their territory. Indigenous people then were able to express Christian faith while remaining completely traditional in their understanding.

This spirituality arising out of the land based on family is able to find expression through a theology of real presence in creation and the sacraments. With an understanding of sacraments as bringing together the spiritual and material world as seen in the Incarnation. Again, the simple observation that the Incarnation shows the value of creation. As noted above, the Cree understanding of land and of salvation affirms what Athanasius also puts forward, that the love of

---

[51] R. M. Grant, *Irenaeus.*, 4.6.6.
[52] Alexander Schmeman, *For the Life of the World: Sacraments and Orthodoxy*, 2nd ed. (Crestwood, N.Y.: St. Vladimir's Seminary Press, 1973), 14.

God, expressed in bringing forth creation, will also move to heal or save creation through the sending of the son.[53] This is in concord with the recorded remarks of plains Cree Chief, Little Hunter, that healing the land would be the result of people coming together under the eyes of the one Great Spirit.[54] The incarnation was seen in this light, that the coming together of the visible and spiritual affirms creation and affirms Indigenous people within the land.

Moving now to think about the sacraments from an Indigenous perspective of having a Spirituality flowing from the land. According to Luther, sacraments were a coming together of the material and the spiritual. The word added to the water, transforms the water to become Christ's baptism. This echoes a reading I have heard from Bishop Mark MacDonald but echoes also a place based or locative reading of Christ's baptism. For Luther, the water with the Word is what makes the sacrament of baptism.[55] It is a coming together of the Word, who is Christ, and the water; the word added to the water. For an Indigenous locative reading of the Jesus' baptismal accounts take Mark's gospel, for example, Jesus Christ baptizes the water, and it becomes Christ-baptism: Jesus, who is the word, is added to the water.[56] A coming together of both the material or creation and the divine or creator.

One of the Indigenous Masters' students at the Vancouver School of Theology observed that the baptismal account of Jesus in Mark 1 could be read like a birth narrative.[57] Jesus comes out of the water, there is the presence of the Spirit or a breath, and the voice of a proud parent affirming that this is the beloved son. It would be

---

[53] Athanasius, *On the Incarnation of the Word*, trans. unknown, Christian Classics Ethereal Library, (Grand Rapids, MI: Calvin College, c296-373), 1.3,4. https://ccel.org/ccel/athanasius/incarnation/incarnation?queryID=10351578&resultID=2038.
[54] Morris, *The Treaties of Canada*, 191.
[55] Luther's Larger Catechism, XIII part four of baptism.
[56] Mark 1:9-11.
[57] Lauren Sanders, Spring, 2019.

possible then to read our baptism as our re-creation story. Rather than setting us free from the material world to pursue some life free from the limitation of creation now or in the future, our baptism, as our re-creation, grounds us in community. It is a picture of our present and our future, and for people in the midst of trauma, a source of hope. Thoroughly human and moving toward becoming who we were created to be, humans in proper relationship with all including the land and the creator. As such our baptism, read as part of our creation or recreation story, affirms our desire to live in good relationship with all. It is a place of unity and of diversity for it does not set aside our own creation stories but fulfills or enhances our own narrative memory as we see Christ baptizing our stories and our Indigenous land in Spirit and in Truth.

Christ present within the waters of baptism and the baptismal covenant has become the basis for living an Indigenous Christian faith within the Indigenous Anglican Church. *A Disciples' Prayer Book*, states:

> In Jesus we know we belong to a Sacred Circle, with the Gospel and Baptismal Covenant in the Center.
> In this Sacred Circle:
> We are all related;
> We live a compassionate and generous life;
> We respect all life, traditions, and resources;
> We commit ourselves to spiritual growth, discipleship and consensus.[58]

This prayer was written as a description for how Indigenous Identity and Spirituality came to be understood by the Indigenous Church as well as prescriptive of how we should continue to live upon the land. This expression of faith was made possible by Indigenous treaty spirituality, learned from the creator through creation, and made it possible to hold Indigenous communal identity and Christian

---

[58] *A Disciple's Prayer Book* (CanadaReprint from 1992), VI, https://www.anglican.ca/wp-content/uploads/A-Disciples-Prayer-Book.pdf.

faith together. And this desire to honour the creator and the land makes it possible for Indigenous treaty spirituality to be affirmed by and affirm the ongoing real presence of Jesus in the gospel expressed by the sacrament of baptism. A presence that presses the Indigenous church and potentially also the non-Indigenous Christian Church to continue to move toward the goal of treaty relationship and the common good by living as relatives within the land.

Turning now to Holy Communion, Irenaeus points out that the bread, which comes forth from the earth, "announces consistently the fellowship and union of the flesh and Spirit."[59] He goes on to say that in the Eucharist there is a coming together of two realities, earthly and heavenly. It is also proclaiming our future, one that begins now with the promise of harmony between creator and creation as is seen in Incarnation of Jesus Christ; fully human, and fully divine. In the Eucharist we take in the broken bread, which is the broken body of Christ, and we are taken into the body of Christ: we in turn are broken and given for the world. Not to escape the suffering of the world, but rather, that the suffering is taken into Christ as we are now on the way to resurrection.

In the real presence of the Christ in the Eucharist, Indigenous people witnessed the incarnation occurring once again. 'Real presence' goes beyond saying that Jesus is somehow present, 'real presence' affirms that in this sacred ceremony, something material becomes a place the creator does something powerful to take in the whole world, bringing together creation and creator. As stated above by Irenaeus creation reveals Christ as saviour. Jesus comes into our midst in a unique and powerful way. It is a communal meal affirming of family and of the land. This is turn gives strength for the journey as we become the broken body of Christ, on our way to the resurrection.[60] It is possible then to see our own trauma as people

---

[59] Grant, *Irenaeus*, 4.18.15.
[60] Henri J. M. Nouwen, *Life of the Beloved: Spiritual Living in a Secular World* (New York, N.Y.: Crossroad, 1992).

shifted and remembered in a different way.[61] Not that what we experienced was justified or acceptable, but despite this we have hope, for we are now moving toward life and healing.

INENIMOWIN

We developed a teaching called *Inenimowin*. It is a word from Oji-Cree and refers to feelings. We developed small group training to help people lead others through the wounds of the past to find strength in our brokenness. We based the whole program on the Eucharist as talked about by Henri Nouwen. As the Eucharist is taken, blest, broken and given, we are taken and blessed – to help Indigenous people see they are the beloved. We are broken – to remember the trauma in a different way – to see that as we embrace our brokenness we find Christ present with us - and healing us. We are given for the world, despite our brokenness, no - because of our brokenness taken in by Christ, our suffering and healing become part of Christ's salvific work. We then are part of the healing work of Christ given for the world.

The Eucharist offers hope by displaying the two natures of Christ and our past and future harmony, where our own land and people can find healing. It is possible to hold up Holy Communion to affirm the treaty ceremony or story. Treaty is a place where the challenges of sharing territory are overcome by the treaty entered into by Indigenous people, newcomers and creator. It was marked by Indigenous and Christian ceremony.

Both Sacraments, being representative of an Indigenous Christology, affirming or running parallel to Indigenous treaty spirituality, also have the possibility of affirming the connection to the earth. Both sacraments point to a past and future of a harmonious relationship between creator and creation that are seen in the two natures within the person of Jesus Christ. This relationship calls us to something higher than merely enduring this life. Our lives are poured

---

out for our relatives, understanding that our suffering is for our relatives. This is closer to the idea envisioned by Vine Deloria, with the Christian West finally learning that being in covenant with the God of all creation would lead to harmonious relationship lived out in community.[62] Not to divide, as some Christians are intent on doing, but to work toward the healing of relationships.

I need to make clear that I do not think that the language of the Church is translatable, completely to the secular world. I understand that the preaching to the world does not look the same as the preaching within the Church.[63] I understand that the Sacraments are part of the grammar of the Christian Church and as such will continue to strike many outside the Church as arcane ceremonies of an institution that is now in decline. I am saying, however, that within the Indigenous communal treaty spirituality, it is possible to see a people who take in the gospel, expressed in the sacraments, as affirming of their relationship with land and others and work toward the healing of relationship with Canada. It fits within their Christian faith and within their Indigenous identity. As my former student, Nisga'a Hubert Barton has put it, "they (Christian faith and Indigenous identity) run parallel within my heart." Christian faith and Nisga'a Identity are not abstract ideas used as thought experiments, they represent who we are. This pushes us, I believe, out of the category of religious phenomenology to talk about our shared ontology or reality upon the earth.

Conclusion

Summing up my thoughts on the matter. In Canada, we need a new shared story that acknowledges the land and the Indigenous people, and the possibility of newcomers being taken into an Indigenous identity. The treaty as covenant offers a place that this

---

[62] Vine Deloria and James Treat, *For This Land: Writings on Religion in America* (New York, N.Y.: Routledge, 1999), 72-73.
[63] Paul Ricoeur is one author who makes this distinction. See Paul Ricœur, *Political and Social Essays* (Athens: Ohio University Press, 1975), 135-148.

kind of collaboration could occur. It takes in land, newcomers, and Indigenous people, and the creator. It is a place of possibility where aspects of repentance could impact not just the Church but also the larger secular society. Indigenous people do this by not succumbing to seeing secular – spiritual opposition. They are all taken in by the treaty as covenant.

In order to turn back to the treaty, repentance is necessary. It is necessary for us Indigenous people since the colonial and neo-colonial thought and practice continue to induce lateral violence, in addition to systemic racism.[64] Taking responsibility by embracing a God-given Indigenous self-determining identity is key to the good of all of the land.

At the same time, repentance by non-Indigenous is understood as taking responsibility for the past. This means embracing failure as part of identity to move forward in humility and embrace treaty as their creation story provides resources to hold these together under the creator, who joins us.

> Jesus Christ is present with us in our Creation stories.
> Reaffirmed in the sacraments.
> Christ's Baptism as our recreation story, as Creator and creation come together.

---

[64] Editor's note, "In a Canadian context lateral violence is believed to exist within many Indigenous communities worldwide with the common causal explanation as oppression, colonisation, racism and intergenerational trauma... According to the Native Counselling Services of Alberta (NCSA) (2008) lateral violence is described as the way powerless people covertly and overtly direct their dissatisfaction inward, toward each other, toward themselves and toward those less powerful than themselves" Yvonne Clark, "What's in a Name? Lateral Violence within the Aboriginal Community in Adelaide, South Australia," *The Australian Community Psychologist* 27, no. 2 (2015), https://doi.org/Network (Australian Psychological Society. College of Community Psychologists) 1320-7741.
https://www.psychology.org.au/for-members/publications/journals/Australian-Community-Psychologist/ACP-Issues.

Affirming the land in the water and in the person of
Jesus Christ come in the flesh.
Water as the first medicine taking us all in.

The Gospel Based Discipleship is then a practical outflowing of how our baptismal covenant is read alongside our treaty showing the possibility of holding Indigenous (human) identity alongside of Christian faith. This is done through gathering around the gospel proclaimed and shaping our people.

The Eucharist, us taking in the real food of Jesus Christ's body and blood – taken, blessed, broken and given. So, our past trauma and our future home are proclaimed as we are taken, blessed, broken and given. So that we can see through practical programs that our brokenness does not amount to our complete failure but finds a place on the way to the resurrection.

This is the gospel of Jesus Christ, and this is the place where life flows out of us despite our brokenness. A place on the land where creator and creation come together in perfect harmony. A place that affirms the treaty or covenant between peoples as good and sacred. As we hold one another, honouring and respecting the distance between us as the place for collaboration and the way forward.

"Walking into the future facing history:" An Introduction to Bicultural Treaty Partnership in a Three Tikanga Anglican Church

REV 'D DR RANGI NICHOLSON

He korōria ki te Atua i runga rawa,
He maunga-ā-rongo ki runga i te mata o te whenua,
He whakaaro pai ki ngā tāngata katoa.

Glory to God on high,
Peace on earth,
Goodwill to all people.

Introduction[1]

BICULTURAL TREATY PARTNERSHIP between Māori and the Crown is highly varied, highly contextual and highly contested in Aotearoa New Zealand. Partnership in the Three Tikanga Anglican Church is the same. At the signing of the Treaty of Waitangi in 1840 tribal chiefs clearly were prepared to share their political and economic power with the British Crown. Without the involvement of reputable Pākehā Anglican and other Church missionaries, who translated, promoted and signed Te Tiriti o Waitangi, as well as the support of Māori chiefs sympathetic to the missionaries, it would have been unlikely that the covenant would have gained any real traction among Māori. While the names Treaty of Waitangi and Te Tiriti o Waitangi are used interchangeably in this paper, it is acknowledged that Te Tiriti o Waitangi (Te Tiriti), the Māori language version of the Treaty, was signed by most Māori chiefs. Within 30 years of the signing, the balance of power had shifted to the rapidly increased number of Pākehā immigrants who advanced the development of a Pākehā settler state and the cause of colonisation. Colonial governments, the judiciary and other key stakeholders, such as the Anglican Church, consigned the Treaty relationship, obligations and responsibilities to the position of historic artefact. Since the mid-1970s the Crown and the Anglican Church have belatedly recognised that injustices have occurred as a result of such a position. Pākehā Anglicans largely oppressed Māori Anglicans for over 130 years from the time of the first Anglican Church Constitution in 1857 until the new Constitution in 1992.

---

[1] This paper was based upon my doctoral thesis entitled "Ko te mea nui, ko te aroha: Theological Perspectives on Māori Language and Cultural Regenesis Policy and Practice of the Anglican Church." Due to limited space, it has not been possible to include a more detailed coverage of referenced writings on bicultural Treaty partnership nor the background to the development of a new constitution for Aotearoa New Zealand. Please refer to chapter 6 of my doctoral thesis for more detail on these including the three constitutional conferences held in 2000: the Building the Constitution Conference, Treaty Conference, and Nation Building and Māori Development Conference.

Tikanga Pākehā bishop, John Bluck, maintains that Māori felt "dishonoured, disenfranchised and ignored for over a century."[2] Some Tikanga Māori Anglicans would assert that such oppression continues today due to an unwillingness on the part of Tikanga Pākehā to share resources justly and equitably. Bluck comments that Tikanga Pākehā continues to be challenged by "the disparity between resources and in particular numbers of stipended clergy across the Tikanga."[3]

For the purposes of this paper, the term *Pākehā* broadly refers to all New Zealanders of British or European descent especially in the nineteenth century and most of the twentieth century. I also acknowledge that the term *Pākehā* is problematic for some New Zealand Anglicans, including more recent migrants, who are not British or European.[4] However, I am unable to explore this debate due to constraints of time and space.[5] Tikanga Māori, Tikanga Pākehā and Tikanga Pasefika, on the other hand, are the names describing the ecclesial arrangements for Anglicanism in its Māori, Pākehā and Pasefika expressions under the 1992 Te Pouhere/Constitution of the Anglican Church in Aotearoa, New Zealand and Polynesia.[6] Given the three major cultural groupings within the Three Tikanga Anglican Church, I underscore the diverse cultural backgrounds of the various commentators by mentioning their ethnic identities. To support the view that most of the public debates are occurring between cultural

---

[2] J. Bluck, "Stunned Mullets, Untested Vehicles and Other Things Anglican," in *Te Awa Rerenga Maha: Braided River*, ed. D. Moffat, Three Tikanga Church Colloquium (Auckland: Anglican Church in Aotearoa, New Zealand and Polynesia, 2018), 5.
[3] Bluck, "Stunned Mullets," 7.
[4] A. Fletcher, "Finding Identity in the Body of Christ," in *Te Awa Rerenga Maha: Braided River*, ed. D. Moffat, Three Tikanga Church Colloquium (Auckland: Anglican Church in Aotearoa, New Zealand and Polynesia, 2018), 198-199.
[5] Further discussions see, J. Bluck et al., *Te Awa Rerenga Maha: Braided River*, ed. D. Moffat, Three Tikanga Church Colloquium, (Auckland: Anglican Church in Aotearoa, New Zealand and Polynesia, 2018, 2018).
[6] https://www.anglican.org.nz/About/Constitution-te-Pouhere

elites, I also mention their occupations. In addition, I have tried to identify those commentators who are known to me to be Anglican.

In 2040 Aotearoa New Zealand, including the Three Tikanga Anglican Church, will commemorate 200 years since the first signing of Te Tiriti. The Church will come under considerable scrutiny at this time regarding its record concerning the Treaty. Will the Three Tikanga Church be well placed to witness the Gospel imperatives of love, justice and peace to the nation as set out in the fivefold international Anglican Consultative Council mission statement?[7] Is the Church well placed to review its own Constitution? Just as the Church contributed towards the Treaty, a biblically conceived covenant and constitutionally foundational document, is the Church well placed to contribute to a new written constitution for Aotearoa New Zealand?

Alongside the Crown, it was the Anglican Church, in its search for justice, peace and reconciliation in the mid-1980s, that assisted the recovery of the concept of partnership which was one of the main Treaty principles supported by the Crown. In this paper I initially venture beyond the church doors into the public square to examine the political, economic and constitutional debates on Treaty partnership. One of the fundamental debates is whether the Treaty ought to be central to the policy and practice of the Crown in Aotearoa New Zealand. Major debates around partnership largely focus on the levels of transparency, authenticity, equality and equity required to meet Treaty obligations and responsibilities, and whether transformation ought to be incrementally pragmatic or radically innovative. Yet another debate is centred on the possible future shape of Treaty partnership and biculturalism including the place of multiculturalism. As a result of these debates, heightened tensions and a straining of relationships between Māori and the

---

[7] See Appendix 1, end of this chapter.

Crown have occurred. The same has occurred in the Anglican Church between Tikanga Māori and the other two Tikanga.

The Three Tikanga Anglican Church has given a central position to the Treaty in its 1992 Te Pouhere/Constitution and some of its subsequent policymaking and practice. Given the Church's Gospel responsibilities and Treaty obligations, it is pertinent to examine contemporary debates on bicultural Treaty partnership. The public square, where these debates are taking place, is the Church's major mission field. The mission and ministry work of the Church is contextual. The Three Tikanga Church cannot ignore contemporary bicultural Treaty debates in Aotearoa New Zealand in the development of its public theologies and policies.

Due to the constraints of this brief paper, I have initially focussed on the major debates on partnership regarding the centrality of the Treaty and partnership transparency in some detail because it raises fundamental issues such as the importance of the Treaty, who exactly are the partners and what are their legal roles and responsibilities. I have then also included from my doctoral thesis a synthesis of partnership debates centred on authenticity, equality and equity as well as incremental or radical transformation in the mission field of Aotearoa New Zealand.[8] In addition, I briefly review a synthesis of the major debates around biculturalism and multiculturalism. Finally, I acknowledge that the focus of this paper is on the Crown principle of partnership. Participation and protection are also important Crown principles which, although not covered in this paper, have a critical contribution to make in terms of justice, peace and reconciliation.

---

[8] R. Nicholson, "'Ko Te Mea Nui, Ko Te Aroha': Theological Perspectives on Māori Language and Cultural Regenesis Policy and Practice of the Anglican Church." (PhD. University of Auckland, 2009).

CENTRALITY OF THE TREATY

In 1984 the Bi-cultural Commission of the Anglican Church on the Treaty of Waitangi circulated a discussion paper regarding the Treaty of Waitangi among members of the Anglican Church in Aotearoa New Zealand. In the Commission's discussion paper, there is a brief section about the principle of partnership which was intended to stimulate reflection and submissions. The Commission tentatively advocated that partnership is an on-going process whereby the government legislates in the interests of the majority while, on the other hand, acknowledging the significant place of Māori as a result of the Treaty. While Article 1 cedes governorship or kāwanatanga, Article 3, in exchange, guarantees protection and the rights and privileges of being a British subject. It is Article 2 which confirms the position of Māori in terms of full chieftainship or tino rangatiratanga regarding lands, villages and possessions.[9] A diverse range of perspectives exist concerning the meaning of tino rangatiratanga. In brief, the Commission believed that the Treaty recognised and established the principle of partnership despite a level of tension in the varying roles of both partners. The initial perspectives on this principle were well received by the majority of those who made submissions and were subsequently confirmed in the Commission's Report in 1986. Furthermore, partnership was defined as involving "co-operation and interdependence between distinct cultural or ethnic groups within one nation" in "a spirit of mutual respect and responsibility." [10] The Anglican Church incorporated these principles into its new Constitution.[11] Clearly the Commission, as well as the majority of the Church's General Synod

---

[9] Bi-cultural Commission, *Te RīPoata a Te KōMihana Mo Te Kaupapa Tikanga Rua Mo Te Tiriti O Waitangi = the Report of the Bi-Cultural Commission of the Anglican Church on the Treaty of Waitangi* (Christchurch, N.Z. : Provincial Secretary of the Church of the Province of New Zealand, 1986).
[10] Bi-cultural Commission, *Bicultural Commission*, 25.
[11] General Synod/te Hinota Whanui, "Constitution/Te Pouhere, Canons and Statutes," (NZ: Anglican Church in Aotearoa, New Zealand and Polynesia, 1990), 6, 10. https://www.anglican.org.nz/Resources/Canons.

which adopted the Constitution, regarded the Treaty as central to the mission and ministry of the Church. All Three Tikanga agreed to the centrality of the Treaty.

Just as there was a good deal of discussion and debate surrounding the centrality of the Treaty and the principle of partnership in Anglican Church forums, the same has occurred in the Waitangi Tribunal, the courts, Parliament and the wider community. I begin by drawing upon the work of Janine Hayward, a Pākehā academic, concerning the Waitangi Tribunal. The Treaty of Waitangi Act 1975 established the Waitangi Tribunal and a decade later its jurisdiction was extended to include claims "... by any Māori or group of Māori prejudicially affected, or likely to be prejudicially affected, by any ordinance, regulation, policy, practice, or action (done or omitted) by or on behalf of the Crown since 6 February 1840 which is *inconsistent with the principles of the Treaty.*"[12] It has, of course, been the Crown who has largely defined what these principles are.

Over more than 40 years the Waitangi Tribunal has focussed on the Treaty in its deliberations on claims. As a result, several principles have emerged including the principle of partnership. Alongside the Tribunal's reports successive governments have passed legislation such as the Environment Act 1986 and the Resource Management Act 1991, where weight is expected to be given to these Treaty principles by government departments and agencies. While the Tribunal initially explored the Treaty text and possible principles in its early claims, it was the State-owned Enterprises (SOE) Act 1986 which acted as a catalyst for major advances in thinking concerning these principles.[13] In this Act the government included a section which declared that "Nothing in this

---

[12] Janine Hayward, "'Flowing from the Treaty's Words': The Principles of the Treaty of Waitangi," in *The Waitangi Tribunal: Te Roopu Whakamana I Te Tiriti O Waitangi* eds., Janine Hayward and Nicola Wheen (Wellington, N.Z.: Bridget Williams Books, 2004), 29.
[13] Hayward, "Flowing from the Treaty's Words," 31.

Act shall permit the Crown to act in a manner that is inconsistent with the principles of the Treaty of Waitangi."[14]

The Court of Appeal in 1987, in a case known as the *New Zealand Māori Council v Attorney-General*, declared in its judgement that the Treaty confirmed the notion of partnership between Pākehā and Māori requiring each to act towards the other reasonably and with the utmost good faith. The relationship between the Treaty partners creates responsibilities analogous to fiduciary duties. The duty of the Crown is not merely passive but extends to active protection of Māori people in their use of their lands and waters to the fullest extent practicable.[15]

The Waitangi Tribunal drew upon these judgements in its own findings in claims such as the Allocation of Radio Frequencies Report in 1990, and the Ngāi Tahu Report in 1991. In the Electoral Option Report in 1994 the Crown's role was defined to the extent that it is reasonable considering the context. The fiduciary nature of its responsibilities was made more explicit in the Te Maunga Railways Land Report in 1994:

> A fiduciary relationship is founded on trust and confidence in another, when one side is in a position of power or domination or influence over the other... Because the Crown is in the powerful position as the government in this partnership, the Crown has a fiduciary obligation to protect Māori interests.[16]

The partnership principle also figured in later claims. Te Whānau o Waipareira Report in 1998 declared that the role of partnership is to assist the Crown to discern the level of Māori self-determination in the management of Māori issues and, more

---

[14] Hayward, "Flowing from the Treaty's Words," 32.
[15] Hayward, "Flowing from the Treaty's Words," 32.
[16] Hayward, "Flowing from the Treaty's Words," 36.

specifically, the nature of its relationship with Māori in the pursuit of resolutions to such issues.[17]

In the 1990s the Tribunal made an important connection between partnership and consultation by the Crown. Indeed, in the Radio Spectrum Management and Development Final Report in 1999 it was the Tribunal's view that the Crown was obliged to consult Māori "as fully as practicable."[18] The Tribunal also acknowledged where the Crown had met its obligations to consult such as in the Kiwifruit Marketing Report in 1995. It is the Tribunal which has recommended to the government the degree to which importance should be attached to the Treaty. Successive governments, with their own political agendas regarding the centrality of the Treaty, have made their decisions about the nature of partnership.

Nevertheless, Hayward believes that the principle of partnership is now "well entrenched and widely accepted." [19] Anglican Māori and professor, Sir Mason Durie, also asserts that the Treaty applies to all Crown developments whether they are "economic, environmental, cultural and social."[20] Durie observes that "At the heart of the Treaty is the promise of a mutually beneficial relationship between Māori and the Crown – a partnership."[21] Such a stance can also be applied to constitutional development.

TRANSPARENT PARTNERSHIP

Some Pākehā and Māori believe that the notion of Treaty partnership is far from being transparent. A lack of clarity exists about who are the partners. The nature of their relationship or their responsibilities is also not easily understood. Nonetheless, an

---

[17] Hayward, "Flowing from the Treaty's Words," 34.
[18] Hayward, "Flowing from the Treaty's Words," 38.
[19] Hayward, "Flowing from the Treaty's Words," 40.
[20] Mason Durie, *Ngā Kāhui Pou Launching Māori Futures* (Huia Publishers, 2003), 262.
[21] Durie, *Ngā Kāhui Pou*, 265.

attempt has been made to elucidate partnership within a constitutional framework.

An initial issue that needs clarification is whether the partnership is clearly between Māori and the Crown or between Māori and non-Māori. The identity of the Crown prompts the question of whether this entity is the government and the courts. Pākehā academic, David Pearson, raises the conundrum of who should be the non-Māori partner: Pākehā or all other New Zealanders including Pākehā. As the population in Aotearoa-New Zealand becomes more diverse, he sees the dangers of racial division.[22] The late Hugh Kawharu, Anglican Māori professor, acknowledged that while the Treaty was signed between Māori and the Crown as a relational covenant, the reality has been that such a covenant has been between Māori and non-Māori in Aotearoa New Zealand.[23] In this paper I acknowledge that the partnership is between Māori and the Crown, in other words, between Māori and the government and the courts. I agree with Kawharu, however, that in practice, the Treaty has emerged as a relationship between Māori and non-Māori.

Anglican Māori and judge, Sir Edward Taihakurei Durie argues that, legally, partnership has not been defined in terms of relationship but rather in the way both Māori and the Crown should relate to each other.[24] In other words, Durie claims that partnership has not been legally defined. It is then not surprising that various

---

[22] D. Pearson, "Rethinking Citizenship in Aotearoa/New Zealand," in *Tangata Tangata: The Changing Ethnic Contours of New Zealand*, eds., Paul Spoonley, David G. Pearson and Cluny Macpherson (Melbourne: Thomson Dunmore Press, 2004), 311.
[23] Hugh Kawharu, "Foreword," in *Waitangi Revisited: Perspectives on the Treaty of Waitangi*, eds., Michael Belgrave, Merata Kawharu, David Vernon Williams (Melbourne: Oxford University Press, 2005), v.
[24] E. Durie, "The Treaty in the Constitution," in *Building the Constitution*, ed. Colin James (Wellington, N.Z.: Institute of Policy Studies, Victoria University of Wellington, 2000), 203.

commentators have expressed concern about this lack of transparency.

One of the earliest Pākehā to express an opinion on the Treaty of Waitangi and partnership was the playwright and publisher Bruce Mason. In 1993 he wrote a paper entitled *The Principle of 'Partnership' and the Treaty of Waitangi: Implications for the public conservation estate*. In this paper he refers to the *partnership myth*: "...Treaty partnership is ill-defined, confused, and misleading - dangerously so in regard to the Crown's obligations to all citizens and the potential for detriment to the majority of New Zealanders."[25] For Mason, the notion of partnership is less than transparent.

Pākehā businessperson and former senior civil servant Roderick Deane contends that partnership "...as a concept appears to be a judicial invention and a complicated and ambiguous one at that."[26] He acknowledges that such a partnership can be complex and not transparent. It can mean different things to different people. Pākehā academic Christopher Tremewan also maintains that a partnership between peoples is a romantic concept when, in his view, it actually takes place between elites.[27]

Pākehā Treaty of Waitangi educators, Robert and Joanna Consedine, talk of government hypocrisy and two-faced actions as examples of a lack of transparency. It is the Crown, in the form of past governments, that has preached partnership and concepts of good

---

[25] Bruce Mason, "The Principle of 'Partnership' and the Treaty of Waitangi: Implications for the Public Conservation Estate," *Dunedin, NZ: Public Access New Zealand, Monograph Series*, no. 6 (1993).
http://www.publicaccessnewzealand.org/files/partnership_abstract.html.
[26] R. Deane, "Globalisation and Constitutional Development," in *Building the Constitution*, ed. Colin James (Wellington, N.Z.: Institute of Policy Studies, Victoria University of Wellington, 2000), 115.
[27] C. Tremewan, "Re-Politicising Race: The Anglican Church in New Zealand," in *Public Policy and Ethnicity: The Politics of Ethnic Boundary Making* (Palgrave Macmillan, 2006), 96.

faith and trusteeship.[28] Yet it is the Crown which has introduced economic policies that have severely disadvantaged the Māori partner. They contend that in the mid-1980s economic reforms impacted on Māori to the extent that about a quarter of them lost their jobs while the top ten per cent, overwhelmingly wealthy Pākehā, were greatly rewarded. A two-fold increase in poverty among children between 1991 and 2004 took place.[29] Given this level of poverty, especially for Māori, the Pākehā political and media criticism of Māori education, health and social welfare funding would appear to be less than justified.

Two commentators refer to partnership as an illusion. Pākehā legal academic Alex Frame argues that to "dangle some illusion that this can be one race, one vote is not only dangerous, but it is in a sense a cruel deception."[30] Evan Poata-Smith, Māori academic, also refers to the illusion of a partnership.[31]

Oppressive colonialism still exists in Aotearoa New Zealand albeit in a more covert form. Some Māori have discerned partnership to be a mask for such colonialism.[32] Māori legal academic Ani Mikaere believes that behind the language of partnership the colonial oppressor continues to devalue Māori customary law or tikanga Māori.[33] Jane Kelsey asserts that it is hypocritical for the government

---

[28] Robert Consedine and Joanna Consedine, *Healing Our History: The Challenge of the Treaty of Waitangi* (Auckland, NZ: Penguin, 2012, 2005), 246.
[29] Consedine and Consedine, *Healing Our History: The Challenge of the Treaty of Waitangi*, 247.
[30] D. Slack, *Bullshit, Backlash & Bleeding Hearts: A Confused Person's Guide to the Great Race Row* (Auckland: Penguin, 2004), 161.
[31] E. S. Poata-Smith, "Ka Tika a Muri, Ka Tika a Mua? Maori Protest Politics and the Treaty of Waitangi Settlement Process," in *Tangata Tangata: The Changing Ethnic Contours of New Zealand*, eds., Paul Spoonley, David G. Pearson and Cluny Macpherson (Melbourne: Thomson Dunmore Press, 2004), 74.
[32] Roger Maaka and Augie Fleras, *The Politics of Indigeneity: Challenging the State in Canada and Aotearoa New Zealand* (Otago University Press, 2005), 299.
[33] Ani Mikaere, "The Treaty of Waitangi and Recognition of Tikanga Maori," in *Waitangi Revisited: Perspectives on the Treaty of Waitangi*, eds., Michael Belgrave,

to claim that "te Tiriti o Waitangi confers no binding rights on Māori, while claiming that private property rights are sacrosanct and negotiating international treaties that require the government to protect the rights of foreign investors and incorporations..."[34]

A major problem for Anglican Māori academic Merata Kawharu is that there has also been insufficient guidance or advice concerning the roles and responsibilities of the partners and as a result the outcomes have been quite uneven.[35] A major impediment to successful partnership for some Māori has been the lack of Māori and Crown clarity concerning the Treaty generally, including a poor understanding of rangatiratanga in particular.[36] Such deficiencies have the potential to accentuate Māori social and economic difficulties.[37] (Please note that sometimes commentators refer to tino rangatiratanga as rangatiratanga which can be translated as self-determination).

Pākehā and Māori have attempted to clarify the nature of partnership. Tremewan asserts that in reality a partnership allows "for re-contestation of 19th century political settlements in the context of 21st century social dynamics."[38] Frame maintains that partnership is an outcome of cooperation, and that cooperation is a better word than partnership. In his opinion cooperation is a more flexible and pragmatic approach.[39] Furthermore, power sharing will

---

Merata Kawharu, David Vernon Williams (Melbourne: Oxford University Press, 2005), 330.
[34] Jane Kelsey, "Maori, Te Tiriti, and Globalisation: The Invisible Hand of the Colonial State," in *Waitangi Revisited: Perspectives on the Treaty of Waitangi*, eds., Michael Belgrave, Merata Kawharu, David Vernon Williams (Melbourne: Oxford University Press, 2005), 1.
[35] Merata Kawharu, "Rangatiratanga and Social Policy," in *Waitangi Revisited: Perspectives on the Treaty of Waitangi*, eds., Michael Belgrave, Merata Kawharu, David Vernon Williams (Melbourne: Oxford University Press, 2005), 114.
[36] Kawharu, "Rangatiratanga," 105.
[37] Kawharu, "Rangatiratanga," 108.
[38] Tremewan, "Re-Politicising Race: The Anglican Church in New Zealand," 96.
[39] Slack, *Bullshit, Backlash*, 97-98.

depend on the context. As an example, in the area of Māori language, the role of Māori will be substantial. However, it has been asserted that issues such as nuclear policy and immigration would be decided along democratic lines.[40]

Pākehā professor of politics Andrew Sharp argues that partnership can be classified under three forms of constitutionalism. The first he terms *legal constitutionalism*. Here, it is mostly Pākehā politicians and lawyers who claim that the law defines the nature of Treaty rights and that the partnership between Māori and the Crown is determined by the government.[41] *Māori constitutionalism*, however, is centred on the Treaty – "a biblically conceived 'covenant.'"[42] Sharp notes that "Māori constitutionalism insists that the Treaty is a record of an agreement between Māori and Crown that set out the basic terms of New Zealand's constitution."[43] It acknowledges that, in the Māori language version of the Treaty, Māori did not cede sovereignty and that the tino rangatiratanga described in Article 2 means control over not only material possessions but also culture, language and customs.[44] The Treaty is still regarded as binding for each partner today. The third form of constitutionalism is called *whakapapa constitutionalism*. Here iwi, hapū and whānau claim that they have the right to self-government which is based on whakapapa and not on legal or Treaty constitutionalism.[45] Sharp summarises mainstream thinking on the constitution as following two paths, namely, the incorporation of tikanga Māori and the Treaty into common law and the move in the direction of a written constitution.[46]

---

[40] Slack, *Bullshit, Backlash*, 160-161.
[41] A. Sharp, "The Treaty in the Real Life of the Constitution," in *Waitangi Revisited: Perspectives on the Treaty of Waitangi*, eds., Michael Belgrave, Merata Kawharu, David Vernon Williams (Melbourne: Oxford University Press, 2005), 313.
[42] Sharp, "Real Life of the Constitution," 313.
[43] Sharp, "Real Life of the Constitution," 315.
[44] Sharp, "Real Life of the Constitution," 314.
[45] Sharp, "Real Life of the Constitution," 320.
[46] Sharp, "Real Life of the Constitution," 324.

A person whose views exemplify Māori constitutionalism, and the centrality of the Treaty is Anglican Māori professor and former President of the Māori Party, Whatarangi Winiata. [47] Professor Winiata was also a member of the Anglican Church's Bicultural Commission on the Treaty of Waitangi. He has attempted to clarify the nature of partnership by exploring the possibility of the co-existence of two sovereignties as a declaration of interdependence. He has linked Māori long-term survival with "the effective Māori retention of tino rangatiratanga over taonga Māori, including mātauranga Māori, which has emerged from unique experience and unique conceptualisation." Winiata alleges that the major disagreement which emerged between the two Treaty partners over the foreshore and seabed issue was a denial of tino rangatiratanga. In his view Māori failed to convince the Crown not to take advantage of their authority. As a result of the 2005 election the Māori Party, which is committed in its Constitution to rangatiratanga, entered Parliament, in other words, into the space described by Winiata as kāwanatanga or government. Winiata's vision for partnership is the reconciliation of kāwanatanga and rangatiratanga.

Some Māori are more focussed on whakapapa constitutionalism. In her discussion regarding Ngāti Mutunga, Māori consultant Evelyn Tuuta (2005) asserts that rangatiratanga is more about everyday decision making by Māori rather than the wording of the Treaty.[48] The major priority which emerges is how to protect the

---

[47] W. Winiata, "The Reconciliation of Kawanatanga and Tino Rangatiratanga," in *Rua Rautau Lecture, Rangiatea Church, Otaki* (Aotearoa New Zealand Radio NZ, 6 February 2005 2005).
https://www.rnz.co.nz/national/programmes/waitangiruarautaulectures/audio/2508851/2005-professor-whatarangi-winiata.
https://www.rnz.co.nz/national/programmes/waitangiruarautaulectures/audio/2508851/2005-professor-whatarangi-winiata
[48] E. Tuuta, "Feast or Famine: Customary Fisheries Management in a Contemporary Tribal Society," in *Waitangi Revisited: Perspectives on the Treaty of Waitangi*, eds., Michael Belgrave, Merata Kawharu, David Vernon Williams (Melbourne: Oxford University Press, 2005), 176.

tribe or iwi, family or whānau and individual at the local level. For coming generations any relationships with the Crown and other outside agencies are primarily aimed at survival. Mason Durie also believes that partnership is at its strongest when whakapapa constitutionalism is evident.[49]

In the context of local government, the need for partnership has become more apparent with tribal Treaty settlements contributing significantly to regional economies. More representation by Māori at the level of such government will become increasingly necessary for a better-informed partnership.[50] Some Pākehā politicians, nonetheless, question the need for such representation. This was revealed in debates concerning the provision of Māori seats on the new council for the proposed supercity of Auckland. The National Party-led government decided against the three reserved Māori seats which a Royal Commission of Inquiry had recommended.[51] This was contrary to the wishes of their political ally, the Māori Party.

A low level of transparency is evident in terms of partnership which has been variously described as ill-defined, confused, misleading, ambiguous, romantic, hypocritical and illusory. In an attempt to provide clarification, the categories of legal, Māori and whakapapa constitutionalism offer a clearer picture of three kinds of partnership that Pākehā and Māori are pursuing. Undoubtedly, a diverse range of Māori and Pākehā perspectives exists regarding the definition or nature of partnership. If there is uncertainty about exactly what partnership means, it could also be argued that there

---

[49] Mason Durie, *Whaiora: Maōri Health Development* (Oxford University Press, 1998), 87.
[50] A. Sullivan, "The Treaty of Waitangi and Social Well-Being: Justice, Representation and Participation," in *Waitangi Revisited: Perspectives on the Treaty of Waitangi*, eds., Michael Belgrave, Merata Kawharu, David Vernon Williams (Melbourne: Oxford University Press, 2005), 127.
[51] D. Fox, "Black Days," *Mana* (2009): 4.

will be real difficulty in attaining a level of authenticity, equality and equity.

AUTHENTIC, EQUAL AND EQUITABLE PARTNERSHIP

Authentic partnership inevitably involves real consultation and power sharing. For some Pākehā, such consultation and power sharing would depend on the context. Māori decision-making regarding international economic agreements, or immigration, or foreign policy, would appear to fall mostly outside the scope of this kind of power sharing and consultation. A seemingly small minority of non-Māori commentators, however, would welcome Māori participation in even these areas of policymaking. It is not surprising that many Māori claim that it is the Crown which imposes its own constraints on any concept of partnership in a continuance of colonisation. Any suggestions that such a partnership is equal is referred to by some Māori as an "illusion" or a "fantasy" when the Crown perceives itself to be the dominant senior partner and Māori to be the minor junior one.[52]

Aotearoa New Zealand's international relations and trade also have significant bearing on the developing nature of equal and equitable partnership.[53] The issue has been raised that neo-tribal capitalism, driven by neo-liberal economic policies, ironically risks remarginalising Treaty rights.[54] One way that this occurs is through decontextualisation which ignores the huge range of Māori contexts. Such decontextualisation attempts to separate the economic from the social, cultural and spiritual. The Crown, through economic treaties, exposes Māori to being exploited by powerful international investors and transnational incorporations. Under the Treaty equitable economic partnership would offer the opportunity to moderate the consequences of such neoliberalism.

---

[52] Maaka and Fleras, *The Politics of Indigeneity*, 273.
[53] Consedine and Consedine, *Healing Our History: The Challenge of the Treaty of Waitangi*, 245.
[54] Kelsey, "Globalisation," 91-98.

INCREMENTAL PRAGMATISM AND RADICAL INNOVATION

Tensions also exist within Māoridom regarding whether any changes and power sharing will be a gradual or an abrupt process; incremental pragmatism or radical innovation.[55] Those who favour the former are concerned that a good working relationship is developed between both partners. Supporters of the latter seek overdue major constitutional change based on the Te Tiriti o Waitangi and Māori sovereign rights to self-determination or tino rangatiratanga. The same kind of tensions exists among non-Māori. Partnership in 1840, of course, essentially involved two major cultural groupings. In the next section I will discuss diverse contemporary viewpoints on biculturalism.

BICULTURALISM

Due to protest, both in Aotearoa New Zealand and overseas in the 1960s, 1970s and early 1980s, the Crown began introducing biculturalism in state agencies to reduce cultural marginalisation and institutional racism. In the 1990s, with the introduction of the new MMP electoral system, which produced more Māori members of Parliament, these bicultural policies became entrenched. In 2015 the Waitangi Tribunal in its Report on Stage 1 of the Te Paparahi o Te Raki concluded that the Ngapuhi chiefs, who signed Te Tiriti o Waitangi in February 1840, did not cede sovereignty to the British Crown.[56] If there are two sovereignties, Māori and Crown, it can be argued that there are two nations in Aotearoa New Zealand. Another debate may emerge which prioritises bi-nationalism over biculturalism.[57]

---

[55] Colin James, *Building the Constitution* (Wellington: Institute of Policy Studies, Victoria University of Wellington, 2000), 21.
[56] Waitangi Tribunal, "He Whakaputanga Me Te Tiriti the Declaration and the Treaty: The Report on Stage 1 of the Te Paparahi O Te Raki Inquiry," *Lower Hutt, New Zealand: Legislation Direct* (2014): 1.
[57] Maaka and Fleras, *The Politics of Indigeneity*, 140-142.

The notion of biculturalism, however, is highly varied, highly contextual and highly contested. Pākehā commentators have distinguished between symbolic biculturalism and resource-based biculturalism.[58] In the former there is a good deal of Pākehā support for the general idea of biculturalism although there is also a level of containment in terms of policies. Singing the national anthem in Māori, or performing a haka at All Black rugby games, are cited as examples of symbolic biculturalism which are acceptable to most Pākehā. In contrast, the latter option of resource-based biculturalism, which involves the distribution and management of mostly financial resources, has met with huge Pākehā opposition. Such opposition has been attributed to cultural conflict in a democracy that privileges individualism and equal opportunity over facing past injustices and intergroup relations. A major reason that governments have had difficulty proceeding from symbolic to resource-based biculturalism is international economic agreements which subordinate indigenous rights to the market economy. It is these rights which could, however, act to restrain globalisation excesses threatening this country's sovereignty as a state.[59]

As a result of biculturalism, there have been changes such as less monoculturalism, more Māori members of Parliament and far more recognition of Māori language, culture and well-being.[60] There has also been an acknowledgement that this notion has failed to deliver an increase in Māori managers in the state sector, or more tino rangatiratanga, or self-determination. In addition, it has been

---

[58] Louise Humpage, "'Liabilities and Assets': The Maori Affairs Balance Sheet," in *Tangata Tangata: The Changing Ethnic Contours of New Zealand* eds., Paul Spoonley, David G. Pearson, and Cluny Macpherson (Melbourne: Thomson Dunmore Press, 2004), 26; J.H. Liu, "History and Identity: A System of Checks and Balances for Aotearoa/New Zealand," in *New Zealand Identities: Departures and Destinations*, eds., James H Liu et al. (Wellington, N.Z.: Victoria University of Wellington. Centre for Applied Cross-Cultural Research, 2005), 76-80.
[59] Maaka and Fleras, *The Politics of Indigeneity*, 95, 299.
[60] Mason Durie, "Nga Tai Matatu: Tides of Maori Endurance," *OUP Catalogue* (2005): 139.

questioned by Māori whether symbolic biculturalism has resulted in anything more than a superficial gloss on monoculturalism.[61] For many Māori, biculturalism has emerged in the twenty-first century as only one issue which sits alongside Treaty claims, self-determination, constitutional review, tribal development and other cultural and economic priorities.[62] Indeed, Māori appear to be increasingly suspicious of biculturalism despite its contribution to raising the profile of Māori political interests and more shared policymaking and implementation.

Several non-Māori reject an uncritical biculturalism for a range of reasons. In their opinion this concept stresses difference rather than recognises commonalities.[63] It also fails to acknowledge the diversity that exists within each cultural grouping as well as growing intercultural fluidity.[64] Other objections to biculturalism include its contribution to ethnic division, its lack of success in eliminating Māori poverty, its support of a new Māori elite and its advocacy of tribalism.[65] Biculturalism is also perceived to oppose democratic ideals and values.

A debate has also emerged between biculturalism and multiculturalism. The question has been posed whether biculturalism is a precursor to multiculturalism.[66] Māori continue to operate from a hermeneutic of suspicion concerning

---

[61] Maaka and Fleras, *The Politics of Indigeneity*, 98.
[62] Maaka and Fleras, *The Politics of Indigeneity*, 140-141.
[63] Shirley Bell, "'Cultural Vandalism' and Pakeha Politics of Guilt and Responsibility," in *Tangata Tangata: The Changing Ethnic Contours of New Zealand*, eds., Paul Spoonley, David G. Pearson and Cluny Macpherson (Melbourne: Thomson Dunmore Press, 2004), 103.
[64] H. B. Levine, "Moving Beyond Cultural Essentialism," in *New Zealand Identities: Departures and Destinations*, eds., J. H. Liu et al. (Wellington, N.Z.: Victoria University of Wellington. Centre for Applied Cross-Cultural Research, 2005), 115.
[65] Elizabeth Rata, "Rethinking Biculturalism," *Anthropological Theory* 5, no. 3 (2005): 1-3.
[66] J. Williams, "The Treaty of Waitangi and Western Democracy in Practice" (paper presented at the Proceedings of Treaty Conference 2000, Auckland, 2000), 88-97.

multiculturalism.⁶⁷ This term is perceived to be a tool of Pākehā to prevent the allocation of resources or the realisation of aspirations.⁶⁸ It has also been argued that without Māori tino rangatiratanga or self-determination neither biculturalism nor multiculturalism will be fully realised in Aotearoa New Zealand.⁶⁹ Not all non-Māori, however, believe that these two notions need to exist in conflict.⁷⁰ There is a claim that biculturalism under the Treaty of Waitangi has a major contribution to make by projecting a local identity in the face of globalisation. Other non-Māori would maintain that multiculturalism would also fulfil the same function.⁷¹ Conservative Pākehā also assert that a national identity is more important than biculturalism. ⁷² Indeed, some predict that the Crown will opt for multiculturalism.⁷³ Another view is that past governments have used biculturalism as well as multiculturalism as forms of containment, in other words, to retain political power.⁷⁴

FUTURE BICULTURAL PARTNERSHIP IN AOTEAROA NEW ZEALAND

Few Pākehā or Māori are prepared to predict the future of partnership and biculturalism. Some Pākehā attempt to imagine a future partnership which honours and fulfils the Treaty of Waitangi. ⁷⁵ Such a situation would require major constitutional change and real power sharing. The problem is that the average New

---

⁶⁷ Maaka and Fleras, *The Politics of Indigeneity*, 140-149.
⁶⁸ R. Walker, *Ka Whawhai Tonu Matou: Struggle without End* (Auckland: Penguin, 1990), 390.
⁶⁹ Maaka and Fleras, *The Politics of Indigeneity*, 275.
⁷⁰ C. Ward and E-Y. Lin, "Immigration, Acculturation and National Identity," in *New Zealand Identities: Departures and Destinations*, eds., J. H. Liu et al. (Wellington, N.Z.: Victoria University of Wellington. Centre for Applied Cross-Cultural Research, 2005), 169.
⁷¹ Ward and Lin, "Immigration, Acculturation," 170.
⁷² Rata, "Rethinking Biculturalism," 13.
⁷³ Sharp, "Real Life of the Constitution," 204; James, *Building the Constitution*, 165.
⁷⁴ Maaka and Fleras, *The Politics of Indigeneity*, 274.
⁷⁵ P. Snedden, The Treaty of Waitangi: Source of Disunity or Template for Cultural Inclusion, 2004, Auckland ; Consedine and Consedine, *Healing Our History: The Challenge of the Treaty of Waitangi*, 254.

Zealander needs to become far more informed about Aotearoa New Zealand history and the Treaty debates and then be motivated to support significant transformation.[76] This will take time. It would appear that there are no short- or medium-term solutions to the current tensions. There are no guarantees that biculturalism will continue to be supported. Some conservative Pākehā argue, as mentioned earlier, that it will be merged into multiculturalism by future governments. Factors which could also impinge on its future include globalisation and the increase of dual-ethnicity and multi-ethnicity New Zealanders.[77]

Yet another complicating factor is those New Zealanders who suffer from Treaty Fatigue and a lack of Treaty Hope.[78] "Three Pākehā...have discerned that the Treaty debates...are becoming progressively influenced by the phenomenon of Treaty Fatigue."[79] The Treaty-Māori problem is seen as divisive. It is only lawyers and consultants who are benefitting from the Treaty industry, not disadvantaged Māori. Māori are blamed for this problem which they need to solve. The Treaty is only an historical artifact which is irrelevant today and in the future. The perceived antidote to Treaty Fatigue is Treaty Hope where the Treaty is a positive document for Aotearoa New Zealand especially for its governance and management.

For Māori, the future of biculturalism is affected by the fact that its credibility has become increasingly suspect in the light of Māori expectations concerning self-determination. Indeed, biculturalism is perceived as a government strategy of containment and concession

---

[76] Consedine and Consedine, *Healing Our History: The Challenge of the Treaty of Waitangi*, 252-253.
[77] P. Callister, "Ethnic Measurement as a Policy Making Tool," in *Public Policy and Ethnicity: The Politics of Ethnic Boundary Making* (Palgrave Macmillan, 2007), 154.
[78] Frances Hancock, David Epston, and Wally McKenzie, "Forging Treaty Hope: The Application and Relevance of Narrative Ideas and Practices in Developing Treaty-Based Policy and Practice," *Community Development Journal* 41, no. 4 (2006).
[79] Nicholson, ""Ko Te Mea Nui, Ko Te Aroha"," 107.

as well as a limited strategy for the advancement of Māori aspirations. Greater acceptance of these aspirations through public policy, social institutions, national identity and new social experiences forms part of Māori visions and plans. Equal and equitable partnerships are more likely to lead to accelerated change which will consist of multiple intergenerational strategies at constitutional and institutional levels.[80] Such change will be undergirded by recognition of the twin sovereignties of Māori and the Crown. In this light, bi-nationalism has the potential to encapsulate a bicultural partnership which is transparent, authentic, equal and equitable. A number of Māori advocate visioning and planning for a future which will include a higher percentage of those with Māori ancestry in the general population. For some Māori, however, local or regional tribal situations will continue to be the top priority rather than the national context.

FUTURE THREE TIKANGA CHURCH DECISION-MAKING

Reputable Pākehā Anglican missionaries translated, promoted and signed Te Tiriti which many Māori believe is a biblical covenant. Without such Pākehā missionary involvement as well as the support of Māori chiefs sympathetic to the missionaries, it would not have gained any real traction among Māori. God takes very seriously covenants entered into by God's representatives. An example is the covenant making in the Book of Joshua. The Treaty is clearly not just a secular agreement. After 135 years of Pākehā oppression, Māori were re-empowered by the new Anglican Constitution in 1992. This was power sharing in that Māori became equal partners with Pākehā. Māori were enabled to make the important mission and ministry decisions for their Tikanga. The problem has been that Tikanga Māori can make as many decisions as they like, but without access to financial and other resources to deliver on these decisions such power sharing is limited.

---

[80] L. T. Smith, *Decolonizing Methodologies: Research and Indigenous Peoples* (Dunedin: University of Otago Press, 1999), 254.

A major problem is that there is a lack of knowledge among Three Tikanga Anglican bishops, clergy and laity about Aotearoa New Zealand and Polynesia's history including its church history. Anglicans, not only in Aotearoa New Zealand, but also in the Diocese of Polynesia, need to become far more informed about Aotearoa New Zealand and Polynesian history as well as that of the Anglican Church. Anglican Māori theologian, Moeawa Callaghan, argues that any theology in Aotearoa New Zealand must base itself on the experience of colonisation and the 1840 Treaty of Waitangi.[81] For many Māori, history is important theologically because they continue to be affected by their collective memory of injustice, oppression and disempowerment. "There can be little understanding of Māori theological perspectives if due regard is not given to the fact that the Māori community walks into the future facing its history."[82] Indeed, it can be argued that Māori history is a critical source for theological interpretation of God's work regarding Three Tikanga bicultural Treaty partnership

This lack of historical knowledge also includes contemporary Treaty of Waitangi debates since 1975. Bishops, clergy and laity in the Three Tikanga Church cannot ignore these Treaty debates in Aotearoa New Zealand and Polynesia because of Gospel responsibilities, including the Gospel imperatives of love, justice and peace, and Treaty obligations. One of the fundamental debates focuses on who are the bicultural Treaty partners in the Three Tikanga Church? According to the 1992 Constitution, the partners are Tikanga Māori, Tikanga Pākehā and Tikanga Pasefika. Yet there is considerable diversity within each Tikanga cultural grouping. Another of the fundamental debates centres on the place of Te Tiriti in the Anglican Church. While the 1992 Constitution placed the

---

[81] Moeawa Callaghan, "Look to the Past to See the Future," *First Peoples Theology Journal* 4, no. 1 (2006): 104-109.
[82] R. Nicholson, "The Theological Implications of Three Tikanga Church," in *Doing Theology in Oceania: Partners in Conversation (Proceedings of Theology in Oceania Conference, Dunedin, 1996)* (Dunedin, NZ: Centre for Contextual Theology, School of Ministry, Knox College, 2000), 37.

Treaty at the centre of the Anglican Church, my research in the early twenty-first century showed that Tikanga Pākehā had largely re-marginalised it.[83] Sadly, Tikanga Māori has also started to move down this same track. Although General Synod approved the new Constitution in 1992, it is doubtful whether Tikanga Pasefika has ever placed the Treaty at the centre in the Pacific Islands because it occurred in the context of Aotearoa New Zealand. However, it can be argued that Tikanga Pasefika agreed to join the Province under the Constitution as a full partner and are therefore fully committed to Gospel responsibilities and Treaty obligations not only in Aotearoa New Zealand but also in the Pacific Islands. Of course, those Tikanga Pasefika worshiping communities situated in Aotearoa New Zealand are more directly impacted by bicultural Treaty partnership. They join the non-Māori Treaty partner, tangata Tiriti. Regrettably, the phenomenon of Treaty Fatigue has also impacted on the Three Tikanga Anglican Church. What is needed as an antidote to Treaty Fatigue is certainly hope but also journeying together towards more love, more justice and more peace.

A major debate is whether the Anglican Church in Aotearoa, New Zealand and Polynesia continues to align with its current 1992 Constitution or whether to undertake a major review and transform it to reflect developments since the 1980s including the emergence of bi-nationalism and the inequitable distribution of resources. Other major debates concerning partnership are focussed on the optimal levels of transparency, authenticity, equality and equity to meet Gospel responsibilities and Treaty obligations. Another debate is positioned around whether transformation ought to be incrementally pragmatic or radically innovative. Just as the 1992 Constitution was radically innovative and subsequently the Church has pragmatically attempted to implement new policies, it may be

---

[83] R. Nicholson, "Theological Perspectives on the Bicultural Partnership and Missional Standing Resolutions of the Three Tikanga Church," in *Te Awa Rerenga Maha: Braided River*, ed. D. Moffat, Three Tikanga Church Colloquium (Auckland: Anglican Church in Aotearoa New Zealand and Polynesia, 2018), 169.

recognised that the reality has been a season for each process. Yet another debate is sited on biculturalism and multiculturalism. A Tikanga Māori perspective is that biculturalism is a precursor to multiculturalism. Many Tikanga Māori Anglicans are suspicious of biculturalism as a form of containment, a form of limited empowerment. A number of Tikanga Pākehā Anglicans appear to support symbolic biculturalism, such the Lord's Prayer and waiata in the Māori language in their church services, but struggle with resource-based biculturalism, in other words, with the just and equitable sharing of financial and other resources. Māori Anglican clergyperson and former Chief Executive Officer, Anglican Missions, Robert Kereopa, states that the challenge is "in order to live in equal partnership with integrity, resources need to be fairly shared.[84]

If the Anglican Church is to make a major theological contribution to the development of a new Constitution for Aotearoa New Zealand, then it will be critical that Anglicans know the history of their lands including the bicultural Treaty partnership debates. The Three Tikanga Church cannot ignore the history of Aotearoa New Zealand and Polynesia as well as contemporary Treaty debates because the Church is affected by such debates in the mission fields of Aotearoa New Zealand and Polynesia. We will only be able to contribute with credibility to a new Constitution for Aotearoa New Zealand if we have our own house in order. This means the possibility of Anglican constitutional change. The emergence of two sovereignties and two nations may mean that bicultural Treaty partnership becomes subsumed by bi-national Treaty partnership. The korowai of rangimarie or peace, underpinned by love and justice, may demand no less.

---

[84] R. Kereopa, "Equal Partnership Enabling New Expressions of Indigenous Mission in a Three Tikanga Church," in *Te Awa Rerenga Maha: Braided River*, ed. D. Moffat, Three Tikanga Church Colloquium (Auckland: Anglican Church in Aotearoa, New Zealand and Polynesia, 2018), 37.

Concluding Remarks

Finally, the Three Tikanga Anglican Church will need to make decisions regarding its position in 2040 at the bicentennial commemorations of Te Tiriti o Waitangi, the future of its bicultural Treaty partnership and its own Constitution as well as the new Constitution of Aotearoa New Zealand. Will the Three Tikanga Church be well placed to witness the Gospel imperatives of love, justice and peace to the nation? Over the next 20 years, just as the Church contributed towards the Treaty, a biblically conceived covenant and constitutionally foundational document, will the Church be well placed to contribute to a new written constitution for Aotearoa New Zealand? As the Anglican Church in Aotearoa, New Zealand and Polynesia walks into the future facing its history, may God give the Church the confidence and the courage to journey together towards more love, more justice and more peace.

Kua paiheretia tātou ki te aroha o te Karaiti.
We are bound together by the love of Christ.[85]

---

[85] Anglican Church, *New Zealand Prayer Book: He Karakia Mihinare O Aotearoa* (Auckland: Collins, 1989), 419. https://anglicanprayerbook.nz/404.html.

Appendices to Chapter 2

Appendix 1: Anglican Consultative Council Fivefold Mission Statement

1. To proclaim the good news of the Kingdom;
2. To teach, baptise and nurture the new believers;
3. To respond to human needs by loving service;
4. To seek to transform unjust structures of society, to challenge violence of every kind and to pursue peace and reconciliation;
5. To strive to safeguard the integrity of creation and sustain and renew the life of the earth.

Appendix 2: Core Values/Ngā Tikanga Rongopai[86]

Cl.60 "The Church recognises a special bi-cultural partnership, founded upon the principles of the Treaty of Waitangi/Te Tiriti o Waitangi, and seeks to express this in its life."

Values are the basis upon which decisions are made. The following list seeks to honour this partnership by naming our core values:

Aroha To live in the love of Christ. "Ko tāku ture tēnei, kia aroha koutou tētahi ki tētahi, me ahau hoki kua aroha nei ki a koutou." (John 15:12)

Rangatiratanga To exercise responsible leadership with integrity, fairness and respect. "Arahina mātou, ngā iwi katoa hoki i ngā huarahi o te tika, o te rangimārie." (Guide us and all people in the way of justice and peace).

Manaakitanga To uphold the dignity of the individual, the whanau and community through the expression of mutual love and kindness. "Kia tīaho ai te āhua o te Karaiti i roto i a mātou." (That the life of Christ may be revealed in us).

Whanaungatanga To respond to and live as a community of faith in recognition of our common goal as disciples of Christ. "Ka aru mātou i a te Karaiti, tui, tui, tuituia mātou." (Called to follow Christ, help us to reconcile and unite).

Kotahitanga To celebrate our unity of purpose and direction and contribute nationally and internationally to the growth and mission of the Anglican

---

[86] Anglican Church, *ANZPB/HKMOA*, 406;425;477;483;488;490;936.

Communion. "Ko tātou tokomaha he tinana kotahi." (We who are many are one body).

Pukengatanga To commit ourselves to strengthen scholarship, research, teaching and ministry in the Anglican community. "Waihangatia mātou, kia rite ki tōu ake te āhua." (Therefore we offer all that we are and all that we shall become, literally: create us into what we are to become according to your likeness).

Kaitiakitanga We commit ourselves to treasure the people and resources of the College. "Mō ngā Tai-mihi-tāngata, mō ngā Moana e hora nei." (We offer thanks and praise for this good land).

We invite the Church to call us out with love and grace if we are not acting in accordance with these values.

Episcopal Fragmentation in Te Pouhere

Ven Dr Lyndon Drake

Introduction

TE POUHERE ESTABLISHED a model of episcopacy where Diocesan/Amorangi bishops have overlapping territorial jurisdiction. The overlaps arise because each of the three Tikanga can have a diocese/pīhopatanga which covers the same piece of land.

In practice, Tikanga Pasefika has its dioceses in the Pacific Islands and the overlaps are primarily between Tikanga Pakeha dioceses and Tikanga Māori Pīhopatanga. For example, the Diocese of Auckland includes all of the same areas as te Pīhopatanga o te Tai Tokerau (although the converse is not true).[1] As a consequence, the same area has two diocesan bishops governing it: one in Tikanga Pākehā (the bishop of Auckland), and the other in Tikanga Māori (te Pihopa o Te Tai Tokerau). Each of these bishops has the authority to ordain and license ministers within the same geographical boundary.

In this paper I make a narrow point: that te Pouhere establishes a model of episcopacy that breaks with canonical and ecumenical coherence. This is, I believe, a theological oversight. The great tradition in which monarchical episcopacy was established and eventually codified in conciliar decisions gives exclusive territorial jurisdiction to a single diocesan bishop within the church. Each piece of land (or each "city" in conciliar terminology) has one and only one diocesan bishop.

In the great tradition the bishop visibly embodies the church and in particular the unity of the church. Having two diocesan bishops destroys the idea that the church is a single, indivisible body.[2] What is more, the visible embodiment of the local church in the person of the diocesan bishop is secondary to an even higher ecclesiological principle where the visible unity of the church militant is vital to maintain because it accords with God's purposes

---

[1] The Diocese of Auckland extends further south, into Waikato and down to Thames. This geographic disparity has resulted in further complications in the past.
[2] It also has various pragmatic problems, where ordination or licensing are subject to a degree of jurisdiction shopping.

and is a demonstration of the Spirit's power in this present age of the world in uniting disparate peoples. This present unity is a foretaste of the eschatological hope of the church which is to be visibly and eternally united under its true head, Christ I.

Singular diocesan bishops embody an ecclesiological principle and the eschatological hope of the church. A pragmatic solution to a problem of structural injustice in the New Zealand church has led to a significant divergence from conciliar orthodoxy. As we shall see later at least one other Anglican response to similar issues of structural injustice has produced a more orthodox solution.

In this paper I will summarise the conciliar symbols which formalised the practice of singular diocesan bishops before stating the ecclesiological and eschatological benefits of the conciliar tradition. I will then turn to the effects of creating overlapping episcopal jurisdictions in Te Pouhere, including by contrasting Te Pouhere with the differing approach taken in Canada.

TE POUHERE'S EPISCOPAL MODEL

In looking back at Te Pouhere's model, I have been unable to discover any theological reflection on this choice. Indeed, personal conversations with those who remember the formulation of the constitution suggest that the decision to have overlapping diocesan jurisdictions was a pragmatic one. In this case, a specific problem was the lack of empowerment for Māori pīhopa to function with the same degree of episcopal authority as their Pākehā counterparts and in similar numbers. Te Pouhere corrected a structural imbalance, in fact a structural injustice, by a pragmatic solution: elevating the various hui amorangi to have the same status as the existing, largely Pākehā dioceses.

It is worth noting in passing that this new constitutional parity of ngā pīhopa with the existing Pākehā diocesan bishops was not accompanied by a redistribution of assets, so nga pīhopatanga have ever since functioned in a state of severe financial disadvantage. For example, even though both te Pīhopatanga o Te Tai Tokerau *and* the Diocese of Auckland should have been regarded as the natural descendants of the pre-1992 Diocese of Auckland, in practice each

Tikanga Pākehā diocese saw itself as an existing body, and ngā pīhopatanga as *de novo* creations. Hence, while the structural injustice of episcopal authority was in one sense remedied, even from a pragmatic point of view it was never given the financial support needed.³

CONCILIAR ORTHODOXY

As is well-known, the scriptural texts addressing ecclesiology and in particular church government do not permit a terminological distinction between bishops and presbyters. Nevertheless, in my view it is well-established that the basic functional difference between a bishop and a presbyter does date to the very early stages of the church.⁴ These differences of function were in due course given terminological distinctiveness by identifying the ordination of presbyters and wider oversight with the title of bishop. This terminological distinction finds its earliest attestation in Clement's words, but by the late second century CE was quite well-established. The practice of monarchical authority has ever since been recognised as a structural formalisation of a looser but still observable scriptural pattern in response to the needs of the church.⁵

A question which was not resolved in council in the earliest centuries of the church concerned the exclusivity of this episcopal jurisdiction over a particular city. The lack of formal decision over

---

³ A straightforward test of this as a matter of necessity rather than ideals can be found in this simple thought experiment: ask a tikanga Pākehā Diocese to give away assets to the poor so that what remains forces them to function on the asset base that each tikanga Māori Pīhopatanga subsists on. If that seems impossible for the tikanga Pākehā Diocese in question — and I note that despite hundreds of millions of investment assets that could be given to the poor in the way I suggest — no tikanga Pākehā Diocese has felt this to be a practical possibility so far.
⁴ Francis A. Sullivan, *From Apostles to Bishops: The Development of the Episcopacy in the Early Church* (Mahwah, New York: The Newman Press, 2001).
⁵ Martyn Percy, *Clergy: The Origin of Species* (London; New York: Continuum, 2006). Percy gives a helpful location of the origins and development of the distinction between the orders of presbyter and bishop in response to theological and social change.

this issue is unsurprising given the marginal status of Christians and churches in the first centuries — the survival of the church was arguably a more pressing issue than episcopal competition for oversight of adjacent cities. In due course, though, this did become a challenge which appears to have arisen over the practice of dispatching presbyters across diocesan boundaries. Conciliar responses to this are evident in the canons of the Nicene (Appendix 1) and Chalcedonian (Appendix 2) councils. I have anachronistically taken the references to the bishop of a "city" to refer to a diocese. I justify this anachronism by reference to the case of χωρεπισκόποι ("rural bishops") in the canons of the Synods of Ancyra (Appendix 3) and Antioch (Appendix 4) later in this paper.

Council of Nicaea

The Council of Nicaea established two canons which are relevant for the present matter. The first, Canon 15, explicitly refers to bishops (along with presbyters and deacons) and rules that they are to remain in the city of their ordination. The second, Canon 16, applies the same rule to the parish church to which a presbyter or deacon has been appointed. Canon 16 helps to give context to Canon 15: Canon 16 speaks of a particular parish and hence when Canon 15 mentions the church of a particular city, it is speaking of the diocese as a whole, which of course is quite properly considered to be the church in a particular geographic location.

Canon 15's ruling mentions the "great disturbance and discords" that occur when bishops and other ministers move from one city to another and requires that any attempt to cross diocesan boundaries should be responded to in two ways: the actions taking by a person who crosses diocesan boundaries are "utterly void" and the person concerned must be compelled to return to their original diocese. The canon formalises and codifies geographic exclusivity for a diocesan bishop. It is evident from the wording that crossing diocesan boundaries was already seen as aberrant behaviour, an aberration that was taking place and which the Council agreed to formally prohibit.

Council of Chalcedon

When we turn to Chalcedon, several canons address the issue of geographic exclusivity for a diocesan bishop. Canon 5 refers back to the Nicene canons and reaffirms their force. The remainder of the relevant canons expand on the principle of geographic exclusivity and apply the principle to a number of specific cases, no doubt in response to particular actions.

So, for example, when Canon 6 prohibits the ordination of a presbyter or deacon "at large," in other words someone not licensed to a particular parish church, the implication is that some diocesan bishops were avoiding the restriction imposed by Canon 16 of Nicaea about presbyters or deacons leaving the parish church they had been assigned. Ordaining someone "at large" meant that they would not have been assigned an individual parish church and hence could not be accused of leaving a church. The penalty for such an ordination "at large" was that the ordination was invalidated. In other words, such ordinations were to be treated not merely as irregular but entirely invalid.

Canon 10 extends this to another edge case: a presbyter or deacon who retained their assignment to a parish church in one diocese while also being assigned to a parish church in another diocese. Such a person was to be compelled to return to their original diocese or to be stripped of their orders if non-compliant. According to Canon 13, the only way to move from one province to another was through an exchange of episcopal letters. Canon 20 makes an exception for ministers forced "by necessity" to move countries. Under Canon 12, the geographic exclusivity of a metropolitan bishop was also to be maintained, a province could not be split into two. Bishops who attempted to divide a province were to be reduced to their original rank.

The Case of χωρεπισκόποι

An interesting additional point of clarification can be found in the case of χωρεπισκόποι ("rural bishops" or more literally "field bishops"). The canons of Nicaea and Chalcedon both refer to the bishop of a "city" only and the idea of exclusive authority belongs to these urban bishops, one urban bishop per city. These bishops held a status broadly similar to a modern diocesan bishop, a point which is made clearer by considering the status of rural bishops.

The canons of two other councils suggest that a city bishop held authority over the city and the adjacent rural areas because rural bishops fell under their authority. Canon 13 of the Synod of Ancyra rules that rural bishops can only ordain presbyters and deacons under written authority from the city bishop. Similarly, Canon 10 of the Synod of Antioch states that while rural bishops on their own authority can ordain "readers, sub-deacons, and exorcists," they can only ordain presbyters or deacons on written authorisation from the city bishop.

This clarifies that χωρεπισκόποι held a status analogous to suffragan or assistant bishops, where the overall authority for a diocese (including a city and its surrounding rural areas) was held by a single bishop with exclusive geographic jurisdiction. This jurisdiction was expressed particularly in the exclusive right to ordain or authorise the ordination of presbyters and deacons. Rural bishops could only act in these matters with written authority from the city bishop.

VISIBLE UNITY OF THE CHURCH

I suggest that these conciliar and synodical canons not only solve pragmatic problems but point to a theological idea. If "the bishop is the church" then the bishop must also embody the visible unity of the church.[6] The unity of the church is a vital aspect of ecclesiology. The church is "one body," its visible and real unity is Christ's own desire, and it points forward to the marriage of Christ to his singular bride at the end of the present age.

---

[6] Peter C. Bouteneff and Alan D. Falconer, *Episkopé and Episcopacy and the Quest for Visible Unity: Two Consultations* (Geneva: WCC Publications, 1999).

This visible unity is damaged if there is more than one bishop for a geographic area. Of course, the splintering of the church, first in the Great Schism between Eastern and Western churches and then in the Reformation, has resulted in a multiplicity of bishops and loss of visible episcopal geographic singularity. Nevertheless, it would be remarkable if these unfortunate schisms became normative *within* a particular church in addition to being visible *between* different churches.

Within a particular church preservation of one diocesan bishop for any given geographic area is a visible marker of the unity Christ sought. In his prayer in John 17.20–23, Jesus desires that a watching world will discern the true discipleship of the church by its visible unity. In an episcopally-led church, this visible unity is marked by monepiscopacy.

TE POUHERE'S CONSEQUENCES

In my view, Te Pouhere's establishment of geographically overlapping dioceses and pīhopatanga creates a discontinuity with the ecumenical tradition of the church, an ecumenical tradition which until now survived both the Great Schism and the Reformation. It also formalises and institutionalises a form that preserves separation of Māori, Pakeha and Polynesian Anglicans from each other through a structural separation that is damaging to the church's present witness to the Spirit's power to unify those whom society separates through its structural prejudices.

Indeed, my sense is that Te Pouhere has achieved one good outcome (the ordination of Māori bishops) at the expense of a loss (abandoning the challenging task of experiencing the Spirit's leading towards ethnic unity in worshipping communities). We have accepted an easier and half-hearted answer to a problem — and while making a pragmatic improvement is commendable in one sense, Christians are called to an idealistic pursuit of the best God offers rather than an acceptance of half-measures, no matter how palatable those half-measures seem.

Episcopal Jurisdiction in Canada

A point of comparison can be found in the Canadian Episcopal church, which like Aotearoa has indigenous Anglicans who have long sought to rectify unjust power structures within the church which have privileged colonial descendants over indigenous church leaders.

With every opportunity to observe the structure of Te Pouhere in practice and in conversation with indigenous leaders within the province of Aotearoa, New Zealand and Polynesia, the Canadian church has chosen instead to carve out geographically exclusive dioceses for the indigenous church. This has created areas which are overseen by an indigenous diocesan bishop who has exclusive jurisdiction within their own diocese. In doing so, the Canadian church has preserved continuity with the orthodox, canonical tradition of the church. By including non-indigenous parishes within the indigenous dioceses, the Canadian church also expresses a visible ecclesial unity that places non-indigenous peoples under indigenous episcopal authority.

Conclusion

Te Pouhere's episcopal theology appears to be pragmatic, with no internal evidence of awareness of the discontinuities it has introduced from the ecumenical great tradition. The novelty of overlapping jurisdictions for Diocesan Bishops and Pīhopa reverses the formal rejection of multi-episcopacy by the church at Nicaea. One consequence of this reversal is a marring of the church's present witness to the eventual unity of those whom society tends to separate.

In the previous volume (*Te Awa Rerenga Maha*), bishop Peter Carrell suggested that what was needed was "to blow up the existing model and do something new.[7] I am arguing that we should blow up

---

[7] P. Carrell, "The End of the Three Tikanga Church? Ephesians on the Unity of the Church.," in *Te Awa Rerenga Maha: Braided River*, ed. D. Moffat, Three Tikanga

the existing model and do something old. In fact, echoing Anashuya Fletcher's chapter in the same volume,[8] we should recognise that the impetus for this is not a novel one but has been part of the challenge of the church since its origins. The church is always faced with the risk of ethnic division and always needs to find the courage to express the cosmic change Christ brings to such ethnic divisions in its ecclesial forms.

I suggest that the Anglican Church in Aotearoa, New Zealand and Polynesia should reconsider its episcopal ecclesiology while recognising that the aberration was well-intentioned. Part of the good intended was to rectify the appalling failure of the church to ordain Māori bishops, a failure which dates back at least to the 1860s.[9] This failure was a significant factor in the splintering of the Māori church into heterodox prophetic movements, such as Rātana and Ringatū. The divergence from trinitarian orthodoxy by the Māori prophetic movements, however, should not become an excuse for the Anglican church to remain committed to a divergence from ecclesiological orthodoxy. This simply places a bandaid over the underlying problem: a systematic rejection of indigenous episcopal leadership in a Pakeha-dominated church. Instead, the Anglican church should rectify the underlying problem by taking two key steps: formation of indigenous dioceses, and the appointment of indigenous bishops more widely in the church.

First, in imitation of the Canadian church, indigenous dioceses/pīhopatanga should be created with exclusive and singular episcopal jurisdiction. This would be part of rewriting a broken story of the stripping of the indigenous church of its status in the land in the late 1800s. Māori pīhopatanga would have a missional focus in reaching areas of the country with larger Māori populations, through

---

Church Colloquium (Auckland: Anglican Church in Aotearoa, New Zealand and Polynesia, 2018), 54.
[8] Fletcher, "Finding Identity," 188–201.
[9] C. Peter Williams, *The Ideal of the Self-Governing Church: A Study in Victorian Missionary Strategy* (Leiden: E.J. Brill, 1990).

the primacy of Māori tikanga and reo in the worshipping communities of the pīhopatanga. There is no reason why these indigenous pīhopatanga would need ethnic exclusivity in their leadership, but they would naturally tend to be a formative environment for such pīhopa/bishops, in a mixed-tikanga setting that would also give considerable formative power for pīhopa/bishops who would then have the potential to be translated to another Pākehā-dominated diocese.

Secondly, the Anglican church needs to recognise that its continued failure to ordain and install Māori bishops in the Tikanga Pākehā dioceses (by continually preferring Pākehā candidates) is an example of systemic racism. In 1 Corinthians 1: , Paul points out that the church is distinguished from wider society by its members and leaders being drawn from the marginalised in wider society. Yet, the Tikanga Pākehā dioceses which still control the vast majority of the Anglican church's parishes and finances are almost universally overseen by Pākehā bishops who represent the privileged of New Zealand society.

The current constitutional arrangements of Te Pouhere allow this situation to persist because the Pākehā church can justify its institutional racism by congratulating itself on creating reservations, albeit poor structurally weak, for Māori to function separately. Separatism is not the unity Christ prayed for or which Paul held out as a marker of the Spirit's power. It is a kind of Christian apartheid. For example, the Diocese of Auckland has only had one Māori bishop in its entire history (Tā Paul Reeves) — and Auckland is remarkable for having had a Māori bishop at all. In the last few months, new bishops have been ordained and installed in the dioceses of Dunedin, Christchurch, and Nelson. Not one of these bishops is Māori. I wonder how long Māori will wait for Tā Paul's example to be repeated?

Appendices to Chapter 3

Citations of the canons in the following appendices are from NPNF.

Appendix 1: Selected canons of the Nicene Council

Canon 15. On account of the great disturbance and discords that occur, it is decreed that the custom prevailing in certain places contrary to the Canon, must wholly be done away; so that neither bishop, presbyter, nor deacon shall pass from city to city. And if any one, after this decree of the holy and great Synod, shall attempt any such thing, or continue in any such course, his proceedings shall be utterly void, and he shall be restored to the Church for which he was ordained bishop or presbyter.

Canon 16. Neither presbyters, nor deacons, nor any others enrolled among the clergy, who, not having the fear of God before their eyes, nor regarding the ecclesiastical Canon, shall recklessly remove from their own church, ought by any means to be received by another church; but every constraint should be applied to restore them to their own parishes; and, if they will not go, they must be excommunicated. And if anyone shall dare surreptitiously to carry off and in his own Church ordain a man belonging to another, without the consent of his own proper bishop, from whom although he was enrolled in the clergy list he has seceded, let the ordination be void.

Appendix 2: Selected canons of the Chalcedonian Council

Canon 5. Concerning bishops or clergymen who go about from city to city, it is decreed that the canons enacted by the Holy Fathers shall still retain their force.

Canon 6. Neither presbyter, deacon, nor any of the ecclesiastical order shall be ordained at large, nor unless the person ordained is particularly appointed to a church in a city or village, or to a martyry, or to a monastery. And if any have been ordained without a charge, the holy Synod decrees, to the reproach of the ordainer, that such an ordination shall be inoperative, and that such shall nowhere be suffered to officiate.

Canon 10. It shall not be lawful for a clergyman to be at the same time enrolled in the churches of two cities, that is, in the church in which he was at first ordained, and in another to which, because it is greater, he has removed from lust of empty honour. And those who do so shall be returned to their own church in which they were originally ordained, and there only shall they minister. But if any one has heretofore been removed from one church to another, he shall not intermeddle with the affairs of his former church, nor with the martyries, almshouses, and hostels belonging to it. And if, after the decree of this great and ecumenical Synod, any shall dare to do any of these things now forbidden, the synod decrees that he shall be degraded from his rank.

Canon 12. It has come to our knowledge that certain persons, contrary to the laws of the Church, having had recourse to secular powers, have by means of imperial rescripts divided one Province into two, so that there are consequently two metropolitans in one province; therefore the holy Synod has decreed that for the future no such thing shall be attempted by a bishop, since he who shall undertake it shall be degraded from his rank. But the cities which have already been honoured by means of imperial letters with the name of metropolis, and the bishops in charge of them, shall take the bare title, all metropolitan rights being preserved to the true Metropolis.

Canon 13. Strange and unknown clergymen without letters commendatory from their own Bishop, are absolutely prohibited from officiating in another city.

Canon 20. It shall not be lawful, as we have already decreed, for clergymen officiating in one church to be appointed to the church of another city, but they shall cleave to that in which they were first thought worthy to minister; those, however, being excepted, who have been driven by necessity from their own country, and have therefore removed to another church. And if, after this decree, any bishop shall receive a clergyman belonging to another bishop, it is decreed that both the received and the receiver shall be excommunicated until such time as the clergyman who has removed shall have returned to his own church.

Appendix 3: Canon 13 of the Synod of Ancyra

Canon 13. It is not lawful for Chorepiscopi to ordain presbyters or deacons, and most assuredly not presbyters of a city, without the commission of the bishop given in writing, in another parish.

Appendix 4: Canon 10 of the Synod of Antioch

Canon 10. The Holy Synod decrees that persons in villages and districts, or those who are called chorepiscopi, even though they may have received ordination to the Episcopate, shall regard their own limits and manage the churches subject to them, and be content with the care and administration of these; but they may ordain readers, sub-deacons and exorcists, and shall be content with promoting these, but shall not presume to ordain either a presbyter or a deacon, without the consent of bishop of the city to which he and his district are subject. And if he shall dare to transgress [these] decrees, he shall be deposed from the rank which he enjoys. And a chorepiscopus is to be appointed by the bishop of the city to which he is subject.

Treaty, Partnership and Covenant Theology

Dr Don Moffat

INTRODUCTION

THIS PAPER IS an attempt to draw together strands of history, biblical studies and contemporary responses to our post-colonial environment.[1] The historical element is the Treaty of Waitangi/Te Tiriti o Waitangi, an agreement signed by the British and number of Māori chiefs in 1840, which set out some broad terms for a bicultural Aotearoa New Zealand. It is an agreement that was heavily influenced by notions of covenant founded in the Old Testament. Contemporary applications of the treaty in a modern legal context have led to the adoption of a number of guiding principles seen to underly it. Partnership is one of those principles. The response of the Anglican Church to its colonial past included the adoption of a new constitution in 1992, Te Pouhere. The Treaty of Waitangi and the principle of partnership and bicultural development are cited as foundations upon which Te Pouhere is built. With that background, it is appropriate to review the relationship between covenant and the partnership principle in the light of contemporary scholarship.

A covenant theology based in the Old Testament was a notable feature in how Te Tiriti o Waitangi was presented and perceived in 1840. That theology needs to be taken into consideration when trying to understand what the treaty meant to those who signed it. However, scholarship's understanding of covenant in the Old Testament has moved on since 1840. Can a contemporary understanding of covenant help us bring theology into dialogue with the principle of partnership and bicultural development in ways that are productive for the church and the society now?

In 1990, Maurice Andrew published a small book where he drew on aspects of Old Testament treaty and covenant to suggest

---

[1] I am using the term "post-colonial" as it is commonly used for our current era that has begun to recognise and address the issues of the overt colonial past. I acknowledge that there are still many legacies of that colonial past yet to be addressed and Aotearoa New Zealand has only begun to walk the path to being truly post-colonial.

principles for applying the Treaty of Waitangi with a particular reference to land.[2] I want to pick up that baton, update it and focus on the implications for bicultural partnership. I'd also like to reflect briefly on how it is that we bring an ancient document into conversation with modern post-colonial social and political issues.

COVENANT

A covenant is usually defined as a solemn agreement formally made between parties. When biblical categories are brought into the discussion then a sacred aspect is added; the agreement either explicitly or implicitly involves God. The key covenants in the Old Testament are between Yahweh and Christian or between Yahweh and significant individuals, such as Abraham or David. Yet even covenants between two human parties often drew Yahweh in as a witness. For example, David made a covenant with the tribes of Christian in Hebron "before the LORD" (2 Sam 5:3), which is usually understood to mean the agreement took place in a temple or sacred space.[3] Similarly the covenant between David and Jonathan is called "a covenant of the LORD" (1 Sam 20:8) and described as "a covenant made before the LORD" (1 Sam 23:18). Given the way Old Testament ideas were associated with Te Tiriti o Waitangi it is important that we recognise that there is a sacred aspect to the treaty. To simply state that we now live in a largely secular society will not do. These documents convey meaning, that meaning is tied to the ideas intended by the words that are used. When those words carry notions of the sacred, those ideas have abiding relevance and cannot be dismissed as irrelevant in a 21st century context. Further, it is important for the church that we acknowledge that such notions imply an accountability before God.

---

[2] M. E. Andrew, *Treaty Land Covenant* (Dunedin: M. Andrew, 1990).
[3] M. Haran, "The Běrît 'Covenant': Its Nature and Ceremonial Background," in *Tehillah Le-Moshe: Biblical and Judaic Studies in Honour of Moshe Greenberg*, eds., M. Coogan, N.L. Eichler, and J.H. Tigay (Winona Lake: Eisenbrauns, 1997), 209.

Waitangi and Covenant

First it is necessary to set the historical context that led to the establishment of a treaty between the British crown and various Māori leaders in the mid-nineteenth century. Treaties were a common tool used by European colonial powers to expand their influence.[4] Missionaries were also a feature of colonial expansion and were among the early European settlers in New Zealand. Their primary purpose was to establish the Christian Church among the Māori people. By the time the treaty was presented, Christianity was growing among Māori, much of the Bible was translated into the Māori language, and many Māori were learning to read. Indeed, biblical and religious texts were often a key means for teaching reading. Missionaries had generally made a good impression on Māori and were respected, none more so than Henry Williams the leader of the Church Missionary Society (CMS). Williams had mana – status and respect – with Māori through his proficiency in Māori language, relationships with Māori chiefs, and his efforts in brokering peace among warring tribes.[5]

Williams was opposed to extensive European settlement of New Zealand but encounters with the New Zealand Company and its purchase of land in the lower North Island and upper South Island in 1839 persuaded him that extensive settlement was inevitable. Because of that, Williams became a champion of a formal agreement between the British crown and Māori.[6] When Governor Hobson arrived to broker the treaty at the beginning of 1840, Williams became one of the main players in the events. Henry Williams' influence in the treaty was in two areas. First, he and his son Edward

---

[4] S. Belmessous, *Empire by Treaty: Negotiating European Expansion, 1600-1900* (New York: OUP, 2015).
[5] Hugh Carleton, *The Life of Henry Williams* (Wellington, N.Z.: A.H. & A.W. Reed, 1948); Lawrence M. Rogers, *Te Wiremu: A Biography of Henry Williams* (Christchurch, N.Z.: Pegasus, 1973).
[6] Claudia Orange, *The Treaty of Waitangi* (Wellington: Allen & Unwin, 1987), 58-59; Carleton, *Henry Williams*, 263-305. See particularly Williams' letter, 286.

were responsible for the translation of the brief three-clause treaty into te reo Māori, to which James Busby, the British Resident, suggested some edits. Second, Williams was an agent who explained the treaty to the chiefs on behalf of Governor Hobson at Waitangi and subsequently travelled with the treaty, seeking the signatures of Māori leaders in various parts of the land.

It was the efforts of the missionaries to explain the treaty in terms Māori could understand that led them to equate the treaty with Old Testament covenants. What Henry Williams said on the matter is unfortunately second-hand. We are dependent on what others have recorded because we do not have William's diaries after 1839. Biblical scholarship of the early 19th century was actively developing a critical approach to the Old Testament. Nevertheless, most scholars still treated it as an accurate historical record and so took the narratives in Genesis and Exodus about Yahweh establishing a covenant with Abraham and Christian at face value. That is, they assumed the notion of covenant was intrinsic to the relationship between God and Christian.

It seems that Williams, in keeping with that scholarship, saw covenant as the factor that bound the Israelite tribes together under Yahweh. Further, Williams incorporated ideas from the Davidic covenant, that just rule over Christian's tribes was provided by God and accountable to God. With that understanding, Williams transposed the Old Testament ideas into in the British context, replacing the Israelite monarch with the British one and equating the British and Māori peoples with Israelite tribes. Thus, the treaty was presented to Māori as uniting British and Māori under one sovereign and one God. As Claudia Orange states, Williams perceived that for Christian Māori "there was an additional spiritual dimension; under one Sovereign, Māori and British could be linked as one people with the same law, spiritual and temporal."[7] The statements of Māori chiefs, like Patuone, indicated the treaty was viewed as a covenant in

---

[7] Orange, *Treaty*, 56.

biblical terms by several of those who signed it.[8] Similarly, Governor Hobson's famous greeting to each Māori chief who signed – "He iwi tahi tātou" ("We are now one people") reinforced the notion. Thus, a missionary emphasis on Old Testament notions of covenant played a significant role in the way the Treaty of Waitangi was perceived by Māori and key Pākehā.

While the treaty does not specifically use the language of covenant, the notion was certainly used to promote it and numbers of Māori then and since have understood the treaty as a covenant. This is evidenced by the comments of Archbishop Whakahuihui Vercoe at the 1990 celebrations for the 150th anniversary of the signing of the treaty. He reminded Queen Elizabeth II that Māori were still waiting for the treaty to be honoured. He said "[w]e come to this sacred ground because our tupuna left us this ground. One hundred and fifty years ago a compact was signed, a covenant was made between two people."[9] The Old Testament and Te Tiriti o Waitangi were merged in 1840 and that co-mingling continues in the way the treaty is understood today.

This has implications for the present because treaty negotiations come down to issues of interpretation. That is, the focus on meaning is on what was understood by the signatories. Where there is difference in understanding, or ambiguity in such treaties, the convention internationally is to give the indigenous version priority. However, the Waitangi Tribunal Act calls on the Tribunal to make determinations that treat the English and Māori language versions of the Treaty equally.[10] That is, the Tribunal has the task of negotiating the space between understandings. It is this requirement that has resulted in the development of a group of guiding principles to aid the negotiation process. Three of those principles have become

---

[8] Orange, *Treaty*, 57.
[9] Whakahuihui Vercoe, "By the Rivers of Babylon," in *Te Ao Mārama. Regaining Aotearoa: Māori Writers Speak Out. He Whakaatanga O Te Ao: The Reality* ed. Witi Ihimaera (Auckland: Reed Books, 1993), 83-84.
[10] Treaty of Waitangi Act 1975. Section 5(2).

common and are often referred to as the three "Ps": Partnership, Participation, Protection. These three principles are regarded as expressions of the underlying tenets of the treaty. Each of those principles, and partnership in particular, is supported by the idea of covenant. Further, I want to argue that advances in the understanding of covenant in the Old Testament can nuance how we understand the notion of partnership and what that means for us as a bicultural church and nation.

COVENANT IN SCHOLARSHIP

Discussion on covenant in the Old Testament has moved through several phases since 1840. The first of those moves, and the most significant, came at the end of the 19th century with the publication of Julius Wellhausen's *Prolegomena zur Geschichte Israels* in 1878, the English translation, *Prolegomena to the History of Ancient Christian* appeared in 1885.[11] One of the implications of Wellhausen's arguments about the development of the Pentateuch was that "the presentation of Christian's relations with Yahweh in terms of covenant was a late development and came about as a result of the preaching of the great prophets."[12] Moses, according to Wellhausen, did not mediate a covenant between Yahweh and Christian, but was the founder of a nation which later produced Torah and prophecy.[13] For Wellhausen, the prophets produced a new religion in which the relationship with Yahweh, based on a natural bond, was severed and a new relationship based on covenant, and therefore conditional, was established. Covenant, for Wellhausen, was not fundamental to the relationship with Yahweh but a new form of relationship brought about by crisis. These conclusions led to debate over four interrelated issues which Ernest Nicholson identifies as:

---

[11] Julius Wellhausen, *Prolegomena to the History of Ancient Israel* (Edinburgh: Adam and Charles Black, 1885).
[12] E. W. Nicholson, *God and His People: Covenant and Theology in the Old Testament* (Oxford: Clarendon Press, 1986), 3.
[13] Nicholson, *God and His People*, 4-5.

- The historicity of the journey to Sinai after the Exodus and the nature of the covenant between Yahweh and Christian.
- The meaning of the term b^{e}rith (the Hebrew word for covenant) when applied to the relationship.
- The nature of early Israelite religion.
- The silence of the 8th century prophets about covenant.

While these issues are interrelated, I want to focus briefly on the first two, which have the most relevance for the topic at hand.

Nicholson notes that the debate about the antiquity of covenant as a defining feature of the relationship between Christian and Yahweh quite quickly rejected Wellhausen's conclusion that the covenant was a late development.[14] There was widespread agreement that the covenant was ancient and intrinsic to the relationship between Yahweh and Christian. Well known scholars like Herman Gunkel, Kurt Galling, Arthur Weiser, and Walter Eichrodt, writing in the early decades of the 20th century, championed the covenant as fundamental and distinct feature of Israelite religion. This view was further refined in the 1950s with the comparison of second millennium Hittite treaties with the form and structure of the Sinai covenant. This reaffirmed the antiquity of the idea while nuancing the understanding of the place of the cult in Israelite life. Mendenhall argued that the covenant was a socio-religious institution, structuring the people of Christian as a nation as well as their worship. Many scholars found his views attractive. All that agreement began to unravel from the late 1960s when scholarship began to re-examine Wellhausen's conclusions. The change came because arguments that covenant was a theological analogy became more convincing and Mendenhall's idea of a socio-religious institution waned. Thus, the covenant was not seen as fundamental to early Israelite religion, but rather a theological construct that was a response to crisis in the late monarchy era. The treaty model evident in Exodus and Deuteronomy is regarded as the

---

[14] Nicholson, *God and His People*, 28.

result of later theological reflection which uses it as an analogy to help Christian understand its relationship with Yahweh. Thus, Yahweh was understood to have made a promise to Christian which, in turn, put Christian under obligation to Yahweh. The notion, it is argued, developed out of prophetic criticism. This is roughly where scholarship is now on this issue. We have returned over about 100 years to Wellhausen's position but in a new form. Covenant is now widely regarded as a late development in Christian's understanding of its relationship with Yahweh. Nevertheless, the significance of covenant as a metaphor of that relationship is recognised for its explanatory power and its widespread use in the final form of the Old Testament. Thus, covenant is still discussed as a theological theme in the Old Testament because it describes the mature reflection of Christian on its faith and is well imbedded in the final form of the Old Testament and in Judaism.

The second question addressed by scholars that Nicholson notes is the meaning of b^erith. The early search for a meaning largely followed an etymological path and aimed to come up with a primary idea from which related notions developed. There are manifold suggestions about the etymology of b^erith, such as, it being derived from "I eat," or from "to see," or from, "to clasp or fetter," or from the preposition "between" or even "to separate." The variety shows there is no clear option and none of those listed has proved to be convincing to the majority of Old Testament scholars. Additionally, using etymology as the primary basis for meaning was severely undermined by James Barr, who argued convincingly that the derivation of a word is not a predictable guide to its usage in later contexts.[15] The result has been that most recent discussions of the meaning of b^erith focus on its usage, not speculation on its possible antecedents.

---

[15] James Barr, *The Semantics of Biblical Language* (London: Oxford University Press, 1961).

One of the most influential discussions of *b^erith* is the argument by Ernst Kutsch that the primary meaning of the word is "obligation."[16] Further, that the original usage was of the "unilateral acceptance or imposition of an obligation."[17] For this reason he excludes the notion of relationship from his understanding of covenant. His ideas were supported by several scholars, as exemplified by Weinfeld's article on *b^erith* in the *TDOT*. Kutsch's definition is assumed by Maurice Andrew in his discussion of covenant in relation to the Treaty of Waitangi. However, more recent scholarship has rejected narrow definitions when the word clearly has a wider semantic range. Kutsch himself admits that there is a secondary meaning of "bilateral agreement" in the Old Testament, while wanting to retain "obligation" as the primary meaning. The failure of Kutsch's narrow definition to adequately reflect the breadth of usage in the Old Testament has, along with the rejection of narrow etymological definitions, lead recent scholarship to accept that *b^erith* has a sematic range which is best recognised by the variety of ways it is used. Thus, it can be translated by words like, treaty, agreement, alliance or covenant depending on context. Further, scholars also note that these ideas all presume relationship, which has to be seen as a fundamental aspect of *b^erith* whichever word is used to translate it.

COVENANT LOYALTY

It is difficult to discuss covenant in the Hebrew Bible without noting another very significant Hebrew word. That word is *ḥesed*, which is variously translated: faithfulness, loyalty, goodness,

---

[16] E. Kutsch, *Theological Lexicon of the Old Testament*, ed. E. Jenni and C. Westermann, trans. Mark E. Biddle, Vol. 1 (Peabody, MA: Hendrickson, 1997), 256-266. This is supported by M. Weinfeld, "ברית berît" in *Theological Dictionary of the Old Testament*, eds. G.J. Botterweck and H. Ringgren, Vol. 2. (Grand Rapids: Eerdmans, 1975), 253-279.
[17] Nicholson, *God and His People*, 104.

kindness, and mercy.[18] It is frequently used of God's actions of steadfast love. While not restricted to the context of covenant, ḥesed is closely associated with covenant and conveys notions that overlap with it. D.A. Baer and R.P. Gordon, when discussing David's plea to Jonathan to maintain loyalty to him (1 Sam 20:8, 14), state that in that context ḥesed "is not an aspect or ingredient of covenant as such. Rather, the covenant comes in to reinforce the commitment to ḥesed in a situation where its exercise is not naturally to be expected to apply or is likely to be strained by future circumstances."[19] Like the idea of covenant, ḥesed is strongly relational and conveys a commitment for the benefit of the relational party. Divine ḥesed, or steadfast love, is characterised by abundance and persistence among other qualities. Referring to ḥesed, John Goldingay states, "[o]n the basis of the conviction that our human action in covenant is an imitation of God's action in covenant one could reckon that these are the qualities of human covenantal living."[20] Thus steadfast love is consistently seen as the highest of values and necessary for the survival of the covenant relationship in the Old Testament.

SUMMARISING COVENANT

What is there about covenant in current understanding that is significant for this discussion? First, that covenant is about a relationship.[21] This element was dismissed by Kutsch, but it is intrinsic in the many contexts in which b^erith is used in the Old

---

[18] D.A. Baer and R.P. Gordon, "חסד Ḥesed," in *New International Dictionary of Old Testament Theology and Exegesis*, ed. W. VanGermeren (Grand Rapids, MI: Zondervan, 1997); *The Dictionary of Classical Hebrew*, ed. David J. A. Clines, Vol. III (Sheffield: Sheffield Academic Press, 1996), 277-281; L. Köhler and W. Baumgartner, *Hebrew & Aramaic Lexicon of the Old Testament*, Vol. 1 (Leiden: E.J. Brill, 1994), 336-337.
[19] Baer and Gordon, חסד Ḥesed, 212.
[20] John Goldingay, "Covenant OT and NT," in *New Interpreter's Dictionary of the Bible* (Nashville, Tennessee: Abingdon Press, 2006-2009), 778.
[21] J.G. McConville, "ברית Berîth," in *New International Dictionary of Old Testament Theology and Exegesis*, ed. W. VanGermeren (Grand Rapids, MI: Zondervan, 1997); Goldingay, *Covenant*, 1.

Testament. Some scholars speak about covenant establishing relationship, but the term is probably more frequently used for the formalising or upgrading of a relationship.[22] Goldingay says, "[it] involves a commitment in a relationship, as opposed to a mere acquaintance without obligation."[23] For example, Abraham already had a relationship with Yahweh prior to the covenant in Genesis 15 but that covenant formalised and added to the relationship. The Sinai covenant established a relationship between Yahweh and Christian, but it has its foundations in the existing covenant between Yahweh and descendants of Abraham. As the discussion about *ḥesed* above noted, covenants set relationships on a formal footing and reinforce the commitment between the parties.

Second, covenant is inherently relational because it involves mutual commitment. J.G. McConville observes that Old Testament covenants paradoxically acknowledge both the "initiative of God" and the "necessity of human choice."[24] Goldingay points out that this mutuality is why there is some ambiguity about divine commitment and human obligation in the Old Testament.[25] Covenants such as that made by Yahweh with Abraham in Genesis 15 look a great deal like a promise where the obligation seems to rest solely with Yahweh who chooses the relationship and makes the promises. Yet there are implicit expectations on Abraham and his descendants which are focused on the sign of the covenant, circumcision. Abraham is also called to be blameless in Genesis 17:1 and there are consequences for not having the sign of the covenant. That is, those without the sign will be cut off from the covenant (Gen 17:14). Similarly, the Davidic covenant looks unconditional, but texts also indicate that the covenant is dependent on each reigning monarch to uphold it.[26] This

---

[22] Cf. John Goldingay, *Israel's Gospel*, Vol. 1, Old Testament Theology, (Downers Grove, Ill.: IVP, 2003), 370-371.
[23] John Goldingay, *Israel's Faith*, Vol. 2, Old Testament Theology, (Downers Grove, Ill.: IVP, 2006), 182.
[24] McConville, ברית *Berîth*, 6, 752.
[25] Goldingay, *Covenant*, 1, 771.
[26] See for example Ps 89:39; 132:12.

ambiguity in covenant obligations is because the mutual commitment is not exactly conditional. Like a marriage, a covenant requires that both parties commit themselves to each other but neither explicitly makes the commitment on the condition that the other also does. Covenant defines a relationship of mutual commitment that implies mutual obligation but is not entirely dependent on that obligation. This is why the idea of *ḥesed* is so important in the Old Testament, steadfast love governs the commitment to the good of the other in the relationship.

Further, covenant calls for some exclusivity of relationship. Both the covenant with Abraham and the Sinai covenant are declarations that Yahweh will be Christian's God and Christian will be Yahweh's people (Gen 17:7-8, Exod 6:7, Ezek 36:28), a stance reinforced with the first article of the Decalogue (Exod 20:3). Ezekiel 34:24 makes a similar claim with allusions to the Davidic covenant. It is arguable that the idea of covenant was foundational to the notion of monotheism because it excludes the possibility of loyalty to any other divinity.[27] It is interesting that the prophets frequently use marriage as a metaphor for Christian's relationship with Yahweh and accuse Christian of spiritual adultery when their worship is not exclusively offered to Yahweh.

Finally, covenants persist, though at times with modifications, through historical changes. This is clear in the continuity we see between the covenant with Abraham and the Sinai covenant and then later with the new covenant in the prophets. However, it is also noteworthy in covenants between human partners. The covenant between Jonathan and David is initiated by Jonathan when he is the powerful one, and endures even when Jonathan's father, Saul, wants to kill David (1 Sam 18-20). Here covenant faithfulness supersedes familial obligation. When David becomes king, he shows mercy to Jonathan's son Mephibosheth, because of the relationship with Jonathan. Further, 2 Samuel 21), claims that Christian incurred blood

---

[27] Goldingay, *Covenant*, 1, 770.

guilt because Saul had killed the Gibeonites, a people who had a treaty with Christian (Josh 9). Even a covenant which was obtained through trickery was regarded as lasting. None of the covenants in the Old Testament are time-limited. What limits them is the covenant faithfulness of the partners.

COVENANT AND CONTEMPORARY PRACTICE

While Maurice Andrew focused on the implications of the Treaty of Waitangi for land issues, he did not address the question of how one brings the Old Testament principles to bear on contemporary social and political issues. Christian ethicists say the first step in applying biblical ethics in contemporary life rests with the Christian community living in accordance with its ethical convictions. It can from that basis engage with the wider public in various ways both individually and corporately.[28] Thus while I think the comments that follow have an application beyond the church, I speak mainly to the church because it is our responsibility, first and foremost, to live out these principles in our relationships. That responsibility not only rests on us as citizens of this country but also because our spiritual forebears, the early missionaries, imbued the treaty with notions of Old Testament covenant that continue to speak into our post-colonial context. I would suggest that a contemporary understanding of covenant in the Old Testament implicitly supports Henry Williams' understanding of the Treaty of Waitangi as a covenant and so supports notions of partnership as an underlying principle of the treaty.

Te Tiriti o Waitangi, like biblical covenants, establishes a fundamental relationship between Māori as the indigenous people of this land and those who originate from later migrations to this land. Williams' analogy with biblical covenants indicates that it is a partnership between the two peoples, to be enacted by the Crown under the supervision of God. Governor Hobson supported that with

---

[28] Thomas W. Ogletree, *The Use of the Bible in Christian Ethics* (Philadelphia: Fortress Press, 1983), 189-190.

his famous greeting, "He iwi tahi tātou." While secular governments may not be so willing to accept accountability to a higher power, Christians who claim to live under the God of the Bible must acknowledge that faithfulness to the treaty is something for which they are accountable. The notion of ḥesed, covenant faithfulness, emphasises the expectation that the church must emulate the divine example of kindness, mercy and love.

It is also worth noting that this is a covenant built on existing relationships. It is likely that many Māori would not have signed the covenant if it was not for the relationship missionaries had with them. It was the persuasive influence of Henry Williams and others that saw many chiefs sign it. Others signed because those chiefs influenced by the missionaries had signed. The treaty is founded on relationship and was intended to formalise that relationship for the benefit of two peoples. Relationship is fundamental, this is why the notion of partnership needs to be at the forefront of all bicultural issues. Our priority should not be economic or political but relational. We need to find ways of strengthening the relationships as the foundation for partnership. This is an area the 2017 conference on the Anglican Three Tikanga structure noted the church needed to put much more work into.[29] It has yet to fully enact the ethics it espouses.

The treaty is about mutual commitment, Māori ceded governorship in return for a government protection.[30] It was about making one nation out of two people groups without destroying the distinctiveness of either group. The emphasis is on partnering together in this country. Both parties have obligations, but the

---

[29] See the papers from that conference in D. Moffat, *Te Awa Rerenga Maha: Braided River* (Auckland: The Anglican Church of Aotearoa, New Zealand and Polynesia, 2018).
[30] Obviously, the issue of what Māori ceded is contentious given the differences between the two versions of the treaty. While the English version cedes sovereignty, the Māori version cedes kawanatanga, which is more accurately translated as governorship in our contemporary context. I am using the more likely Māori understanding given I am referring to what they ceded.

obligations should be motivated by the partnership because they are implied by the mutual relationship. As the notion of covenant faithfulness emphasises, each party should respond generously for the sake of the other. This is where the Old Testament analogy with marriage is helpful, it puts the emphasis on the commitment of the partners to the relationship, as the central factor. When the focus falls on the obligations, the relationship is already in trouble. When the relationship is good, obligations are naturally fulfilled as part of the commitment of the partners to each other. The tragedy of the colonial era is that there was no partnership, rather one party took control. In our Anglican church context, a valid critique of the three Tikanga structure is that the church has yet to work out ways of expressing partnership beyond its bureaucratic levels.

The treaty is also fundamentally bicultural because it established an exclusive relationship. This is the reality in a multicultural world. As a covenant the treaty established a fundamental relationship between tangata whenua and later migrants. Again, at the 2017 conference at St Johns College about the Anglican three Tikanga structure, we had considerable discussion on how unhelpful the often narrow use of the word Pākehā is for this idea. We tend to use the word primarily for New Zealanders of European origin but that is a contraction of its meaning, which is more generally a word for non-indigenous people. The church should know that others can be incorporated into covenantal relationships. The Sinai covenant, while based on the earlier covenant with Abraham, involved more than blood descendants of Abraham; they were a "mixed crowd" (Exod 12:38). Further, the new covenant opened the door to a new society where Jews and Gentiles were made one people under God.[31] When new migrants commit themselves to this country and its Christian community, they take on the community responsibility of this church. Maybe we need a way of recognising and acknowledging that.

---

[31] E.g., Gal 3:28-29, Eph 2:11-22, Col 3:11.

The treaty calls on both parties to commit themselves to each other for mutual benefit. Further, the powerful partner has particular obligations toward the more vulnerable party. In the relationship between David and Jonathan we see the relationship and the obligations change over time. Yet the powerful always acts to support the less powerful, even when it means acting against self-interest and familial loyalties.

Christian communities cannot leave Treaty of Waitangi responsibilities to the government and related political bodies. Christians have a responsibility before God to honour the commitment. This is because this treaty established a fundamental relationship at a spiritual level. Neither can we shrug off responsibility by relegating the treaty to history now passed because covenants persist. Covenants are not limited by time, but by faithfulness. They can be upgraded and superseded but not dropped because each party is accountable to God.

Conclusion

The history of Te Tiriti o Waitangi makes it clear that Old Testament notions of covenant were important in the way it was originally understood by both Māori and Pākehā. While modern scholarship has moved in its views on the ideas of covenant, contemporary scholarship reinforces much of what missionaries, Māori and Governor Hobson understood about the nature of the relationship. It is a relationship of mutual obligation which is dependent on faithful intent and action by all parties to ensure a healthy relationship that benefits all. Given the significant involvement of the missionaries and biblical ideas, the church has a particular responsibility to live according to the treaty committments and to advocate for them in the public sphere.

A Commonwealth of Koinōnia: A New Testament Concept with which to Weave Te Korowai o te Rangimārie

Rev'd Dr Derek Tovey

INTRODUCTION

A COMMON THEME emerging from the Colloquium "Three Tikanga Church: Reflecting Theologically" held here in October 2017 was the need for our partnership as a Three Tikanga church to be built on relationships. A perception of the Three Tikanga relationship also expressed then was that the idea of partnership, expressed in the Constitution/Te Pouhere adopted in 1992, lacked a good theological articulation.

In this paper I wish to explore the New Testament concept captured in the word *koinōnia* (and its cognates) to provide a least the outline of a theological foundation to the idea of partnership and then to see what implications this has for our relationships in a Three Tikanga church. Although I am considering a particular word – or word-group – I prefer to speak of *koinōnia* as a concept for it is a word that has a fairly wide range of meanings and is found in a variety of contexts.

In the Hellenistic world of the New Testament and in the period leading up to it *koinōnia* was used of various types of association and partnerships, one of the main ones being the marriage partnership.[1] In a very full study of the term, Julien Ogereau provides instances from everyday documents, both epigraphical inscriptions and papyri, of *koinōnia* and its cognates being used in a wide variety of contexts from political and treaty alliances to joint business ventures such as share-cropping, joint ownership of land, houses, animals, workshops and even slaves.[2] The noun *koinōnos* could refer to a partner in business and this is probably the sense in which it is used in Luke 5:10 where James and John the sons of Zebedee are described as "partners" (*koinōnoi*) of Simon. In Galatians 2:9 Paul writes of how

---

[1] John M. McDermott, *The Biblical Doctrine of Koinōnia* Vol. N.F.19 (1975), 67; See also J. Y. Campbell, *Three New Testament Studies* (Leiden: Brill, 1965), 8.
[2] Julien M. Ogereau, *Paul's Koinonia with the Philippians: A Socio-Historical Investigation of a Pauline Economic Partnership*, Vol. 377 (Mohr Siebeck, 2014). See chapter five, and especially e.g., 169–73, 199–208.

James, Cephas and John give "the right hand of fellowship" to Barnabas and himself when they recognise "the grace that had been given to" Paul. Here the word *koinōnia* may simply mean the hand of friendship, that is, they accept Paul as a fellow-Christian. However, given that an agreement is made about spheres of mission (Paul and Barnabas to the Gentiles, the others to the Jews) it probably signifies acknowledgement of a partnership. Indeed, Grosvenor and Zerwich in *A Grammatical Analysis of the Greek New Testament* translate it as "association, partnership" and also as an "agreement" and write: "shook hands with me and B[arnabas] in token of our partnership, [namely] in spreading the gospel."[3]

The basic meaning of *koinōnia* is the sharing in something with someone. It is used in the New Testament mostly by Paul. He gives this term a rich and varied sense given the types of contexts in which he uses the word. He also provides a strong theological and christological flavour to its use, out of which I suggest we may construct a theology of partnership.

In Philippians 1:5 Paul thanks God for the Philippian Christians because of their sharing (*koinōnia*) with him in the gospel. This certainly entailed a sharing by providing financial and physical support, as well as spiritual and moral support, for his ministry of evangelism and teaching. We shall come back to the financial aspect later. But it was also a sharing – a partnership – in the grace and salvation brought to them, as to Paul, through the death and resurrection of Jesus Christ. For Paul this is a fundamental basis for all Christian partnership and unity: So, for instance, in writing to the Corinthians (1 Corinthians 1:9): , Paul states that they have been called into the "partnership" (NRSV, "fellowship"; Greek *koinōnia*) of God's Son, Jesus Christ the Lord.

---

[3] M. Zerwick and M. Grosvenor, *A Grammatical Analysis of the Greek New Testament*, 4th revised ed. (Rome: Editrice Pontificio Istituto Biblico, 1993), 567.

This fundamental partnership is expressed above all in the "sharing" of the Eucharist. So, Paul says in 1 Corinthians 10:16 - 17: :

> The cup of blessing that we bless, is it not a sharing (*koinōnia*) in the blood of Christ? The bread that we break, is it not a sharing (*koinōnia*) in the body of Christ? Because there is one bread, we who are many are one body, for we all partake of the one bread.

We may recall that Paul later uses the body imagery specifically to make the point that we need one another, that all our varied gifts and talents are required for the proper functioning of Christ's body, and those who may seem less important or less "presentable" should be treated with the greater consideration and respect.[4]

Indeed, the passage about the body begins with the statement that "in the one Spirit we were all baptised into one body – Jews or Greeks, slaves or free – and we were all made to drink of the one Spirit." Not only are we baptised into one body, so that we become "sharers" in the life of Christ, but we also "drink of the one Spirit." Paul will sign off his second letter to the Corinthian Christians by blessing them thus: "The grace of our Lord Jesus Christ, the love of God, and the *koinōnia* of the Spirit (NRSV has "communion of"/RSV "fellowship of") be with all of you" (2 Corinthians 13:14). There is debate about whether we read an objective genitive here (that is, this is a participation in the Holy Spirit, we all share the Spirit's presence in our lives, if you will), or whether it is a subjective genitive: that is our participation with each other (our communion or fellowship, our common life, if you will) is derived from the Holy Spirit. Whatever the case, we may say that the Holy Spirit animates our participation both in our shared experience in the life of Christ, and the resulting shared life as those brought into Christ's body, the church.

---

[4] For a treatment of 1 Corinthians 12:12 – 26 in connection with our Three Tikanga church, see Fletcher, "Finding Identity," 188 – 201, and specifically 190 – 194.

The partnership that is established by being baptised into Christ, and sharing in – being a participant in Christ's death (an aspect we will return to) – and being drawn into a single "community" of participants in the Spirit and by the Spirit, is captured differently by Paul in Romans 11:17 when he addresses the Gentiles as having been grafted into the olive tree of God's people Israel. Gentiles are, he says, *synkoinōnos*, "sharers with," "partners with" the Jewish branches in the "rich root of the olive tree," that is, those branches that remain when others are broken off so that the Gentile believers may be "grafted in."

This statement of the interrelationship of Gentiles and Jews as joint partners opens up the aspect of the two groups (though the term Gentiles includes a wide range of cultures and ethnicities) belonging together in one "commonwealth" or a common citizenship in the kingdom of God. Paul introduces this idea in Philippians 3:20 where he reminds these citizens of a Roman colony that their true "citizenship" (*to politeuma*) is in heaven from where their Saviour Jesus Christ will come.[5] This concept of "citizenship" is developed wonderfully by Paul in Ephesians where he states that Gentiles, who were formerly strangers or aliens in regards of the "commonwealth of Israel" (*tēs politeias tou Israēl*), have with their Jewish fellow believers been made into "one new humanity." Divisions between them have been brought down and they are now reconciled to God into "one body" through the death of Christ. So, Paul goes on, "you [Gentiles] are no longer strangers and alien but you are citizens (*sumpolitai*), or fellow-citizens with the saints and also members of the household of God..." (Eph. 2:19).

Now, it is important to state that this partnership, this *koinōnia* in Christ does not mean uniformity. It is a unity in diversity. Several writers I have read have emphasised this point, but it is nicely

---

[5] See also Phil. 1:27. On this see further Andrew Lincoln, "Communion: Some Pauline Foundations," *Ecclesiology* 5, no. 2 (2009): 153–154.

captured by Cecily Boulding who, reflecting on "the Church as essentially corporate personality with Christ," states:

> This profound perception justifies the presence of pluriformity, diversity in the Church; without it *koinonia* cannot be realised, for relationships demand not sameness but complementary diversity; as in the Trinity itself, the many actually constitute the one. But, as in the Trinity, it is an ordered complementarity.[6]

It is important to consider the sociological context into which Paul's letter writing is to be set. Quite apart from the fact that scholars are now recognising that we cannot regard Second Temple Judaism as a monolithic system, we must recall that Paul would have encountered much ethnic and cultural variation among and within the different geographical regions to which he travelled, and in which the churches to which he wrote were set. Paul would not have tried to homogenise the cultural variations which he encountered: and indeed, we might say that in some of his letters he is trying to bring an "ordered complementarity" to the differences in custom and culture that existed. So for instance, in 1 Corinthians he is concerned to ensure that former Gentile idol worshippers (or worshippers of the Greco-Roman gods) can live together whether or not they are able to get beyond scruples about eating meat that has been offered to idols (1 Corinthians 8). In the context of the Roman church this was, perhaps, a matter of ensuring that kosher-food eating Jews and non-kosher, anything-goes eating Romans accepted each other's habits without judging (see Romans 14: 1 – 4). If Luke's account of Paul's actions are to be believed, then Paul was quite prepared to have Timothy circumcised (presumably because his mother was a Jew; see Acts 16: 1 – 3), despite his strong, one might almost say violent, opposition in the letter to the Galatians to circumcision being required of Gentile converts (see Galatians 5:2 - 12). Note, however,

---

[6] M. Cecily Boulding, *The Church Makes the Eucharist and the Eucharist Makes the Church* (St. Mary's College, University of Durham, 1993), an "occasional" printed lecture 6.

that even in the midst of his strong denunciation of circumcision, he is still able to say, "For in Christ Jesus neither circumcision nor uncircumcision counts for anything; the only thing that counts is faith working through love" (Gal 5:6). Later he states that whether one is circumcised or not is immaterial (if we may read it like this) but what is important is that we are part of a new creation (Gal 6:15).

My point here, then, is that being in partnership with one another, and enjoying unity as a church did not entail that cultural and ethnic differences ceased to be factors in the relationship of one church with another, or indeed with one Christian believer and another. Indeed, insofar as there was no conception of a "universal" church but rather local "churches" or groups of believers in different localities throughout the regions where they had been established, it might be argued that the churches Paul and others worked with had both a bi-cultural (Jew and Greek) and a multicultural (Jew and Gentile) character.[7] Distinguishing thus between a bi-cultural and multicultural character to the early Christian churches by using these distinctions may be a bit of a stretch, and should be understood as a kind of "metaphorical" representation of such a mix. However, it is doubtless true that the cultural and ethnic make-up of the early church was very varied, so we should beware of thinking too generally or broadly when speaking of the "Gentile" component.

What drew these diverse and varied Christian groups into a unity, or a "oneness" of being – captured gloriously in the rich imagery of a passage like Ephesians 2:11 – 22, or the "body" image – was not an erasure of cultural and ethnic difference but a

---

[7] The terms here are *Ioudaios* (for Jew); *Hellēn* (for Greek), and *Ethnos* (for Gentile). *Ethnos* could refer to either a "nation" or "people" or to someone of non-Jewish ethnicity, i.e. a Gentile. *Hellēn* and *ethnos* are probably used more or less interchangeably for "non-Jews" or "Gentiles." Sometimes Paul does identify types of non-Jew more specifically, e.g. in Romans 1:14, he writes of Greeks and barbarians; and in Colossians 3:11 (assuming Pauline authorship here) he specifies Greeks, barbarians and Scythians. Why Paul makes these differentiations is a matter for speculation.

reconciliation to God and one another through the death of Christ, and a "sharing" or partnership in Christ's death and life (symbolically captured in partaking of the holy communion together), and a common experience of the Spirit. This is a foundational, theological aspect of *koinōnia*. It is this *koinōnia* that forms our common life. Boulding concludes her lecture by quoting Jean Marie Tillard, and this nicely captures much of what a theological underpinning of partnership, *koinōnia*, is all about. "Salvation is essentially a matter of communion. *Koinonia* is the form which the life of grace takes of its own nature, and because of its ultimate origin in the Trinitarian life of God...*Koinonia*, received as a gift is the very content of the grace of salvation."[8]))

Out of this foundational aspect of *koinōnia*, namely a sharing in the life of Christ, and the gift of the Spirit, a *koinōnia* that establishes us individually as children of God and corporately as the church, flows a number of further aspects of *koinōnia* and implications for how this form of partnership affects our life together.

A Partnership in Self-Giving and Suffering with Christ

One of these aspects of *koinōnia* is what may be called a partnership in self-giving and suffering with Christ. Exploration of this aspect takes us back to Philippians. Here Paul wishes to promote a spirit of humility and common concern among the Philippian believers: he wishes them to look after each other's interests not just their own. He appeals to the fact of their "sharing in the Spirit" (2:1): : their common participation in having the Spirit to enable their compassion and sympathy, to bring them to the mind of Christ. Then he sets before them the example of Christ, in that well-known "hymn" (Phil 2:6–11). Christ did not seek to cling onto his position and status with God, but rather he "emptied himself" and became a slave in human form, ready to die on the cross in fulfilment of obedience to God's plan and purpose.

---

[8] Boulding, *The Church Makes the Eucharist*, 7.

In Philippians 3:10 Paul states how he himself wants to know Christ, the power of his resurrection and partnership (*koinōnian*) in his suffering by becoming like Christ in his death. Whatever Paul means by this – and perhaps in the light of what has gone before, the Christ hymn and his statement that all he might consider worthwhile in worldly terms, he counts as rubbish – he means that he wants to be like Christ in a self-sacrificial death. Paul began his letter by saying how he thanked God for the Philippians who shared in the work of the gospel with him. One of the ways they did this was by sharing in his sufferings. They themselves are going through their own sufferings for Christ which Paul describes as "having the same struggle that you saw I had and now hear I still have" (Phil 1:29, 30). Whatever the nature of the Philippians suffering was, Paul later thanks them for their concern for him. Although he says he has learned to be content in whatever state he finds himself, he goes on, "In any case, it was kind of you to share (*koinōnēsantes*) in my distress" (Phil. 4:14).

During the Waikato war (1863–64), called "the Great War for New Zealand" by Vincent O'Malley, the Kingitanga forces heard that (or believed) the British were running short of supplies. So Wiremu Tamihana sent a gift to the commander of the British forces, Lieutenant-General Duncan Cameron "of goats, turkeys and other provisions." This was done through a loyalist chief, Wiremu Te Wheoro, who carried with him a letter from Tamihana citing Romans 12:20: "if thine enemy hunger, feed him; if he thirst, give him drink."[9]

How might this sharing in the work of the gospel be effected today? A number of Pākehā diocese have "cluster-groups," or such-like groups, that bring clergy in ministry units in a given locality together for discussion and fellowship from time to time. Perhaps

---

[9] Vincent O'Malley, *The Great War for New Zealand: Waikato 1800–2000* (Wellington: Bridget Williams Books, 2016), 237-238. As an aside, I think that great gain and illumination, not to mention encouragement, would be brought to our discussions of partnership, if we were to reflect on historical instances of partnership between early Māori and Pākehā Christians.

where Tikanga Māori rohe are contiguous with these, these could become cross-tikanga "cluster-groups." (As noted below, the Diocese of Waikato and Te Hui Amorangi o te Manawa o te Wheke already have biennial joint ministry schools.)

A Partnership in the Work of Liberation

Paul calls upon the idea of a partnership in the faith when he writes to Philemon regarding Onesimus, whom Paul wishes Philemon to receive back as a fellow believer. At the outset of the letter, Paul prays that the sharing or partnership (*hē koinōnia tēs pisteōs sou*) of Philemon's faith "may become effective when you perceive all the good that we may do for Christ" (Philemon 6).[10] McDermott sees the use of the term *koinōnia* here "as an example of Paul's indicative-imperative usage. The κοινωνία with God and with other Christians in which Philemon participates must show its fruit in activity, for Paul will ask him to receive back Onesimus."[11]

With reference to Philemon 17, where Paul writes, "So if you consider me your partner (*koinōnon*), welcome him as you would welcome me," McDermott writes: "Here the real goal of v. 6's κοινωνία is expressed: if Paul is a κοινωνός to Philemon, Philemon should also receive Onesimus as one."[12]

J.Y. Campbell sees the use of the term "*koinōnos*" in Philemon 17 as an instance of its use in the sense of "business partner" and writes: "In this whole passage, Paul makes half-playful but very effective use of business terms in writing of the spiritual relationship between Philemon and himself." [13] Whether we consider Paul engaging in "half-playful" or somewhat manipulative rhetoric in the letter, there are two features of the letter that speak to our situation as a Three Tikanga church.

---

[10] Some manuscripts read "you" (plural) instead of "we."
[11] McDermott, *Biblical Doctrine*, N.F.19, 228.
[12] McDermott, *Biblical Doctrine*, N.F.19, 228-229.
[13] Campbell, *Three NT Studies*, 10.

First, Paul approaches Philemon as an equal partner in the gospel; and this may account for the manner and tone of his request to Philemon. Furthermore, Paul is surrounded by a team of partners, whom he refers to as sharing with him in some particular circumstance or enterprise. So Archippus, in Philemon's own household, is a "fellow-soldier" (v. 1), while Epaphras is a "fellow-prisoner" (v. 23) and Mark, Aristarchus, Demas and Luke are "fellow-workers" (v. 24). This speaks to the fact that in all Paul's interactions with his churches, or with people within them, he always met them on level ground, as it were. They were his equals.

One of the advantages, I believe, of our Three Tikanga setup is that our *koinōnia*, our partnership in the gospel, and in the work of mission and ministry is worked out within the conditions of equity and of meeting each other as, at least potentially, on equal terms. The structures of coloniser and colonised, of "Settler" church and "Te Hahi Mihinare" church in a relationship of inequality have been removed. Now, the challenges of working together in partnership take place between people of equal standing structurally, and politically, whatever barriers of material wealth and opportunity may still hamper a given Tikanga.

A PARTNERSHIP OF MUTUAL SHARING OF RESOURCES IN THE SERVICE OF THE GOSPEL

One of the most fruitful partnerships in the New Testament to consider in the context of our reflections on the bi-cultural and three Tikanga nature of our church is the partnership that Paul had with the church in Philippi. In his very comprehensive study of *Paul's Koinonia with the Philippians*, Julien Ogereau shows, from a survey of documentary evidence in inscriptions and papyri, the economic connotations that the *koinōn* word-group had in Paul's Greco-Roman context. Given that this language was found in documentary evidence drawn from everyday life, and the high concentration of financial and economic terms found in Phil 4:10 – 20, Ogereau argues that *koinōnia* should be understood in economic terms in Philippians 1:5 – 7 and

4:10 – 20.[14] More specifically, building on the proposals of J.P. Sampley (and a French scholar Jean Fleury), Ogereau maintains that Paul's relationship with the Philippians was in the nature of a *societas*, a Roman term for various kinds of partnership, for which the Greek term *koinōnia* was used in Greek documents.[15]

A *societas* was a "legal entity" that could exist in various forms.[16] The type of *societas* (*koinōnia*) that Paul established with the Philippians approximated, according to Ogereau, to a *societas unius rei*, which was a partnership that was formed towards the goal of achieving a profitable, or non-profitable, objective or course of action. Indeed, such a partnership might have as its objective a non-commercial, non-profitable (in terms of financial profits, that is) end. In the case of Paul's partnership with the Philippians, it was a *koinōnia* (*societas*) formed for the preaching and propagation of the gospel. It was what Ogereau terms a *societas evangelii*;[17] or as Paul puts it himself, a *koinōnia eis to euangelion* (Phil. 1:5).

A *societas* was established in informal ways, by consensus rather than by legal agreements, and depending upon the mutual

---

[14] The terms in Phil. 4:10 – 20 are "gift" (NRSV; Greek: doma; perhaps "contribution" in view of Ogereau's overall argument?), "the matter of giving and receiving" (Greek: *ho logos doseōs kai lēmpseus*; more literally, "the account of payments and receipts"), "profit" (*ho karpos*), "received in full" (*apechō*) and "paid in full" (*plēroō*). See Ogereau, *Paul's Koinonia*, 377, Chapter 3, 270–289.

[15] See Ogereau, *Paul's Koinonia*, 377, 216–219. On the form of the *societas* with the Philippians generally, see chapter eight. Cf. J. Paul Sampley, *Pauline Partnership in Christ: Christian Community and Commitment in Light of Roman Law* (Philadelphia Fortress Press, 1980). Ogereau seeks to put Sampley's argument on a firmer footing by providing more documentary "hard evidence" of *koinōnia's* denotation of *societa* (216). Fleury's article (which I have not consulted) is "Une société de fait dans l'église apostolique (Phil. 4:10 à 22)." In *Mélanges Philippe Meylan*. Vol. 2 (Lausanne: Université de Lausanne, 1963), 41–59.

[16] I call it a "legal entity" as it was recognised in Roman law, though "legally recognised entity" might be a better description, for, as my description above indicates, a *societas* could be formed in fairly informal ways, if judged by modern legal standards and expectations.

[17] Ogereau, *Paul's Koinonia*, 377, 338.

trust and faithfulness of the partners. No more was needed than for partners to agree together to work towards a common end or join in a common enterprise. No formal contract, nothing in writing, no witnesses were required; and the consenting parties did not need even to be physically present as long as they indicated their willingness to join in partnership somehow. As Ogereau puts it: "...what distinguishes *societas* from modern forms of partnership the most, is that it could be established for the pursuit of non-capitalistic aims and lacked entirely contractual formalism."[18] A *societas* was terminated, moreover, when one party requested or initiated the termination; though it would also be ended with the death of a partner or through a breach of trust.[19] "[T]he *societas* lasted as long as the partners remained of the same mind ...true to their original agreement."[20]

The partners in a *societas* need not all contribute the same kind of thing to the partnership. For instance, one party in the partnership might provide the finances, the other might give time and skills, or provide the labour. In the case of Paul's *koinōnia* with the Philippians, the Philippians provided the finances, while Paul provided his energy and effort, skills and time in the preaching of the gospel, to the *societas evangelii* (so Ogereau). I would argue that the Philippians may well have contributed some personnel as well. One would assume that Ephaphroditus, "my brother and co-worker and fellow-soldier, your messenger (*apostolos*) and minister to my need" (Phil. 2:25) – and the one by whom the Philippians monetary contribution came to Paul (Phil 4:18) – was one such. While he was in Philippi, Euodia and Syntyche also worked with Paul in the cause of the

---

[18] Ogereau, *Paul's Koinonia*, 377, 333.
[19] The *societas* rested upon the legal and moral obligations incumbent upon the partners. Lawyers could, it seems, be called in to settle disputes, but the *societas* fundamentally depended upon the mutual trust and consensual agreement of the parties (and a *societas* could well have many members, or parties to it); see Ogereau, *Paul's Koinonia*, 377, 332-336.
[20] Ogereau, *Paul's Koinonia*, 377, 334.

gospel.[21]Ogereau argues that Paul followed his usual custom while in Philippi which was to refuse the support of the local church, but willingly entered into a partnership with them for the support of his evangelistic activities elsewhere, for example in Thessalonica (Phil. 4:16).[22] Paul's *koinōnia* (viz. *societas*) – partnership/"sharing in the gospel" (1:5) with the Philippians thus took on quite a concrete, and one might also say, "business-like," character. It demonstrates that *koinōnia* was understood to operate not merely at a "theological" level of shared faith and salvation in Christ, nor at a "communal" level of "fellowship" in common belief and religious practices (e.g., sharing in Holy Communion together), but also in practical, economic terms of sharing monetary resources and one's physical labour.

What I find helpful in the notion of *koinōnia* (*societas*) as a formal and "legal" entity (though by our modern standards we might be inclined to think of it as "informal" and "quasi-legal") is that it highlights the fact that our partnership need not be understood purely in "theological" terms, or even as a kind of "spiritual fellowship" based on a common faith in Christ, but that it also takes shape within the structures of formal agreements and "contractual/consensual" parameters, and flows out into practical and economic outcomes such as sharing of resources, finances and expertise. While we cannot correlate our three Tikanga church entirely with a first-century *koinōnia* partnership, we also find ourselves within a legal and formal relationship established by our 1992 Constitution, a constitution which itself looks to a treaty, the

---

[21] Clement and "my loyal companion" (who may have been the returned Ephaphroditus, unless *Syzygus* should be taken as a proper name) and other "coworkers" are also mentioned but it is not clear whether they were members of the Philippian church or came from outside. (See Phil. 4:3; also Phil 2:25 which mentions the return of Ephaphroditus, who may, indeed, have come back to the Philippian congregation bearing Paul's letter, and would, therefore, have been on hand to help mediate between Euodia and Syntyche).

[22] One purpose of Ogereau's study is to examine how Paul funded his mission, and why he accepted finances from Philippi, when he seems to have wanted to assert his financial independence from other churches (e.g. the Corinthian church).

Treaty of Waitangi which, while not entirely legally entrenched, yet witnesses and calls us to a consensual partnership. In some ways, given that the Constitution also points us to our scriptures and formularies in its fundamental provisions, we have all the theological resources we need.

What now is needed is to continue to work out (continue because we don't come to this without prior work having already been done) how we translate that partnership into the concrete realities of our church's life in all its aspects and in view of all its resources – economic, physical, personnel, and structural. As an example of one arena where this has already begun, I refer to the Report of the Commission on Resource Sharing to the Standing Committee of the General Synod/te Hīnota Whānui – November 2010.[23] There we read that, among other things, the Diocese of Waikato and Te Hui Amorangi o Te Manawa o Te Wheke hold a joint ministry conference every second year; the Diocese of Auckland and Te Tai Tokerau share "some buildings and other resources at ministry level" and there is some income sharing; and the Diocese of Christchurch transferred some property, and some entities and estates handed over various amounts of money to Te Wai Pounamu.[24] The question is, how are some of the other perceived needs for resource sharing working out? What of the other observations made or recommendations provided: how have they progressed? What further has been implemented since the Report was published?

A PARTNERSHIP IN FINANCIAL AID

There is one further use of the term *koinōnia* by Paul which we should touch on briefly. It is used in a sense that, as Ralph P. Martin states, moves the meaning from "participation in" into the sphere of

---

[23] Proceedings of the *Sixtieth General Synod/Te Hīnota Whānui* (Nadi, Fiji: The Anglican Church in Aotearoa, New Zealand and Polynesia, 2012), B-163 – B170.
[24] *Proceedings*, B-165, 166.

"sharing with."²⁵ This gives rise to the idea of "generosity" and is used concretely in reference to the collection taken up among Paul's Gentile churches for the relief of poor Jewish fellow-Christians back in Jerusalem(see 2 Cor 8:4; 9:13 and Rom. 15:26, where Martin maintains *koinōnia* specifically means "collection"). It is interesting that Paul in Romans 15:27, the very next verse after that in which he speaks of the Macedonian Christians' eagerness to contribute to the needs of the Jerusalem saints who are poor, provides a theological rationale by saying that, if the Gentile Christians have shared (*ekoinōnēsan*) in the spiritual benefits of the gospel delivered by Jewish Christians, they are obligated to provide material help.

Paul put a lot of effort into the collection for the poor saints of Jerusalem (see Rom. 15:25 – 31; 1 Corinthians 16:1 – 4; 2 Corinthians 8, 9 – where he especially holds up the Macedonian Christians as exemplars [8:1 – 5]; cf. Gal.2:10 which provides some rationale for Paul's energetic pursuit of this project).²⁶ Paul's efforts in this regard arose not simply out of a concern for fellow-Jews in need, but also because he was concerned to cement relations between Jewish and Gentile Christians, and saw this collection as a way of Gentiles expressing Christian solidarity with Jewish Christians. George Panikulam sees the collection as a "direct expression of Christian fellowship" and states that *koinōnia* in this context is "the community's response to the Gospel."²⁷ An important feature of the collection in Paul's mind was that it should promote "socio-economic

---

[25] Ralph P. Martin, *The Family and the Fellowship: New Testament Images of the Church* (Exeter Paternoster Press, 1997), 42.
[26] If extending "the right hand of fellowship" (Gal 2:9) amounted to some sort of formal agreement (a *societas*, even?), then Paul's "remembering the poor" would be an obligation upon him, as well as something he was eager to do.
[27] George Panikulam, *Koinonia in the New Testament a Dynamic Expression of Christian Life* (Rome: Biblical Institute Press, 1979), Analecta Biblica 85, 49-50, 56.

equality" or "equity" between the Gentile and Jewish Christians (2 Cor 8:13, 14: "fair balance" [NRSV];[28] Greek: *isotēs*).[29]

The reference to the *koinōnia* of the early church in Acts 2:42 whose practical effects are spelt out in v. 44, is relevant here. This way of life, where the needs of all are met out of the common sharing of resources, is also described in Acts 4:32 – 37, where private ownership of possessions gave way to holding "everything in common" (*apanta koina*). Even if this is a somewhat idealised picture drawn by Luke (or might we say an "aspirational" description?), it points to a sense that Christian belonging must express itself in concrete acts of mutual care and provision for needs.[30]

CONCLUSION: A COMMONWEALTH OF *KOINŌNIA*

Our current Colloquium, or Hui, has been called to enable us to reflect on the nature of partnership. I trust that what has been developed above, looking at the *koinon* word-group, and especially *koinōnia* itself, has begun to point the way to some biblical principles for a theological foundation for our considerations of bicultural and three Tikanga partnership.

By way of conclusion, let me draw together a few threads. Our *koinōnia* as Christians is derived from, and based upon, our initial *koinōnia* with Christ, through the Holy Spirit, on the basis of Christ's death and resurrection. We share the life of Christ, and are drawn together as members of his Body, his *ekklēsia* (church). Our

---

[28] If extending "the right hand of fellowship" (Gal 2:9) amounted to some sort of formal agreement (a *societas*, even?), then Paul's "remembering the poor" would be an obligation upon him, as well as something he was eager to do.

[29] Julien M. Ogereau, "The Jerusalem Collection as Κοινωνία : Paul's Global Politics of Socio-Economic Equality and Solidarity," *New Testament Studies* 58 (2012): 373; Also John Koenig, *New Testament Hospitality: Partnership with Strangers as Promise and Mission* (Philadelphia: Fortress Press, 1985), 76-77.

[30] Some have surmised that perhaps this mode of operating by the early church in Jerusalem gave rise to their subsequent need for aid from elsewhere! Be that as it may, the early church – both Jewish and Gentile – understood that *koinōnia* was to be expressed in very concrete, practical terms.

participation together in the Eucharist, sharing the body and blood of our Lord, is a visible and tangible reminder of our *koinōnia*, both with the triune God and with each other. The use of *koinōnia* language in 1 John, which I have not explored here, is in a very real sense an encapsulation of this spiritual, what we might also call "salvational", *koinōnia* (see 1 John 1:1–7; especially for *koinōnia*, verses 3,6,7).[31] We are called to partnership as citizens in a new "commonwealth" (*to politeuma*; Phil. 3:20).

But belonging to this new "commonwealth" does not erase our ethnic, cultural differences; nor does it require a necessary removal of cultural mores (except where these are injurious to human well-being, and contrary to the values of the new commonwealth). Rather we are called to a *koinōnia* that encompasses, as well as moves across tikanga boundaries, and, if anything, should strengthen our respect for, and valuing of, different ways of being and living. This "commonwealth" gathers up all that is best from our separate "wealths," as it were: and creates from these a partnership for the flourishing and wellbeing of all.

Our *koinōnia* as brothers and sisters in Christ is not only to be understood in spiritual and "theological" terms, but it has to be worked out concretely and practically. *Koinōnia* is expressed as the mutual sharing of resources, whether these be monetary, material (in various ways: buildings, educational materials, and so forth), personnel, and even institutional. And where the need expresses itself, the *koinōnia* may well take the form of aid: financial or other

---

[31] On *koinōnia* in the Johannine epistles, see John Reumann, "Koinonia in Scripture: Survey of Biblical Texts," in *On the Way to Fuller Koinonia: Official Report of the Fifth World Conference on Faith and Order [Santiago De Compostela]*, eds., Thomas F. Best and Günther Gassmann (Geneva: WCC Publications, 1993), 54–55; Panikulam, *Koinonia* 130–140.
Regarding koinōnia in verse 3: "The word indicates the setting aside of private interest and desires and the joining w. another or others for common purposes." Fritz Rienecker and Cleon L. Rogers, *A Linguistic Key to the Greek New Testament* (Grand Rapids, Michigan: Zondervan Publishing House, 1976), 785.

resources. But even in these situations, *koinōnia* always carries with it the sense of reciprocity.

Koinōnia, this broad concept of sharing, partnership, joining together and being joined together, "fellowship" even, can I believe provide us with a rich, and deep mine of biblical reflection and guidance, to help us develop our own partnerships within our three Tikanga church.

6

Partnership as Validating Voices: Reading Relational Faithfulness in Matthew's Judgment Parables[1]

KAREN DAVINIA TAYLOR

---

[1] A collection of sayings and parables preparing the final judgment, NRSV titles: 'The Necessity for Watchfulness,' 'The Faithful or the Unfaithful Slave,' 'The Parable of the Ten Bridesmaids,' 'The Parable of the Talents' and 'The Judgment of the Nations.

Introduction

CONVERSATION DURING THE 2017 Three Tikanga colloquium observed a need to strengthen interaction and build partnership across Tikanga at the parish level.[2] This chapter provides a practical theology contribution to this need to strengthen relationships across tikanga. It introduces an appreciative inquiry methodology designed for integration into the ongoing life of congregations and communities, a methodology that would encourage partnership in the Three Tikanga church among individuals and communities. The methodology, named WisdomCafé, aims to validate voices among and between multi-ethnic congregations. Begun as a doctoral project with roots in the islands of Melanesia, the Pacific and Aotearoa NZ, WisdomCafé is a methodological process developed to strengthen relationships and partnerships across ethnic and generational boundaries in conversation with experience and scripture. It is a form of relational discipleship that offers insight from the margins of cultures into the challenge of welcoming minority voices to speak and provoking the majority culture to listen.

I introduce the project and my use of the terms - culture, high- and low- context communication styles, judgment and discernment. I then illustrate the methodology in conversation with Matthew 24:36-41 and a worked example that connects with the quest for partnership within and beyond the borders of a multi-ethnic congregation. At the same time, I argue for a reading of the judgment parables through a hermeneutic of relational accountability. This hermeneutic may be more familiar to some cultures than to others.

Leadership in our Province call for creativity and focus in a rapidly changing world, and in how we grow one another up into

---

[2] D. Moffat, "Ezra and Separate Development," in *Te Awa Rerenga Maha: Braided River*, ed. D. Moffat, Three Tikanga Church Colloquium (Auckland: Anglican Church in Aotearoa, New Zealand and Polynesia, 2018), 69.

maturity, into Christ and so into flourishing communities.³ I saw this gap as not the *what* so much as the *how*. It is what I think Bishop Victoria Matthews, in her charge to the Christchurch Synod in 2017, described as, not so much, "more programmes and strategies," as valuable as they are, but reaching beyond to a culture shift in congregations.⁴ This turn to being is, at its core, a turn to the other, to relationship, evidenced more in our nation's minority cultures than its Pākehā majority.⁵ One example of this is Frank Smith's discussion of four Samoan cultural concepts to illustrate "a relational way of being premised on a theology that God is a relational God."⁶ Smith invites a Three Tikanga church to explore theologies that acknowledge relational interconnectedness with God, others, and creation, so that we strengthen relations across these three culturally based structures of the Anglican Church in our Province.

WisdomCafé is one response to the observed need for a shift towards the relational discipleship essential to enhancing partnership across Tikanga at the parish level. It incorporates "World Café" into scriptural concepts of gratitude,⁷ story, reflection, and

---

³ "A Voyage of Faith – the Charge," Anglican Taonga, The Anglican Church in Aotearoa, NZ and Polynesia/Te Haahi Mihanare ki Niu Tireni, ki Nga Moutere o Te Moana Nui a Kiwa, 2012, http://www.anglicantaonga.org.nz/news/general_synod/voyager "A Summary of Te Runanganui's Three-Day Conference in Wellington," Anglican Taonga, 2015, both accessed 28 July, 2018.
http://www.anglicantaonga.org.nz/features/extra/to_achieve_full_maturity.
⁴ "Synod Charge, Christchurch, NZ," Anglican Taonga, 2017, accessed 28 July, 2018, http://www.anglicantaonga.org.nz/features/extra/synod2017.
⁵ For discussion on definitions of Tikanga Pākehā as anyone not Māori or as only the NZ European majority see Fletcher, "Finding Identity," 188 – 201, and specifically 198-199.
⁶ F. Smith, "Relational Hermeneutics in the Three Tikanga Context as the Anglican Church in Aotearoa, New Zealand and Polynesia," in *Te Awa Rerenga Maha: Braided River*, ed. D. Moffat, Three Tikanga Church Colloquium (Auckland: Anglican Church in Aotearoa, New Zealand and Polynesia, 2018).
⁷ World Café sits within Appreciative Inquiry, both are strengths-based methodologies that support communities in collaborative change. See Juanita Brown and David Isaacs, *The World Café: Shaping Our Futures through*

response, to indirectly build bridges across difference towards practices of partnership. In its original context, the project explored how scriptural themes and personal stories might validate voice among a multi-ethnic congregation within Tikanga Pākehā, Auckland Diocese in 2017. WisdomCafé was also offered in the three Tikanga environment of theological training. Essentially, WisdomCafé involves personal stories provoked by scriptural themes while enjoying food together.

In conversation with Matthew's Judgment Parables, scholars and lived experience, I identified a collection of relational themes:

Matthew 24:36-25:46	WisdomCafé: Theme
As in the days of Noah	Acknowledging relationships
Householder and the Thief	Acknowledging acceptance
Faithful or Unfaithful Slave	Acknowledging accountability
Ten Bridesmaids	Acknowledging responsibility
Talents	Acknowledging trust
Judgment of the Nations (Sheep & Goats)	Acknowledging our neighbour

These themes framed the development of questions following World Café's facilitative style. These themed questions aim to generate community stories (not bible studies) of faithfulness from a position of gratitude.

WisdomCafé uses simple yet transformational practices of storytelling to encourage a community to reflect on ordinary activities in the light of those scriptural themes. In their stories, they move from daily activities to reflection and back to daily activities. Stories of ordinary activities became sacred spaces, as God's presence was recognised in those historic situations, invoked in re-telling and gratitude. To illustrate, I summarise an interpretation of Matthew 24:36-41, the theme identified alongside a worked example

---

Conversations That Matter (San Francisco, CA: Berrett-Koehler Publishers, 2005); and Mark Lau Branson, *Memories, Hopes, and Conversations: Appreciative Inquiry and Congregational Change* (Lanham: Alban Institute, 2016).

of questions and group conversations, beginning by clarifying my use of 'culture' and the related direct and indirect communication styles.

CULTURE AND COMMUNICATION

Culture overlaps with ethnicity and is learned in our households of origin. Health educator, Dianne Wepa defines culture as "our way of living," influenced by our family heritage, central to how we perceive and interpret those around us, always shifting, and shaped by other cultures. She writes:

> It's our taken-for-grantedness that determines and defines our culture. The way we brush our teeth, the way we bury people, the way we express ourselves through our art, religion, eating habits, rituals, humour, science, law, and sport; the way we celebrate occasions (from 21sts, to weddings, to birthdays) is our culture. All these actions we carry out consciously and unconsciously.[8]

Culture influences how we see and act, think and speak, read scripture and tell stories, what we value and what blinds us. Our culture is evident in how we practice hospitality, the preparation, style and quantity of food selected, the guests present and the ways we welcome. We learn our culture from the inside, taking what and how we 'do life' as normal, the way it is done as well as who we are.

"Culture is like gravity: you do not experience it until you jump six feet into the air."[9] Central to critical reflection on one's own cultures are the opportunities to gain distance offered by time immersed in cultures distinct from our own, whether by travelling across oceans or being welcomed into homes in neighbouring

---

[8] D. Wepa, "Chapter 5: Cultural and Ethnicity," in *Cultural Safety in Aotearoa New Zealand*, ed. D. Wepa (Melbourne, VIC, Australia: Cambridge University Press, 2015), 66.
[9] Alfons Trompenaars, *Riding the Waves of Culture: Understanding Cultural Diversity in Business*, 2nd ed.. ed. (London: Nicholas Brealey Pub. , c2000, c1993), 4.

tikanga. By sitting at table with another culture we may begin a journey of self-examination and critique of our own cultural values, perspectives and interpretation of the bible. Such self-critique is necessary for each tikanga if we are to avoid ethnocentrism. [10] Cultural ethicist, Bernard Adeney argues that a first step in overcoming ethnocentrism is the recognition that my own

> values are not necessarily the same as God's. All
> Christians hold many values derived from their culture.
> A second step is to understand that our own
> interpretation of Scripture comes from a particular
> cultural context. A third step is to see that God's values
> may be "enfleshed" differently in another culture from
> how they are in my own.[11]

Adeney's words remind us that we each approach scripture with lenses shaped by our culture and life experiences, and that what we see there is also provoked by encounter with the Holy Spirit, one another and ourselves.

Cultures shape our communication styles. Jesus' parables reflect their roots in oral and high-context traditions making high- and low- context cultural communication styles relevant to this discussion (Malina, 2001, pp. 2-5). In high-context cultures, while speech and gifted orators are valued, context and action speak more loudly. Dame Joan Metge, in her work on whakamā, illustrates a high-context culture when she describes how te reo Māori had no phrase equivalent to the English language's, "I'm sorry," because members showed repentance by their actions. [12] In contrast, low-context cultures depend more on spoken words for meaning; verbal

---

[10] Moffat, "Ezra," 70-71.
[11] Bernard T. Adeney, *Strange Virtues: Ethics in a Multicultural World* (Downers Grove, Ill.: InterVarsity Press, 1995), 23.
http://catalog.hathitrust.org/api/volumes/oclc/32132816.html.
[12] Joan Metge, *In and out of Touch: Whakamaa in Cross Cultural Context* (Wellington, N.Z.: Victoria University Press, 1986), 97-98.

articulation of a phrase like "I'm sorry" risks being disconnected from attitudes and actions of repentance. It also risks low-context cultures like that of Pākehā missing culturally contextual cues and misinterpreting meaning. In reverse, high-context cultures may read meaning not intended by Pākehā communications. Subsequent misunderstandings only multiply where a culture holds other cultures in contempt.

This contextual aspect of cultural communications is significant in contemporary communication between the Three Tikanga as well as when reading scripture. In considering the high-context cultures of scripture, acknowledging both context and relationship is significant to understanding relational accountability in the judgment parables.[13]

JUDGMENT AS DISCERNMENT

The *New Dictionary of Biblical Theology* notes that in the OT, judgment refers to "setting things to rights."[14] Matthew's gospel is noted for its Jewishness, evident in how it takes ethical daily living for granted, articulates a practical wisdom with integrity of heart and action, and recognises faithful living by its fruit - all of which inherently form part of Matthew's understanding of judgment. I interpret judgment not with its popular meaning of condemnation, but its alternative meaning as a process or practice of discernment required when holding another to account for their responsibility. Reading judgment as accountability I identify criteria for faithfulness as a lived acknowledgement of relational responsibilities.[15] The judgment parables describe household and community relationships

---

[13] Bruce J. Malina, *The Social Gospel of Jesus: The Kingdom of God in Mediterranean Perspective* (Minneapolis, Minn.: Fortress Press, 2001), 2-5.
[14] T. D. Alexander and B. S. Rosner, *New Dictionary of Biblical Theology* (La Vergne, U.S.A.: IVP, 2020).
http://ebookcentral.proquest.com/lib/stjohns/detail.action?docID=6201852.
[15] Stephen Travis, *Christ and the Judgement of God: The Limits of Divine Retribution in New Testament Thought* (Milton Keynes, U.K.: Paternoster Hendrickson Publishers, 2009), 52.

where one party is responsible to another, and thus they illustrate our responsibility to God and others. In several of these parables, Jesus' stories describe masters calling slaves to account with some commended as good and faithful servants. It follows that these parables illustrate aspects of faithfulness for which God will hold humanity to account in the Final Judgment.

Like David Ford's "wisdom interpretation of scripture," my reading of scripture in conversation with cultures and daily life includes a *"primary desire ... for the wisdom of God in life now."*[16] While my doctoral thesis rereads each of the judgment parables in their context of personal, household and community accountability, this chapter considers the introduction to Matthew's judgment parables (Matt 24:36-41) and its worked example from WisdomCafé. I now briefly explore Matthew 24:36-41, arguing that its succinct yet vivid word pictures illustrate that acknowledgement of relationship with our Creator and one another are foundational criteria for faithfulness.

MATTHEW 24:36-41

> [36]'But about that day and hour no one knows, neither the angels of heaven, nor the Son, but only the Father. [37]For as the days of Noah were, so will be the coming of the Son of Man. [38]For as in those days before the flood they were eating and drinking, marrying and giving in marriage, until the day Noah entered the ark, [39]and they knew nothing until the flood came and swept them all away, so too will be the coming of the Son of Man. [40]Then two will be in the field; one will be taken and one will be left. [41]Two women will be grinding meal together; one will be taken and one will be left.

---

[16] David Ford, *Christian Wisdom: Desiring God and Learning in Love* (Cambridge; New York: Cambridge University Press, 2007), 52.

Jesus responds to the disciples' request for "signs" of his appearing by acknowledging that the timing is known only to the Father (v. 36) and that there will be no signs announcing his return. Jesus cannot give the disciples the certainty they request regarding timing. Instead, he indicates that confidence and hope are based in how we live in relation to God and others in this life. His stories build on the disciples' existing faith in the God he enfleshes to illustrate circles of responsibility; faithfulness is a willingness to meet those responsibilities and give account with ensuing inclusion or exclusion – household, community and coming kingdom of God.

Matthew introduces a theme of being prepared by contrasting the faithful and unfaithful of two generations, Noah's (vv. 37-39) and the last generation (vv. 40-41). For most commentators, the description of Noah's generation in verses 37–39 refers to banal daily life, although they wonder at a seeming arbitrariness regarding who is taken and who remains (vv. 40-41). France concludes: "the example of Noah suggests that it is not purely arbitrary, and the rest of the discourse will explore the basis of the division between the saved and the lost."[17]

I agree that the subsequent stories unpack the foundations of faithfulness, but I suggest that by choosing a low-context interpretation of a high-context text we risk losing alternative interpretations. For the gospel's initial high-context audiences the verses emphasis on the ordinariness of daily life echoes Jewish celebration of the sacred in the ordinary. This reflects cultural values and faith practices rooted in a grateful acknowledgement to the Creator for the gift of life and relationship; an acknowledgement that invokes a joyful response of lived obedience.[18] Writing for *My Jewish Learning* website, Abusch-Magder considers how

---

[17] R. T. France, *The Gospel of Matthew* (Grand Rapids, Mich.: William B. Eerdmans, 2007), 939, 941.
[18] Rabbi Ruth Abusch-Magder connects weekly with Jews worldwide over challah baking and "is passionate about helping Jews find ways to connect their personal

the concept of gratitude is fundamental to Jewish life and practice. The miracle of opening the eyes deserves a prayer of thanksgiving, as does our ability to put our feet on the floor and going to the bathroom. Following the structures of our liturgy, much of life becomes worthy of gratitude. Gratitude is powerful stuff.[19]

Alongside these contemporary reflections, Jon Douglas Levenson considers historical connections of God's love, human gratitude and faithfulness in Judaism, practices that open the self to wonder in the daily activities of life.[20]

In the words, "they were eating and drinking, marrying and giving in marriage" (v. 38), Jesus succinctly highlights daily community life, people doing what they are created to do. When Jeremiah comforts Hebrew exiles with similar imagery we see the fruit of this awareness of the sacredness of daily life. The prophet encourages the exiles to carry out these daily household practices with generosity and faithfulness. He reassures them that this will result in an abundance and flourishing that blesses those it touches, the exiled community as well as their oppressors (Jer 29:1-9).

For a devout first-century Jewish audience, familiar with their Scriptures, Jesus' images of daily life – the acts of putting bread on the table - resonate with the Psalmist's gratitude for life sourced in God. If this context of gratitude to God for daily life introduces the judgment parables, then it offers a foundational criterion for faithfulness that can also be described as the practice of the presence of God in daily life.

---

stories and experiences to that of the Jewish collective through writing and ritual." "Rabbis without Borders," n.d., accessed 19 June, 2021, https://rabbiswithoutborders.org/ruth-abusch-magder/.
[19] Abusch-Magder, "Rabbis without Borders," para. 3.
[20] Jon Douglas Levenson, *The Love of God, Divine Gift, Human Gratitude, and Mutual Faithfulness in Judaism* (Princeton: Princeton University Press, 2016).

In Matthew 24, Jesus' concise word pictures bring to mind two judgment contexts that are familiar to those early high-context audiences (24:38-41), one past and the other still to come. Noah's acknowledgement of God is evident in his daily actions and obedient relationship with his Creator. He exemplifies the faithful and is saved from the flood's destruction. Jesus does not highlight, not pious versus debauched activities but the ordinary shared daily life for Noah and his neighbours. What differentiates these groups is the recognition that life is a gift from a Creator who requires them to live, neither in dull obedience nor flaunted carelessness, but grateful joy. This nonverbal acknowledgement of accountability is evident in Noah's actions, it is a lived acknowledgement.

Verse 39 tells the judgment on Noah's neighbours as they are swept away. In verses 40-41, two are working in the field and two milling grain; people working together to feed their households, living the life they have been given, where "one will be taken, and one will be left." I suggest that through these word pictures, Jesus recognises that a lived acknowledgement expressed in daily life depicts faithfulness.

When Jesus says of Noah's neighbours that they "knew nothing" (v. 39), Luz reads this as a lack of awareness, a surprise at an unexpected judgment; and further that Christ's return is a "catastrophe" for the final generation as it catches them unaware.[21] Yet for Noah's generation, the surprise is due more to refusal to pay attention to the warnings given. Illustrating a high-context culture, Genesis tells of Noah's obedience in building the ark and leaves readers to fill in details, as for example, the curiosity, questions and visible warning that months of building a large ark offered to Noah's neighbours. Despite these warnings, Noah's generation did not repent, but chose to know nothing (Genesis chapters 6-8; Matt 24:39; Heb 11:7). Earlier in Matthew, Jesus has talked about a kind of

---

[21] Ulrich Luz and Helmut Koester, *Matthew 21-28*, Hermeneia - a Critical and Historical Commentary on the Bible, (Philadelphia, Pa.: Fortress, 2005), 211-215.

ignorance in connection with the crowds' unwillingness to acknowledge God's call to repentance, "seeing they do not perceive, and hearing they do not listen, nor do they understand" (Matt 13:13; cf. Jer 5:21). It is possible that Jesus refers to a generation who saw the warning signs but chose to look without seeing, to know "nothing," much as Noah's generation looked without seeing and "knew nothing." They watched the ark being built yet ignored its warning. Their denial of knowledge equates with a denial of the responsibility essential to human relationship and community. John Inge observes that "living is a communal act, whether or not its communality is acknowledged."[22]

Matthew's Jesus is known for his prophetic calls to both leadership and people, reminding them that faithful practices must be integrated with ethical action. Unlike Luke, Matthew does not include the parable of Good Samaritan to do this. Yet in the judgment parables, Jesus tells a collection of stories where how well we love God and neighbour is demonstrated in how well we fulfil our daily responsibilities. These stories paint pictures that emphasise the two most important commandments: love God and love your neighbour as yourself. This theme is obvious in the culminating parable of The Last Judgment with its clear example of love of Christ in our neighbour. Its position at the end of Matthew's final discourse identifies it as a hermeneutical key. It is possible to recognise this same theme of lived acknowledgement in Jesus' introduction to the Judgment Parables. Together, the phrases "as in days of Noah" (v. 37) and "eating and drinking, marrying and giving in marriage" (v. 38), refer to the presence or absence of this lived acknowledgement in both Noah's generation and Jesus' audience (vv. 37, 40-41). Ritual practices of faith are part of cultural taken-for-grantedness for Jesus' first audiences. For them, as for us, it "might well be that deep down we are still substituting a kind of magic for faith …. We cajole God to

---

[22] John Inge, *A Christian Theology of Place* (Aldershot, England: Ashgate, 2003), 131.

save us from ourselves and call it devotion."[23] These parables begin by declaring that how God is acknowledged in the ordinary activities of daily lives, beyond ritual practices, is fundamental to faithfulness.

Having reflected on Matthew's text, the next step in the WisdomCafé methodology is to identify themes that will frame the questions for the community conversations. Reading judgment as accountability in these parables, I identified a theme of a givenness in mutual responsibilities across relationship, one that is essential to generating life-giving partnership. In contrast to entitlement, its concise word pictures illustrate criteria where daily life is lived with grateful acknowledgement of our relation to God and others. This theme of *Acknowledgement* is carried forward into WisdomCafé#1.

Adeney's prompts towards overcoming ethnocentrism, mentioned earlier, are timely here. As a Pākehā, I recognise that my culture could learn much from the relational values of the minority cultures around it, especially in reading these parables. I, like many Pākehā, have still to recognise and value the depth of acknowledgements of relationship and hospitality that are exemplified in, for example, the greeting protocols of Māori or the Oceanic willingness to listen to story that is essential to *talanoa*. These sorts of failures to see and value another's culture impact decision-making, communication and partnership. I will shortly outline a worked example from WisdomCafé#1, but first I trace the development of WisdomCafé's facilitative methodology through its roots in Matthew's parables and appreciative inquiry.

WisdomCafé Methodology

In line with World Café protocols, I chose a name related to Matthew's judgment parables with its themes that illustrate relational faithfulness learned and practiced as practical wisdom.[24]

---

[23] Joan Chittister and Rowan Williams, *Uncommon Gratitude: Alleluia for All That Is* (Collegeville, Minn.: Liturgical Press, 2010), 8.\
[24] Brown and Isaacs, *The World Café*.

Christ's use of stories and my desire to cultivate the stories of each community led my methodology search to World Café, a facilitative method within appreciative inquiry (AI) that incorporates hospitality.[25] AI in practical theology emphasises a gratitude stance and strengths-based questions.[26] World Café retains the narrative and transformative components of AI, the appreciative position, collaboration and participation, but turns aside from AI's focus on systems, paying more attention to relations and conversations about things that matter.[27] Wisdom Café's prioritising of personal story emphasises relationship further to shift from direct goals of organisational or community change to indirect and organic growth. Its methodology combines the welcome of both story and hospitality and is conducive to the goal of cultivating relational strength among multi-ethnic communities.

Like storytelling, hospitality is both widely valued and understood differently across cultures. For example, when asked about welcome in hospitality settings, Aotearoa NZ born Māori, Samoan and Chinese congregation members equated welcome with food and relationship, describing food as synonymous with welcome, family (relationship) and honour.[28] When Pākehā described that they too value hospitality, their definitions of welcome, family and hospitality were less encompassing. WisdomCafé uses stories of daily life to visit across cultural divides. Such stories offer insights into one another's values without identity lost to or consumed by the majority culture.[29] To share stories and reflect theologically on faith and lives in multi-ethnic communities involves making space for difference. It

---

[25] Brown and Isaacs, *The World Café*.
[26] Branson, *Memories, Hopes, and Conversations*.
[27] Brown and Isaacs, *The World Café*. Jeanie Cockell and Joan McArthur-Blair, *Appreciative Inquiry in Higher Education: A Transformative Force* (San Francisco: Jossey-Bass, 2012), 14.
[28] K. D. Taylor, "Dwelling with Honour: Perspectives on Honour, Shame and Human Dignity Today, from Luke 7: 36-50" (MTheol. University of Otago, 2015), 84, http://hdl.handle.net/10523/5598.
[29] Moffat, "Ezra," 68.

is transformative dialogue, akin to the robust conversational give and take of *talanoa*, "used in several of the native languages in Oceania ... (as) a point of intersection."[30]

As initially designed, WisdomCafé offers:

- an appreciative position that reflects elements of biblical practices of gratitude, the robust grounded gratitude that includes lament, evident in the psalms[31]
- provocative questions, shaped in WisdomCafé by the parable themes of community and family living
- a relaxed hospitality setting and small groups (like café tables), and group rotation to encourage deeper shared communication,
- opportunity for participants to find voice through their stories (telling and listening) and to reflect together on shared stories, learning and practicing a simple form of personal and corporate reflection.

For WisdomCafé, we held 90-minute sessions that followed a shared meal in private homes. Each café "table" had a "host" who stayed at the table and facilitated stories and reflection with two to three "guests." Guests moved to different tables for each of the three question sets.

A WINDOW INTO PRACTICE

I turn now to an illustration of this methodology through a glimpse of WisdomCafé#1. Although WisdomCafé is not a bible study, its congregational settings resulted in interest and conversation around the parable texts. My reading of the text as "stories of faithfulness" generated ongoing discussions, especially concerning what judgment might look like when given a neutral definition of accountability. Judgment as accountability required a context of

---

[30] J. Havea, "Welcome to Talanoa," in *Talanoa Ripples: Across Borders, Cultures, Disciplines...* ed. J. Havea (Auckland: Masilamea Press, 2010), 11.
[31] Branson, *Memories, Hopes, and Conversations*.

relationship, which in turn suggested connections with God's covenantal faithfulness to Israel and the relational responsibility given to humanity in the creation narratives (Genesis 1-2).

In WisdomCafé#1, I reference Matthew 24:36-41 and briefly outline the theme of *Acknowledgement* and its interpretive route. Then I introduce the appreciative stance and the World Cafe facilitative style, leading into three questions provoking personal stories followed by reflection questions. Each café table group received a handout with the theme and questions:

WisdomCafé#1, Acknowledgement and Question Set 1

Jesus' example of Noah's generation focuses on the ordinary tasks of living. We discover sacredness in daily life as we acknowledge our relationship with God in the way we carry out ordinary tasks.

Think about the day-to-day activities in your household (growing up or anytime since then): the ordinary jobs that need to get done for the household to run smoothly. *Remember a time when a member of your family or household carried out an ordinary task in a way that made a significant difference to you, or your sense of wellbeing.* What made that possible? What was it that impacted you?

Worked Example

I include one example from a WisdomCafé session with a group of young adults in Auckland in 2017. Tony (pseudonym) was new to the group, the church and in his first year of university study. He had arrived with his family from Asia and grown up through the Aotearoa NZ school system. For this question, the first of the WisdomCafé series, group members allocated themselves into groups and Tony sat listening to three other young men as they exchanged stories and reflected. When the table host invited him to tell a story, he responded, "I'm just struggling to think of one myself." He stayed silent as the other three contributed stories and reflected. I was about to change the groups and question set when Tony responded to the stories and reflections.

> That actually reminds me. When I was in - during my whole school days, from intermediate [students aged 10, 11, 12 years] to high school [students 13 to 16-18 years], Mum always packed me a lunch. That wasn't just like, lunch, like, ordinary ham sandwich, nothing like that ... Of course, when I was a kid growing up, I'd taken it for granted, but looking back it was, like, such an effort you know, just to get up early, because her son needs lunch when he goes to school. Listening to these stories that this group are telling me, just reminded me of that. Yeah, it was the kind of lunch that when you take it...out at lunchtime, all your mates come around and trying to grab a bite of it ... And it actually makes me think that, like, my mum actually, maybe she was lacking in other parts - to actually express her interest in me - it might be that - but then, looking back, it kind of shows me how she always cared.

In listening to others' stories, Tony found a way past his particular place, with its shield of silence. He found a safe place to tell his story. He found voice and validation. Over the following weeks, his confidence grew, and he shared stories more easily, finding a level place to receive and to give stories. In telling his stories, he gave those around him a way to welcome and affirm him.

Tony belongs to a "third space" generation, children growing up on the boundaries of multiple cultures, negotiating identity in ways different from their parents and peers, ways that for some (including myself) found safety in reserve, or as I reflect on it now, a wall of silence.[32] In the ordinariness of the stories told that night, Tony discovered difference and commonality. In Aotearoa NZ, children often take a packed lunch to school, made by their caregiver or themselves. The content varies by household, socio-economic

---

[32] Homi K. Bhabha, *The Location of Culture* (Routledge Ltd, 2012), Chapter 1, https://www.dawsonera.com:443/abstract/9780203820551.

context and culture. Tony's school lunches had always been the envy of his friends. His mother offered them out of a culture that valued food as a way of communicating the heart of the family, welcome and acceptance, as Tony phrased it, showing him, "how she always cared." Like his Auckland school friends, Tony enjoyed the quality of the food, but until he recounted this story and reflected on its significance for himself and his mother, he had not recognised his mother's cultural way of communicating her care. In that WisdomCafé, Tony listened to other stories about parents carrying out ordinary household actions, stories told by these young adults who, as they reflected, recognised their parents' thoughtfulness and generous care. In the light of these reflections, Tony saw similar care in his mother's previously taken-for-granted actions.

His story is one among many that illustrated how the WisdomCafé process validates voice and creates room for future partnership. I turn now to reflections on these first sessions.

REFLECTIONS ON WISDOMCAFÉ#1

Responses to WisdomCafé#1 revealed that its small group focus on personal story and reflection with a lightly structured facilitative process made room for those who had rarely spoken. They found a voice to tell their stories. These personal stories of ordinary daily activities gave insights into perspectives on life, family, culture and values, personal joys and challenges, all of which have increased acceptance and strengthened relationships, with greater engagement by minority voices in majority voice contexts. Another new immigrant to Aotearoa New Zealand who participated in a WisdomCafé#1 session commented, "Funny how hearing those little stories makes you feel closer to the person."[33] Growing insights like these invite more understanding and grace for one another. Not everyone had positive stories, some responded to these questions with historic stories of weakness, failure and pain. These occurred in

---

[33] Held in Auckland, mid 2019.

groups who had known and cared for one another for some years and were met with responses of empathy and gentleness.

Collaboration and Responsibility

There were several surprises, the most relevant to this chapter concern collaboration to empower others and theological reflection. In line with an Action Research methodology, I had hoped to see the primary community take ownership, to collaborate on the project itself, for individuals and communities to be empowered. Talking with the vicar after having held a pilot and three sessions, I expressed surprise because I could not see indications of collaboration or empowerment. The research community continued to describe WisdomCafé as my research, their concern was to do what I needed for the project to succeed. It was additionally puzzling to me because of the theme of relational responsibility threaded through the parables. Even within limitations imposed by the context of PhD research I had anticipated some collaboration. I wondered about this aloud to the vicar, Paul, curious as to what I might do differently to inspire collaboration and responsibility.

Paul encouraged me to stay with the process and passed on his observations as the church leader who supported the research but was not part of that initial WisdomCafé group. Shortly prior to our conversation, he had himself been puzzled by seemingly unconnected individuals approaching him to ask how they could be more involved in church life. He had not initiated any change that might have triggered these responses. On reflection he realised they were all involved in WisdomCafé:

> Firstly, there is a real sense of a positive shared experience, and this is manifest by an excitement around the WisdomCafé community both leading up to and post-WisdomCafé. Overall, there would appear to be a positive shift in the individuals' personal confidence and confidence in their personal faith and beliefs. Especially those who have tended to be quieter in the past. Particularly those not native to NZ or where English is their second language. They have expressed

to me as the church leader that they want to be more involved in church life, asking what they can do to help. This is a recognition of what they bring themselves. There has also been a greater community buy-in to St Matthias gatherings, and in the general life and ministry of the church. One member has asked to be baptised. As well as the growth in confidence, there appears to be deepening in relationships within the Wisdom Café community. I would summarise this by a gentleness and tenderness and deep respect expressed and given to each other verbally and non-verbally. Overall, I have witnessed a positive shift towards and commitment to developing a community rather than just meeting for church on Sundays.[34]

Paul's feedback was encouraging, and I observed this increased sense of belonging as people who had kept silent told their stories and received affirmation and validation.

Personal and Corporate Theological Reflection

One thing that stood out in the stories was the commitment of skilled hosts to the reflection process. Despite planning for facilitators and working with communities familiar with small groups, I was surprised at the discipline needed to follow through the reflection process. WisdomCafé required a type of personal and corporate reflection that was unpractised by enough of those taking part for them to struggle with it. The first community had been invited to take on voluntary journaling and web-based group reflection but without any take-up. It had needed the face-to-face gentle encouragement, vulnerability, and personal and corporate reflecting (named in hindsight as a form of theological reflection) of these skilled practitioners to carry others with them in treasured journeys of discovery.

---

[34] Personal email from Paul Ashman, Auckland, May 2017.

Reasons for hesitancy and lack of follow-through in the reflection process may be due to a missing skill set. It could result from cultural values, such as these six pairs of *Positive*/Negative values prioritised by Kiwis:

Earthy/Unsophisticated,
Modesty/Unintentionally misleading,
Restraint/Overcautious,
Fairness/Hyper-democratic,
Ingenuity/Close enough is good enough; and
Informality/Disrespectful.[35]

Personal and corporate reflection is significant to WisdomCafé, where its indirect approach offered a relaxed space that validated voice and nurtured organic growth, while at the same time risked loss of the ground recovered: it can be difficult to value and hold what has not been named. The initial plan had been for WisdomCafé to have multiple layers of reflection. This has not happened, and in retrospect, it needs more intentionality, clarity and modelling of both theological reflection and gratitude (its appreciative stance), while retaining its indirect approach.

Beyond the research phase, I am exploring the WisdomCafé process as part of congregational services, held within liturgies from Morning Prayer and the communion service. While WisdomCafé has only been used with the judgment parable themes, the process is one that allows for other themes. Through a returning each year for a season of food, stories and reflection, drawing on different scriptural content, I anticipate that communities would more easily incorporate new members, and would continue to strengthen practices of gratitude, theological reflection and voice. And that the indirect

---

[35] There is debate over a "NZ" culture, see Stephen Turner, "'Inclusive Exclusion': Managing Identity for the Nation's Sake in Aotearoa/New Zealand," *Arena Journal*, no. 28 (2007); Cathrin Schaer, "She's Right, Mate (on Falconer & Watson's Cultural Detective)," *New Zealand Herald* (Auckland) 2006, Canvas, https://natlib.govt.nz/records/20605173.

empowerment as voice is validated would enable communities to generate growth in unforeseen and multiple ways, with growth overflowing in ever-widening circles of fruitfulness.

Conclusion

Exploring relational faithfulness in local congregations using the lens of these parables has revealed a uniting thread, the essential relational context of both settings. When discussing community, whether the early or contemporary church, a relational context is no surprise, yet this project's relational hermeneutic has emerged from and is vital to its South Pacific context. My decision to use storytelling was a response to Jesus' choice of stories and the research community's 21st century Pacific, yet cosmopolitan context. In keeping the question and reflection structure simple, giving a subject guide, yet also room to tell the stories people wanted to tell, the result has been an organic process that is a shift away from World Café. In its focus on stories, storytelling, and reflection, WisdomCafé takes a turn away from the formulae of "programs" and "courses" historically popular with my Pākehā culture, but which for many of my Māori and Pasefika neighbours, is uninspiring in its blindness to relationship, respectful dialogue and play.

The relational nature of both the process and content of WisdomCafé has made a hospitable space, one in which marginal voices have made themselves heard with surprising enthusiasm creating room for partnership to grow. WisdomCafé hopes to build community by encouraging everyone's voice and by modelling personal and corporate reflection. It takes biblical themes, an appreciative stance, and personal stories to reflect together on the significance of daily activities. In doing so it encounters the sacred in ordinary life. It is still in its infancy stages, yet the hope that birthed it was always to build community within and across cultures. WisdomCafé offers an indirect and organic way to build partnership amid cultural differences at the parish level, and in the face of a majority culture that blindly assumes the rightness of "our way of living." A Three Tikanga Church is uniquely placed to lead that challenge.

7

Friendship, Aotearoa, and the Anglican Church

Dr Anne-Marie Ellithorpe

Kia ora tātou
Ko Maungawhau te maunga
Ko te Waitematā te moana
Nō Tāmaki Makaurau ahau
Ko Anne-Marie Ellithorpe tōku ingoa
No reira, tena koutou, tena koutou, tena tatau katoa

ACKNOWLEDGEMENTS

I acknowledge my gratitude to Atua (God), tāngata (people), and whenua (land).[1] I am grateful for the countless blessings of the Creator and for the sustenance of the unceded Coast Salish territory by the Salish Sea, on the colonised continent known as Turtle Island. It is there that much of my writing has taken place. Yet this paper is primarily shaped by the people of Aotearoa New Zealand —where I was born and where much of my formation has taken place. My ancestors immigrated to Aotearoa from 1842 onwards, from England and elsewhere, settling in a variety of locations including Motueka, Waiharakeke (Blenheim), and Te Upoko o Te Ika a Maui (the Wellington region).[2] While the ongoing dishonouring of Te Tiriti o Waitangi negatively impacted friendship possibilities, my ancestors John Marple and Evangeline Tindill lived amongst Māori in Rūātoki where I expect they became at least somewhat bilingual and bicultural.

The landscape of Tāmaki Makaurau contributed to my early formation. Te Upoko o Te Ika a Māui, most specifically Te Awa Kairangi, contributed to my formation as a young adult. Here I was privileged to learn from the wisdom, hospitality, and spirituality of Māori and Polynesian leaders and friends, and to develop an awareness of Māori and Treaty issues through conversations, course work, reading, and participation in a variety of hui and noho marae.[3]

---

[1] As Catholic Māori theologian Dr. Henare Tate asserts, Māori recognise relationships between Atua, tangata, and whenua as constituting who we are. H. A. Tate, "Towards Some Foundations of a Systematic Māori Theology" (PhD, Melbourne College of Divinity, 2010), 36.

[2] My ancestors include the Newport, Kinzett, Dodge, Woolley, Hunter, Tindill, Marple, Fawcett and Merriman families from England, the Hunter family from Scotland, Margaret McMullen from Ireland, Jean Baptiste Grondin from the Reunion Islands, James Brown from the United States, John Maindonald from Guernsey, and George McDonald from parts currently unknown.

[3] Those I have learned from include Dr. Monte Ohia and Sir Kim Workman. Highlights include learning from Matua Sam Chapman, Matua Muri Thompson, and

More recently, I have been encouraged that my work to develop a practical theology of friendship is relevant to personal, ecclesial, and political life in Aotearoa New Zealand. For this I am particularly thankful to Māori elder, priest, and scholar Rev'd Dr Rangi Nicholson. Yet before articulating the shape of such a theology, I acknowledge that I bring blind spots to this work. I have not experienced life within each of the Tikanga, nor the oppression of colonisation with its negative impact on friendship possibilities. Due to constraints of time and space, I have given inadequate attention to the Polynesian Tikanga throughout this paper. A more fully developed practical theology of friendship appropriate to the Anglican Church in Aotearoa, New Zealand, and Polynesia will draw on the theological, relational, and practical wisdom of each of the Tikanga and honour Māori as first nation by paying particular attention to Māori kaupapa, including those of whanaungatanga and manaakitanga.

Matua Norman Tawhiao during a noho marae at St Michael's Anglican Church and Marae and participating in the Inaugural World Christian Gathering of Indigenous People, organised by Dr. Monte Ohia, in 1996.

Introduction

WITHIN THIS PAPER I advocate for a practical theology of friendship to inform the practices and the social and theological imagination of the leadership and laity of the Tikanga of the Anglican Church in Aotearoa, New Zealand and Polynesia, as well as relationships within and between Tikanga. I begin by exploring the terminology of the social imagination, friendship and practical theology. I then introduce the four sub-movements of a fundamental practical theology that structure the body of this paper and identify themes relevant to each of these sub-movements. While I do not focus on issues of church structure, a practical theology of friendship may nevertheless prove valuable to the Anglican church in Aotearoa, New Zealand and Polynesia, as it seeks to structure itself in ways that are "theologically defensible and contextually appropriate," and to consolidate gains and address concerns that have arisen as a result of the current Tikanga structure.[4]

This focus on friendship may seem to be in some contrast to the stated purpose of the Te Korowai o te Rangimarie colloquium, that is, the development of a theology of *partnership*, especially as expressed in bicultural relations established by Te Tiriti o Waitangi. The terminology of partnership has already been challenged by theologians who advocate instead for attentiveness to the language and relationship of friendship. For example, Bishop John Bluck asserts that: "The theology of a bicultural church and a three Tikanga constitution is all about building community and forming friendships rather than partnerships."[5] Bluck emphasises that partnership can be negotiated, while the kind of friendship Jesus offers "is born out of mutuality where both sides feel equality, respect and regard for the well-being of the other."[6] While I concur with Bluck in advocating for relationships of mutuality, I am convinced that the language of partnership and friendship can co-exist, with a theology of friendship

---

[4] Moffat, "Introduction."
[5] Bluck, "Stunned Mullets," 14.
[6] Bluck, "Stunned Mullets," 14.

deepening our understanding of what it means to be bound together as Treaty partners within Aotearoa.

Relational practices and opportunities for partnership and friendship are shaped by the social imagination. In referring to the *social imagination*, I draw on the concept of the social imaginary identified by Charles Taylor and others as a way to talk about shared life.[7] The social imagination refers to the ways in which people envision their social existence, including how they relate with others and is transmitted socially. The social imagination of various communities may be healthy or diseased. As African-American systematic theologian Willie Jennings laments, many Christians within the West live and move "within a diseased social imagination."[8] Yet there is potential for the social imagination to be transformed through the use of new metaphors and different practices.

Theological insights, metaphors, and analogies also shape the imagination and the way in which we envision our existence and our relationships. Thus, we may also speak more specifically of the *theological imagination*. Again, distortions of the theological imagination are possible, for example, in the ways in which we imagine God, and seek to image God, yet transformation and healing of these distortions are also possible.

The relationship between practices and the imagination is reciprocal. While "a transformative understanding might enter a *social imagination* to unsettle and shift its 'seeing' of the way things

---

[7] Charles Taylor, *A Secular Age* (Cambridge: Harvard University Press, 2007), 172.
[8] Willie James Jennings, *The Christian Imagination: Theology and the Origins of Race* (New Haven: Yale University Press, 2010), 6. Accordingly, any proposed practical theology of friendship "must ultimately grapple with the healing of diseased social imaginations." Anne-Marie Ellithorpe, "Towards a Practical Theology of Friendship" (PhD, University of Queensland, 2018), 3.

are," changes in practices may also provoke changes in the social (and theological) imagination.[9]

Relationship and practice of friendship have the potential to transform the imagination. Friendship is a relationship of mutuality that has been understood in somewhat differing ways in various contexts and cultures. Essentially, however, friendship can be identified as being characterised by mutual affection *and* by reciprocity in willing and doing good for the other. This characterisation can be used to describe relationship with God. A friendship-like relationship with God can be expected to spill over into concern for and friendship with others, expressed through both personal and civic expressions of friendship.[10]

While contemporary friendship is typically perceived of as a personal relationship, friendship also serves as a model for civic relationships within the broader community. Whereas personal friendship involves willing good for the friend, civic friendship involves "willing good for all (the wider community, the other, and beyond)."[11] The ideal of civic friendship includes those activities which community members reciprocally perform for one other as they seek to nurture "civic relationships and their social union as a whole."[12] Civic friendship may include those in need in times of crisis or advocating for the rights of marginalised people. Civic friendship retains essential aspects of personal friendship, "including mutual awareness, good will, and action" as citizens demonstrate care for one another's well-being and are proactive on behalf of others.[13]

---

[9] Taylor, *Secular Age*, 175.
[10] Ellithorpe, "Theology of Friendship," 155.
[11] Ellithorpe, "Theology of Friendship," 157.
[12] Sibyl A. Schwarzenbach, "Fraternity, Solidarity, and Civic Friendship," *AMITY* 3, no. 1 (2015): 12.
[13] Ellithorpe, "Theology of Friendship," 59. Aristotle (384–322 BCE) understood civic friendship (*politike philia*) to be the concern of fellow citizens for one another's "good character" (Politics 1295b23). While some contemporary writers use the term civic friendship narrowly, focusing predominantly on friendship

In the pursuit of self-determination, some Māori reject Western terminology including that of friendship as Pākehā concepts.[14] My intention in advocating for a practical theology of friendship is not to endorse contemporary Pākehā relational practices and understandings, but rather to bring different traditions into dialogue to enrich our understandings of the right-relatedness to which we are called as treaty partners, as communities of faith, and as te whānau o te Atua. Friendship, defined expansively and not in Pākehā terms of personal relationships alone, is another way to understand and talk about right-relatedness.

I acknowledge that kinship is primary in traditional Māori society. However, kinship and friendship are not mutually exclusive. Rather, the Māori idea of friendship is intertwined with that of whānau (extended family) and "the idea of a social universe of *whanaunga* (relatives, relations) that are connected vertically by *whakapapa* (genealogy) and horizontally by *whanaungatanga* (kinship in its widest sense)."[15] The Māori concept of whanaungatanga has the potential to enrich both personal and civic dimensions of friendship.

While Māori communities place greater emphasis on multi-dimensional right-relatedness and social cohesion (implicit within

---

within the context of government, others use it more broadly. Political philosopher, Schwarzenbach, for example, describes civic friendship as "that form of friendship whose traits operate via a society's constitution, its public set of laws, its major institutions and social customs." Schwarzenbach, "Civic Friendship," 11. I concur, whilst acknowledging the possibility for civic friendship to contribute to communities challenging unjust constitutions and laws, and reshaping institutions.
[14] Agnes Brandt, *Among Friends? On the Dynamics of Māori-Pakeha Relationships in Aotearoa New Zealand* (Göttingen: V&R Unipress, 2013), 256.
[15] Brandt, *Among Friends?*, 254. Thus, as Brandt asserts: "In order to understand the meaning of friendship, or the place of *hoa* within Māori society, we need to understand Māori social organisation and kin categories." Brandt, *Among Friends?*, 44. Victor Mokaraka describes whanaunga as "a special and intense connectedness which mediates all other types of relations" (personal communication, 3 February 2020).

civic friendship), Māori also value friends and friendship.[16] Further, the faithfulness of friendship was expected of leaders, according to the saying: He rangatira he hoa matenga mōu, kia kore koe e whakarērea (A chief will be a friend in disaster, and will not forsake you).[17]

From the terminology of friendship, I turn now to the terminology of practical theology. Practical theology, broadly speaking, refers to the work or practices of people as they seek to "sustain a life of reflective faith in the everyday," thereby bearing fruit (whaihua) in everyday life.[18] Practical theology also refers more specifically to an academic discipline that seeks to "enrich the life of faith for the sake of the world," and in so doing, to contribute to restoration and renewal.[19] The term *practical theology* is perhaps not needed within indigenous contexts, where there is not the same dichotomy between theory and practice. Within te reo Māori, one perhaps could speak simply of atuatanga or ahorangi.[20]

---

[16] Brandt, *Among Friends?*, 41. The reo of friendship includes hoa and whakahoa, with hoa being a "Māori friendship idiom of reference and address" that implies affection and reciprocity. Hoa is used across gender and age, although typically within the same generation. Brandt, *Among Friends?*, 42. The word āpiti has a similar meaning. Whakahoa implies befriending and companionship, and carries connotations of partnership. Brandt, *Among Friends?*, 276. Whakahoanga appears to be "a relatively recent linguistic construction derived from the term *hoa* (friend, mate) that fills the lexical gap of 'friendship' in *te reo*." Brandt, *Among Friends?*, 255.
[17] Sidney M. Mead and Neil Grove, *Ngā Pēpeha a Ngā Tipuna: The Sayings of the Ancestors* (Wellington, NZ: Victoria University Press, 2003), 114.
[18] Bonnie J. Miller-McLemore, "Introduction: The Contributions of Practical Theology," in *The Wiley Blackwell Companion to Practical Theology*, ed. Bonnie J. Miller-McLemore (Malden: Wiley-Blackwell, 2012), 5.
[19] Bonnie J. Miller-McLemore, *Christian Theology in Practice: Discovering a Discipline* (Grand Rapids: Eerdmans, 2012), 103–104. See also Gerben Heitink, *Practical Theology: History, Theory, Action Domains*, trans. Reinder Bruinsma (Grand Rapids: Eerdmans, 1999), 4–5.
[20] Ahorangi is an ancient word meaning "a teacher of the highest standing" which may be used metaphorically to speak of theology. Victor Mokaraka (personal communication, 29 January, 2020).

A practical theology of friendship is concerned with the faithful practice of personal and civic dimensions of friendship in the present and on behalf of the future that God is calling us into. Resources for a practical theology of friendship include biblical, Indigenous, and philosophical understandings of relationality, right-relatedness, love and friendship.

What shape then could a practical theology of friendship relevant to the Three Tikanga church take? While there are a number of ways to develop and shape such a theology, I suggest that such a theology follow the four sub-movements of a fundamental practical theology outlined by practical theologian Don Browning: descriptive, normative, systematic and strategic.[21] The remainder of this paper articulates themes that are appropriate to explore within each of these sub-movements.

Within the descriptive sub-movement, I consider several ways in which friendship and particularly civic friendship has featured or been lacking within the history of Aotearoa and the Anglican church since the early 19th century. Within the normative sub-movement, I consider the relevance of the Deuteronomic call to the covenant community to image a befriending God. The systematic sub-movement explores the mutuality of love and of creation. The fourth and final sub-movement focuses on the more fully informed practice of friendship within and between Tikanga.

PART I: FRIENDSHIP WITHIN AOTEAROA AND THE ANGLICAN CHURCH

The descriptive sub-movement of a fundamental practical theology seeks to develop a thick description of a situation: "What, within a particular area of practice, are we actually doing?"[22] What norms, metaphors, and visions underlie our actions and our

---

[21] Don S. Browning, *A Fundamental Practical Theology* (Minneapolis: Fortress, 1996), 8. While Browning more typically uses the term *historical theology*, the focus is on *normative* texts and traditions.

[22] Browning, *Fundamental Practical Theology*, 48–49.

practices? Within this descriptive section I focus on several ways in which friendship has played a part in Aotearoa since the arrival of Anglican missionaries and subsequently since the establishing of the Anglican province of New Zealand as well as ways in which friendship and befriending currently feature within Anglican contexts in Aotearoa. My aim is to be illustrative rather than exhaustive as I highlight ways in which willing and doing good for the *other*, most specifically between Pākehā and Māori, have been evident or absent. [23] I acknowledge both personal and civic friendship, that is, the form of friendship that wills good for the wider community and beyond.

Early European settlers would have struggled to survive without the compassion, care and friendship of Māori communities, and relationships of mutual friendship and respect between missionaries and Māori were integral to the early history of Christianity in Aotearoa. Friendship between Samuel Marsden and Ruatara led to the invitation to Marsden to "preach the gospel" in 1814. Personal friendships between Māori leaders and early missionaries (including Henry Williams, leader of the Church Missionary Society), paved the way for the 1840 Te Tiriti o Waitangi between the Māori and the British Crown. This treaty with its covenantal implications may be seen as an early expression of civic friendship. As Don Moffat notes, it appears that "the treaty was presented to Christianised Māori as uniting British and Māori under one sovereign and one God."[24]

Yet this early expression of civic friendship was subsequently followed by land wars, and the unjust confiscation of land. Of course, the fact that the English version stated that Māori gave

---

[23] I use the term *other* positively, to indicate someone who is distinct and unique from the subject at hand.
[24] Don Moffat, "Treaty, Partnership and Covenant Theology," in this volume. See also Claudia Orange, *The Treaty of Waitangi* (Wellington: Allen & Unwin, 1987), 56. In signing Te Tiriti, Māori gave kawanatanga (governance) to the Queen, expecting that such governance would ensure that Māori land was safe from settlers.

rangatiratanga (sovereignty) to the British Crown did not help. Neither did the subsequent devaluing of the treaty or the diseased social imagination of many settlers.

The social imagination that historically contributed to the colonisation of Aotearoa was diseased in ways that ultimately constrained authentic friendship possibilities. There were of course exceptions and many early missionaries sought to protect the interests of Māori.[25] But overall, the social imagination of the settlers was not one that contributed to authentic friendship. Rather, many white settlers considered Māori to be uncivilised, and such perceptions contributed to the many forms of injustice that accompanied the process of colonisation within Aotearoa including the inappropriate appropriation of land and policies of assimilation.

I suspect that such prejudice contributed to the constitution of the Anglican Church in New Zealand being first formulated in 1857 without Māori representation even though the Anglican church in Aotearoa in the early decades of the 19th century was predominantly a Māori church known as Te Hāhi Mihinare. Despite the covenantal implications of Te Tiriti, the writing of the first New Zealand Anglican constitution did not reflect a sense of covenant friendship between settlers and Māori.[26]

Octavius Hadfield, Anglican missionary and Bishop, left a mixed legacy of friendship. While he contributed to the first constitution which excluded Māori voices he was proactive in learning te reo, envisioned the colony as an integrated society with equality of rights and opportunity for all and subsequently

---

[25] E. Prebble, "Incarnational Theology and the Constitution," in *Te Awa Rerenga Maha: Braided River*, ed. D. Moffat, Three Tikanga Church Colloquium (Auckland: Anglican Church in Aotearoa, New Zealand and Polynesia, 2018), 98.

[26] Further, subsequent calls for a Māori bishop were declined in order to protect the (so-called) unity of the church. When eventually a Māori bishop was permitted in 1928, his powers were limited. See J. Bluck, *Wai Karekare Turbulent Waters: The Anglican Bicultural Journey 1814–2014* (Auckland: Anglican Church in Aotearoa, New Zealand and Polynesia, 2012), 53.

encouraged Māori to exercise their constitutional right to register as voters. A friend of the Ngāti Toa chief Te Rauparaha, Hadfield was outspoken against war in Taranaki and "a widely respected peacemaker."[27] He has been called "Friend of the *Tangata Whenua*."[28]

Unfortunately, however, the ruling on Hadfield's behalf within the now infamous court case "Wi Parata vs. the Bishop of Wellington" in 1877 contributed towards ongoing injustice. Māori had given land to the Anglican church to be used for a school for their children. A school had not been built and Māori justifiably wanted the land back. Yet the Chief Justice, James Prendergast, refused to acknowledge the existence of Māori customary law. In his ruling, Prendergast cited the absence of "civilisation" among Māori tribes as justification for denying Māori both sovereignty and property over their land, and declared that the treaty was a "legal nullity." [29] Not only did Prendergast's decision in favour of the bishop demonstrate a lack of civic friendship, it also created a legal precedent for the ongoing appropriation of land, thus perpetuating injustice. This same judge sanctioned the invasion of Parihaka in response to Māori non-violent resistance to colonial oppression.

In stark contrast to this ecclesial and judicial injustice, however, a vision of civic friendship is depicted through the words of Te Whiti, one of the Parihaka prophets instrumental in leading non-violent resistance to oppression within Taranaki. Upon appearing before a magistrate and several justices of the peace on 12 November

---

[27] Bluck, *Anglican Bicultural Journey*, 26.
[28] See Christopher Lethbridge, *The Wounded Lion: Octavius Hadfield, 1814-1904, Pioneer Missionary, Friend of the Maori & Primate of New Zealand* (Christchurch: Caxton Press, 1993).
[29] Quoted in Grant Morris, "James Prendergast and the Treaty of Waitangi: Judicial Attitudes to the Treaty During the Latter Half of the Nineteenth Century," *Victoria University of Wellington Law Review* (2004): 125. In Prendergast's view, the Māori were "savages" who had no sovereignty to cede, nor body of law that could be legally recognised.

1881, and being charged with disturbing the peace.[30] Saunders quotes Te Whiti's clear statement that his vision was for all, Pākehā and Māori, to live "peacefully and happily on the land."[31] His ideal was for Pākehā and Māori to live side by side, with Māori (as dominant ruler) learning from the white man's wisdom, without becoming "subservient to his immoderate greed."[32] Yet Te Whiti's ideal was not to be. Rather, state-imposed policies of assimilation (until after World War 2), integration and, more recently, biculturalism have disempowered Māori and have largely failed to provide the opportunities for self-determination sought by Māori.

After almost a century in judicial limbo, Te Tiriti o Waitangi was recognised as "a still valid compact of mutual obligation" in 1987.[33] Eventually, also, the Anglican Church committed itself to re-examining the principles of bicultural development and partnership in light of a reconsideration of the Treaty. This re-examination contributed to the adoption of a revised constitution in 1992, Te Pouhere. Friendship was integral to the creation of this revised document. John Bluck notes that Te Pouhere "only came about because of a relatively few longstanding and hard forged friendships

---

[30] More precisely, Te Whiti was charged with: "wickedly, maliciously and seditiously contriving and intending to disturb the peace, inciting insurrections, riots, tumults, and breaches of the peace, and, to prevent by force and arms the execution of the law did wickedly declare false, wicked, seditious and inflammatory words." Waitangi Tribunal, *The Taranaki Report: Kaupapa Tuatahi* (Wellington: GP Publications, 1996), 239. These "inflammatory words" allegedly included phrases such as "naku te whenua" (the land belongs to me) and "naku nga tangata" (the people belong to me).
[31] Alfred Saunders, *History of New Zealand 1642-1861* (Christchurch: Whitcombe & Tombs, 1899), 467. Quoted in Bernard Gadd, "The Teachings of Te Whiti O Rongomai, 1831-1907," *The Journal of the Polynesian Society* 75, 4 (1966): 450, http://www.jps.auckland.ac.nz/document//Volume_75_1966/Volume_75,_No._4/The_teachings_of_Te_Whiti_O_Rongomai,_1831-1907,_by_Bernard_Gadd,_p_445_-_457/p1. See also Waitangi Tribunal, *Taranaki*, 239.
[32] W.R. Te Kuiti, "Where the White Man Treads," *New Zealand Herald*, November 30, 1907, 1. Quoted in Gadd, "Teachings," 450.
[33] Bluck, *Anglican Bicultural Journey*, 43.

between some Māori and Pākehā lawyers, bishops, priests and lay leaders who learnt to trust each other" throughout the process of negotiating the new Constitution.[34]

Yet not all celebrate the 1992 Constitutional Revision. Jenny Te Paa Daniel, previously Tikanga Māori Dean of St John's Theological College, describes it as "systemically flawed and politically and theologically bereft." [35] Positively, Te Pouhere allowed for three "Tikanga" (Māori, Pākehā, Polynesian) to exercise mission and ministry to God's people within the context of their own cultures.[36] Negatively, in some contexts at least, it contributed to division and "competition for finite resources rather than... selfless Gospel driven commitment to solidarity with those who are the least in any given situation."[37]

Ideally, Te Pouhere was to provide a base for partnership, power-sharing and mutual respect, and to "promote a three Tikanga church in order to build common ground."[38] It was anticipated that these self-governing Tikanga would share a common life "under the umbrella of a synod that relies on consensus between the tikanga and between the houses of lay, clergy, and bishops." [39] Yet common ground, a common life, and care for the common good have not eventuated. Te Pouhere has not been fully implemented in practice.

---

[34] Bluck, "Stunned Mullets," 15.
[35] "To Say My Fate Is Not Tied to Your Fate Is Like Saying, 'Your End of the Boat Is Sinking': A Heartfelt Critique of the Three Tikanga Church," Progressive Christianity Aotearoa, 2014, https://progressivechristianityaotearoa.com/2014/03/24/critique-three-tikanga/.
[36] Prebble, "Incarnational Theology," 101–102. Prebble notes that Te Pouhere refers to a post to which a waka is tied for safety.
[37] Te Paa Daniel, "A Heartfelt Critique," 3.
[38] Bluck, "Stunned Mullets," 3. Bluck further notes that a resistance movement developed subsequent to the passing of this legislation. See also Brian Davis, *The Way Ahead: Anglican Change & Prospect in New Zealand* (Christchurch: Caxton, 1995), 38.
[39] Bluck, *Anglican Bicultural Journey*, 61.

An expected process of decolonisation and the deconstruction of oppressive systems has not eventuated. Rather, disparity has become normalised.[40]

In addition to the stalemate in implementing the constitution, some mistakenly viewing the Tikanga structure as the *cause* of division within the church.[41] In this regard it is worth noting, as Edward Prebble asserts, that separate structures were in place from the beginnings of Christianity in Aotearoa, "as missionaries and subsequent church leaders attempted to incarnate the gospel within the context of Māori culture."[42]

Further, the current Tikanga structure is not impermeable. Pākehā have become congregants within Māori Tikanga parishes, and Pākehā becoming deacons and priests within Māori Tikanga is not unheard of. Māori are involved in Pākehā Tikanga initiatives such as the Ngatiawa River Monastery.

Māori and Pasefika have benefited from the Tikanga structure in terms of participation and at least somewhat improved access to resources. The restructuring has allowed for Māori self-

---

[40] Speaking most specifically to the relationship between Te Hāhi Mihingare ki Te Tai Tokerau and the Anglican Diocese of Auckland, Rev. John Payne describes 1992-2012 as an era of normalised disparity, with Pakeha parishes enjoying "continued use and control over" established facilities, while north of the Auckland Harbour Bridge there were no church buildings with kitchen or toilet facilities in the control or title of Te Hāhi Mihingare. John Payne, "He Whakapapa O Te Rangapū I Waenga I Te Hāhi Mihingare Ki Te Tai Tokerau Me Te Anglican Diocese of Auckland, Mai I 1814 Ki 2018" (paper presented at the Te Korowai o Te Rangimarie – The Cloak of Peace Colloquium, St John's Theological College, 2019).
[41] Bluck, "Stunned Mullets," 3. Bruce Davidson, cited in L. F. C. Liava'a, "*Felupe* Theology: A Theological Reflection on the Three Tikanga Church and Ministry," in *Te Awa Rerenga Maha: Braided River*, ed. D. Moffat, Three Tikanga Church Colloquium (Auckland: Anglican Church in Aotearoa, New Zealand and Polynesia, 2018), 219.
[42] Prebble, "Incarnational Theology," 101.

determination.[43] Indigenous governance has allowed for indigenous mission innovations.[44] Yet desired changes have been challenged by the legacy of colonial oppression, including a disparity in resources and in stipended clergy across the Tikanga.[45]

Some congregants and leaders have expressed grief at a lessening of contact between Māori and Pākehā at regional and local levels. Yet building bridges between Tikanga that lead to common ground has proven challenging.[46] Nevertheless, where there is genuine and sustained contact, friendship (in both its personal and civic forms) and whanaungatanga are fostered.

What then of the broader community? Anthropologist Agnes Brandt's analysis of empirical data demonstrates that despite Aotearoa providing "a culturally diverse social environment," the rhetoric of culture diversity does not translate easily into every day social practices.[47] As part of their everyday existence, Māori are more likely than Pākehā to need to move between friendship worlds, that is, between contexts within which the inherent rules and obligations of friendship may vary, thus contributing to diverse ways of being in relationship.[48] Pākehā, however, tend to stay within their own social worlds.[49]

---

[43] Self-determination is "a principle that Indigenous peoples insist upon in forming relationships with other parties" and "requires careful attention to power and control issues." Lynne Davis and Heather Yanique Shpuniarsky, "The Spirit of Relationships: What We Have Learned About Indigenous / Non-Indigenous Alliances and Coalitions," in *Alliances: Re/Envisioning Indigenous-Non-Indigenous Relationships*, ed. Lynne Davis (Toronto: University of Toronto Press, 2010), 336.
[44] Kereopa, "Equal Partnership," 33.
[45] Bluck, "Stunned Mullets," 7. The Māori church had only "a handful of stipended clergy across 38 rohe (ministry units)." Bluck, *Anglican Bicultural Journey*, 64.
[46] Such bridges have been described as elusive. Bluck, "Stunned Mullets," 8.
[47] Brandt, *Among Friends?*, 257.
[48] Brandt, *Among Friends?*, 58, 240.
[49] Brandt, *Among Friends?*, 257.

Clearly there has been inconsistency in authentic friendship, and in willing and doing good for the *other* within the Anglican Church in Aotearoa, as well as in the broader community. Yet is friendship integral to the theological imagination and practices that communities of faith are called to foster? Are we called to befriend the *other*?

PART II: IMAGING A BEFRIENDING GOD

The second sub-movement of a fundamental practical theology involves confronting the scene set in the first movement with central *normative* texts of our faith tradition. [50] Here I confront the inconsistency of friendship evident in the first movement with the Deuteronomic exhortation to the covenant community to image a befriending God. Māori understandings and insights from Aristotle regarding the relationship between friendship and justice are also acknowledged.

The book of Deuteronomy provides "a literary account of the renewal of the covenant with God on the plains of Moab." [51] Intriguingly, given our context, Deuteronomy seeks to preserve the identity of a community whose identity and existence is under threat, whilst also fostering an inclusivism that is central to the identity of the community.[52]

Theologically, this ethic of inclusion is based on the inclusiveness of God's actions and character. Within Deuteronomy 10 we read that God shows no favour, and takes no bribes, but rather upholds the cause of the fatherless and widow, *befriending* the stranger and providing the stranger with food and clothing.[53] The

---

[50] I acknowledge the challenges posed by issues of authority and power when it comes to identifying specific texts as normative.
[51] Peter C. Craigie, *The Book of Deuteronomy* (Grand Rapids: Eerdmans, 1976), 24.
[52] Mark R. Glanville, *Adopting the Stranger as Kindred in Deuteronomy* (Atlanta: SBL Press, 2018), 2, 270.
[53] Jeffrey H. Tigay, *Deuteronomy: The Traditional Hebrew Text with the New Jps Translation* (Philadelphia: Jewish Publication Society, 1996), 108.

covenant community is to likewise befriend the stranger. In doing so, they not only image God, but extend empathy based on their own formative narrative: "You too must befriend the stranger, for you were strangers in the land of Egypt."[54] The Hebrew word translated as "befriend" is *'āhāb*. While *'āhāb* is often translated into English as "love," *befriend* more appropriately captures its implication of affection expressed in action.[55] Within the Māori translation of Deuteronomy, *'āhāb* is translated as aroha. Aroha is elsewhere described as the essential element in interpersonal relationships, and as encompassing "respect, friendship, concern, hospitality and the process of giving.[56] Clearly, the covenant community is called to image a God of love, friendship, and justice. Further, the covenant community is exhorted to be an intentional community that goes beyond the natural community of the extended family, through what may be described as a friendship, sibling or kinship ethic.

As Glanville notes, "the social matrix that forms the background to the Deuteronomic vision was conceived in terms of kinship."[57] (Some parallels can be seen between the Hebrew social organisation of extended family, clan, and tribe and the Māori social organisation of whānau, hapu and iwi). Yet kinship was not restricted purely to blood relations. Rather, strangers were to be loved and befriended through being incorporated into households, and thus into extended families, clan groupings, and ultimately the covenant community as a whole. In Deuteronomy, befriending the stranger, is characterised by willing good and doing good for the other, at both personal and civic levels, to the extent that the *ger* (translated into English as alien, sojourner, foreigner, or *other*) is no longer a stranger.

---

[54] Tigay, *Deuteronomy*, 108.
[55] Tigay, *Deuteronomy*, 108.
[56] John Clarke and et al., He Hīnātore Ki Te Ao Māori: A Glimpse into the Māori World, 151 (Wellington, NZ 2001).
[57] Glanville, *Adopting the Stranger*, 1.

The way of life of the covenant community is to be shaped by imaging God, with all citizens proactively involved in fostering the well-being of the broader community. This relational perspective with its emphasis on affection expressed in action is in keeping with Māori understandings and theology and the recognition that a person is never without "*whanaungatanga* and friendship ties to others."[58] Further, it is in keeping with the moral responsibilities upon whānau and friends to act on behalf of those who cannot care for themselves.[59]

As we consider the relevance of the theological mandate to image God through affection expressed in action to the colonial history of Aotearoa, similarities in power dynamics (rather than similarities in social organisation) most appropriately provide the basis for an analogy between the ancient Israelite agrarian contexts and contemporary postcolonial contexts. This analogy then challenges those of us with greater power and privilege to befriend and to actively confront and overcome inequalities in power, privilege and access to resources.

Befriending the stranger, as depicted within Deuteronomy 10, is an essential aspect of justice. Aristotle also identifies a link between friendship and justice. Not only does Aristotle recognise the practice of *philia* (friendship) as holding "states together" (*NE* 1155a22), he asserts that the cultivation of friendship is more important than the cultivation of justice. For when people are friends "they have no need of justice, while when they are just, they need friendship as well, and the truest form of justice is thought to be a friendly quality" (*NE* 1155a25). Friendship then is integral to genuine justice, and justice contributes to establishing and sustaining friendship.[60]

---

[58] Tate, "Māori Theology," 97.
[59] Tate, "Māori Theology," 159.
[60] See also Sibyl A. Schwarzenbach, *On Civic Friendship: Including Women in the State* (New York: Columbia University Press, 2009), 56.

Befriending and friendship are clearly a key aspect of the ethic that the covenant community are called to live by and integral to the pursuit of justice. Further theological grounding for friendship may be found within the mutuality inherent to love and to creation; it is to a discussion of these themes that I now turn.

PART III: THE MUTUALITY OF LOVE AND CREATION

The *systematic* sub-movement of a fundamental practical theology involves the examination of encompassing themes in order to gain a more comprehensive understanding of ideals that have emerged from the normative task.[61] I approach this stage of theological reflection alert to the truth of Māori theologian Henare Tate's observation that the coming of the Gospel message to Aotearoa "did not nullify indigenous thought forms and forms of life, but rather challenged them to extend themselves."[62] For example, Tate notes that the concepts of Atua (God, Supreme Being) and aroha (affection, love, compassion) were already present in pre-contact Māori culture but were developed and linked in new ways through dialogue with the Christian message. Thus, this sub-movement explores themes of mutuality inherent within ideals of love as expressed through *agapē* and aroha and within creation.

The Mutuality of Love

As previously noted, within Deuteronomy the covenant community is exhorted to image a befriending God, a God of love whose affection is expressed in action and through the promotion of justice. Within both Testaments, God's people are exhorted to imitate this love not only by loving their neighbours, but by extending love to strangers, foreigners and even enemies. Love emerges from

---

[61] Don S. Browning, *Equality and the Family: A Fundamental, Practical Theology of Children, Mothers, and Fathers in Modern Societies* (Grand Rapids: Eerdmans, 2007), 14.
[62] Tate, "Māori Theology," 11.

various Biblical texts as a socio-ethical love with social and political implications.

While a variety of images of love may be found throughout the history of Christianity, the ideal of Christian love (*agapē*) is ultimately reciprocity in love, both giving and receiving. The equal regard inherent within "You shall love your neighbour as yourself" (Matt 19:19) implies that "one respects the selfhood, the dignity, of the other as seriously as one expects the other to respect or regard one's own selfhood."[63] Similarly, the reciprocity inherent within such love implies that both parties want the best for each other and seek the good of the other. I am convinced that the reciprocity of friendship as expressed in both its personal and civic dimensions fosters the mutuality and equal regard that is the goal of Christian love.

Christian love is also characterised by self-giving in mutual accompaniment. But the purpose of self-giving is ultimately to restore mutuality.[64] The purpose of sacrificial action including sacrificial resistance to oppression (through "going the second mile," for example), is to seek to restore a situation of imbalance to equal regard.[65] Within the context of personal and civic friendship mutual self-giving is a natural overflow as friends and communities provide support to one another, take risks on behalf of the other and extend practical care through various seasons of life. While there are times when love demands self-sacrifice, the norm is reciprocity.[66]

Reciprocity is also evident in the Māori concept of aroha (love, affection, compassion), one of three principles governing the

---

[63] Don S. Browning et al., *From Culture Wars to Common Ground: Religion and the American Family Debate*, 2nd ed. (Louisville: Westminster John Knox, 2000), 101, 153.
[64] Ellithorpe, "Theology of Friendship," 134; Browning et al., *Culture Wars to Common Ground*, 271.
[65] See also Browning, *Fundamental Practical Theology*, 199.
[66] Ellithorpe, "Theology of Friendship," 134.

relationships among Atua, tangata, and whenua (God, people and land). As described by Tate, the specific focus of aroha is on "the communion in relationship among Atua, tangata and whenua that needs to be brought about by pono (perceptive) and tika (right) action [thus, aroha also] governs action dedicated to bringing about, enhancing or restoring communion among *Atua, tangata* and *whenua.*"[67] Aroha, then, is concerned with promoting, protecting, and where necessary, restoring the inherent mutuality and reciprocity of creation.

The Mutuality of Creation

Creation is comprised of a community of God's creatures "who share the earth in mutual dependence."[68] The mutuality and interdependence of creation is evident experientially and in Hebrew and Māori creation narratives. The second creation account of Genesis depicts human beings as being designed to live in an intimate relationship with God, with healthy relationships with one another (*ish* and *ishah*) and with the earth (*adam* and *adamah*).[69] All human beings are interconnected – to God, to the cosmos and to one another.[70] An emphasis on the connectedness of God, land, and people is inherent to a biblical doctrine of creation. Similarly, the Māori creation story interweaves whenua (land, with its spiritual dimension), with Atua (God, its source and fulfilment) and tangata (people). Tate describes the "totality and fullness" of whenua as taking place in and through its relationship with Atua and tangata.[71]

---

[67] Tate, "Māori Theology," 137. "If our aroha is to be *pono* (to have any truth, honesty or integrity), there must be action behind our words; otherwise, our words are mere empty words." Tate, "Māori Theology," 141.
[68] Richard Bauckham, "Introduction," in *Jürgen Moltmann: Collected Readings*, ed. Margaret Kohl (Minneapolis: Fortress Press, 2014), 5.
[69] See Anthony A. Hoekema, *Created in God's Image* (Grand Rapids: Eerdmans, 1986), 75–82, 102.
[70] John H. Walton, *Ancient near Eastern Thought and the Old Testament: Introducing the Conceptual World of the Hebrew Bible* (Grand Rapids: Baker, 2006), 208.
[71] Tate, "Māori Theology," 77.

Acknowledging the mutuality of all creation, German systematic theologian Jürgen Moltmann identifies creation as "an intricate relationship of community – many-layered, many-faceted, and at many levels."[72] Tate depicts a similar relationality in his description of rangimārie as the somewhat fragile "state of peace and tranquillity within a person, among people, between people and Atua, and between people and creation."[73]

Mutuality is expressed through the acknowledgement of connectedness between God, people and land. Māori have shown significant resiliency in refusing to lose sight of a world where people, land and God are interconnected. Willie Jennings implies that Western Christianity must recover a sense of connectedness between people and land in order to be fully Christian.[74] Tikanga Pākēha have much to learn from Tikanga Māori in this regard.

Clearly there is a need for reconciliation and restoration of relationships of mutual love and reciprocity among people, between people and Atua and between people and the land.[75] Further, the restoration of relationships *between* human beings will require challenging racism, overcoming threats to friendship and honouring sacred friendship treaties.[76]

---

[72] Jürgen Moltmann, *God in Creation: A New Theology of Creation and the Spirit of God* (Minneapolis: Fortress, 1993), 2.
[73] Tate, "Māori Theology," 217. Tate also speaks of *te tapu o*, referring to the mutually enhancing, restorative and empowering "relationship that one being has with other beings, created and uncreated." Tate, "Māori Theology," 50.
[74] Jennings, *The Christian Imagination: Theology and the Origins of Race*, 248.
[75] Tate identifies rongo as peace, specifically peace after conflict, and hohou rongo as the means by which rangimārie can be regained. Tate, "Māori Theology," 217.
[76] Such sacredness may not always have been recognised by colonisers. Canadian colonisers, for example, may not have recognised that indigenous protocols "converted the product of the talks into a covenant to which the Great Spirit was also a party." J. R. Miller, *Compact, Contract, Covenant: Aboriginal Treaty-Making in Canada* (Toronto: University of Toronto Press, 2009), 295. Nevertheless, Miller encourages non-natives to acknowledge that they too are treaty people,

I am convinced that a truly Christian doctrine of creation nurtures relationships of reciprocity and friendship, especially in the midst of diversity and seeks restoration and healing where mutuality has not been acknowledged and honoured. Yet many of us do not imagine ourselves relationally; "our sense of connectivity and belonging tends to be incredibly thin."[77] Without a genuine "doctrine of creation" our imaginations have become diseased and in need of healing in terms of the kind of community we imagine.[78]

A lack of mutuality within the relationality of creation will ultimately contribute to social destabilisation and potentially even cosmic destabilisation. Within the Hebrew prophetic writings, the violation of the vulnerable is portrayed as having "unavoidable cosmic implications."[79] In Amos 8:8, for example, the land is described as trembling in response to injustice. While the current Tikanga structure was developed in response to injustice, it continues to linger along with lack of genuine mutuality. Thus, I turn now to the strategic sub-movement, and consider ways in which consider justice, mutuality and friendship may be fostered.

PART IV: NURTURING FRIENDSHIP IN AND THROUGH THE THREE TIKANGA

The final sub-movement of a fundamental practical theology involves returning to the original issue with ideals that have become more clearly understood, developing a deeper understanding of the specific context in which we must act, and considering ideal praxis within this context, along with means and strategies for use within this context. Consideration is given to where are people currently at

---

participating in and benefiting from treaties. Miller, *Aboriginal Treaty-Making in Canada*, 306, 309.

[77] Willie James Jennings, "New Winds," *Pneuma* 36, no. 3 (2014): 451, https://doi.org/https://doi.org/10.1163/15700747-03603047, https://brill.com/view/journals/pneu/36/3/article-p447_9.xml.

[78] Jennings, "New Winds," 451.

[79] John Brueggemann and Walter Brueggemann, *Rebuilding the Foundations: Social Relationships in Ancient Scripture and Contemporary Culture* (Louisville: Westminster John Knox, 2017), 43.

and what initial steps can be taken towards transformational practices.[80] As Browning asserts, a critical test of clarified ideals and norms is related to their capacity to foster healing within specific contexts.[81] As with each previous sub-movement, I cannot do justice to this sub-movement in this paper, but rather explore select themes.

Whether theologians, priests, or laypeople, the specific context in which we must act includes a country that has been deeply impacted by the dishonouring of Treaty, by Pākehā inconsistency in authentic friendship and by injustice. Further, the specific context in which we must act includes a Three Tikanga church structure guided by Te Pouhere, a church constitution significantly influenced by Crown concepts of biculturalism.

Changes in practices, relationships, terminology, and in the social and theological imagination are needed to foster healing, friendship, and ultimately the unity in diversity that our faith calls us to. *Ideally* faith communities within each Tikanga "image" a befriending God, expressing affection through their actions and through the promotion of justice, and fosters relationships characterised by mutuality and reciprocity. Fostering friendship is integral to the pursuit of justice and is in keeping with imaging a befriending God and honouring the mutuality of creation. Covenantal relationships of mutuality and reciprocity are also in keeping with Te Tiriti o Waitangi. Through the nurturing of theologically inspired and grounded friendship, it is to be hoped that people of all Tikanga will be encouraged and enabled to extend the willing good and doing good inherent in personal friendship to other Tikanga, and to the broader community.

It is clearly appropriate to nurture theologically inspired friendship and whanaungatanga within and between all three Tikanga through the constitution, structures, customs, and practices

---

[80] See Browning, *Fundamental Practical Theology*, 55–56, 69.
[81] Browning, *Equality and the Family*, 396.

of the Anglican church. How then are the understandings and practices this research identifies as vitally important to be encouraged and nurtured? Whose role is it to promote personal friendship, civic friendship, whanaungatanga, and a widespread culture of friendship, within, between, and beyond Tikanga? All have a part to play in this regard, whether laity, clergy, or bishops. As Danielle Allen asserts, all of us are implicitly "founders of institutions," as we all contribute to and affect "the shape of life" in our communities.[82] Thus, all can contribute to cultivating a pervasive culture of friendship, through attitudes and actions towards others, and through interaction with various institutions that shape life within communities.

As Bluck suggests, bishops and others who "meet across the Tikanga to argue about canons and cash" can "invest nationally in building partnerships and friendships." [83] Those involved in theological research and education have particularly important parts to play. Their relationships, practices, and teaching contribute to the shaping of the social and theological imagination of communities of faith.[84] The content of theological education must be rethought given the legacy of colonisation and the complicity of the Church in colonisation. Diversity in knowledge has the potential to contribute to friendship, as well as unity.

The social imagination of many Pākehā congregants of settler ancestry has yet to be captured by a theological vision of friendship,

---

[82] Danielle S. Allen, *Talking to Strangers: Anxieties of Citizenship since Brown V. Board of Education* (Chicago: The University of Chicago Press, 2004), xxi.
[83] Bluck, "Stunned Mullets," 14.
[84] While currently "the wider cultural milieu does not foster a deep understanding of friendship, neither does a great deal of theological education." Anne-Marie Ellithorpe, *Towards Friendship-Shaped Communities: A Practical Theology of Friendship* (Wiley, Forthcoming).

mutuality, and reconciliation.[85] Sadly, it is not unusual for non-indigenous people to "manifest profound ignorance in relation to indigenous history, spiritual practices, ... and knowledge," and unwittingly "do and say things that are offensive, disrespectful, and hurtful."[86] Church leaders cannot force the transformation of social imaginations, nor legislate cross-Tikanga encounters. Nevertheless, leaders can consider the nature of the social and theological imagination that is fostered in and through Pākehā parishes and seek change. Leaders can engage in the challenging work of decolonizing their own thoughts and actions as well as strategizing towards all Anglicans developing a greater awareness of the history of Aotearoa, and the role that the Church has played in this history.[87]

Practices of befriending and of friendship can be enacted. Practices emerge from our theological commitments; they also "contribute to our perception of and ability to live out from such convictions." [88] Greater priority can be given to "building relationships, partnerships, and friendships" [89] and to "actively learning relationality from Māori." [90] For many Pākehā this may require a slower pace of life.

---

[85] Some Pākehā perceive the status or mana of Māori language and culture as low, don't want to learn, and reject even symbolic acts of biculturalism, such as the insertion of the Lord's Prayer in Māori.
[86] Davis and Shpuniarsky, "The Spirit of Relationships," 344.
[87] See Rangi Nicholson, "'Walking into the Future Facing History': An Introduction to Bicultural Treaty Partnership in a Three Tikanga Anglican Church" in this volume.
[88] Kent Eilers, "New Monastic Social Imagination: Theological Retrieval for Ecclesial Renewal," *American Theological Inquiry: A Biannual Journal of Theology, Culture & History* 6, no. 2 (2013): 51.
[89] Bluck, "Stunned Mullets," 14.
[90] This was an important theme in the colloquium, for example, Courtney Menary, "Whakahāngia: Grounding an Aotearoa Theology of Relationship" (paper presented at the Te Korowai o Te Rangimarie – The Cloak of Peace Colloquium, St John's Theological College, 2019).

For Tikanga Pākehā, the Treaty of Waitangi has to a large extent been remarginalised since the new constitution in 1992.[91] Nevertheless, theologically inspired civic friendship may contribute towards new understandings and appreciation of Te Tiriti as a sacred covenant. As Don Moffat notes, the Treaty is about relationship and *mutual* commitment, and was significantly influenced by Scriptural notions of covenant.[92]

As Anglicans seek the best for one another, terminology changes may be required. Given the considerable angst expressed about the name assigned to the Pākehā Tikanga, it appears that a change in terminology would be beneficial. A word that once meant simply *other* and was subsequently used to refer primarily to settlers of European ancestry, is now a "catch-all" covering a multitude of backgrounds. Anashuya Fletcher notes that Pākehā is now understood by scholars to be a relational term, acknowledging that "one lives in the land of the Māori and seeks to live in relationship with them."[93] Yet Fletcher expresses concern that with the current broad understanding that Pākehā implies "white," harm will be done to "new and emerging ethnic minorities within New Zealand."[94] Renaming this Tikanga as *Tangata Tiriti* would be in keeping with a recognition of the treaty as a sacred friendship covenant, given that all non-indigenous immigrants are indeed "people of the Treaty."

Nurturing civic friendship within and between each Tikanga of the Anglican Church in this Province will involve laity, clergy and bishops learning about and from the other, whether of Māori, Polynesian, Asian, European, or mixed descent. It will include a commitment to learning more about shared history, putting aside preconceptions and prejudices, allowing one's social imagination to

---

[91] See Rangi Nicholson, in this volume.
[92] See Don Moffat, in this volume.
[93] Fletcher, "Finding Identity," 198.
[94] Fletcher, "Finding Identity," 198.

be reshaped, and seeking, where possible, to put right injustices of the past.

Further expressions of civic friendship include providing space for healing from the damage done by colonisation, the sharing of resources, and restitution. Seeking the best for the other will include non-Māori supporting Māori in their quest for self-determination, and in their resistance to various forms of colonisation, including neoliberalism. Seeking the best for our host nation will include making greater use of Māori language in liturgical and other settings. As Rangi Nicholson asserts, "the Anglican church has a crucial role to play in the revival and revitalisation of the Māori language."[95] Further, "the Māori language has a crucial role to play in the revival and revitalisation of the church."[96]

Various metaphors and theologies from ethnic groups within the various Tikanga may be drawn on in developing a practical theology of friendship most appropriate to Aotearoa. For example, *felupe* theology, drawing on the Tongan cultural metaphor of a mother who has many children yet "holds together" various obligations, may be appropriately interwoven with or incorporated within a practical theology of friendship.[97]

Wanting the best for the other must ultimately be expressed in the sharing of power. This may well prove challenging, as while the power relations conditioned by colonialism are pervasive, they are also invisible to many non-Indigenous citizens.[98]

Summary

Within this paper I have advocated for a practical theology of friendship to inform the practices and the social and theological imagination of the leadership and laity of the Tikanga of the Anglican

---

[95] Nicholson, "Theological Perspectives," 186.
[96] Nicholson, "Theological Perspectives," 186.
[97] Liava'a, "*Felupe* Theology," 217.
[98] See Davis and Shpuniarsky, "The Spirit of Relationships," 335.

church. It is historically, ethically and theologically appropriate for friendship, in its personal and civic dimensions, to inform relationships within, between, and beyond Tikanga in Aotearoa, New Zealand and Polynesia. Friendship has been at the heart of critical events within the history of Aotearoa, including the signing of the covenant Te Tiriti o Waitangi and the formation of the constitution Te Pouhere. Friendship is integral to justice. It is consistent with the call to the covenant community to image a befriending God in all its aspects. While a diseased social imagination has contributed to oppression and racism, there is potential for transformation throughout Aotearoa and Polynesia, as communities are captured by a theological vision of friendship, mutuality, right-relatedness, and reconciliation, and outwork this vision through wanting the best for, and working on behalf of one another.

8

Theologising *Solesolevaki* as a Form of Social Capital for Partnership in a Three Tikanga Church

REV'D DR ESETA MATEIVITI-TULAVU

Introduction

SOLESOLEVAKI IS A Fijian concept of working together for the benefit of the group rather than for monetary or individual gain. Sustainable tourism researcher Apisalome Movono reframed the indigenous concept of *solesolevaki* as a form of social capital so that communities and villages can respond better to development.[1] The connections involved in *solesolevaki* often embody specific relationships which harness trust and emphasise reciprocity. Connecting is integral to developing partnership and as missional theologian, Cathy Ross, asserts there must be acceptance and a commitment of trust by the other.[2] This paper seeks to demonstrate how *solesolevaki* contributes to a better understanding of partnership within a Three Tikanga church. The bonds of affection cultivated through theology can only become a reality when people work together.

Throughout the world we see and hear people working together by listening to one another, by communicating freely, by doing things together and knowing that success is not individual but rather communal. We are all brought up in environments which involve individuals working collaboratively together to get us where we are today. None of us would be here if it was not for our parents, extended family and friends working together. There are always things which bring people together, from those basic informal special moments to very formal gatherings. From birthdays, funerals, and weddings to gatherings bringing together different institutions and even nations. The church is an institution which embraces and seeks to bring out the spirit of individuals who through their knowledge of each other work collaboratively through various partnerships towards a safe environment. The church I am referring to here is the

---

[1] Apisalome Movono and Susanne Becken, "Solesolevaki as Social Capital: A Tale of a Village, Two Tribes, and a Resort in Fiji," *Asia Pacific Journal of Tourism Research* 23, no. 2 (2018).
[2] Cathy Ross, "The Theology of Partnership," International *Bulletin of Missionary Research* 34, no. 3 (2010).

Three Tikanga Anglican Church in Aotearoa, New Zealand and Polynesia.

I begin with a brief history of how relationships within this church, across the region was formed, as I locate myself in the Fijian Anglican Church, then discuss how significant *solesolevaki* is to the Three Tikanga church by showing how it works on the ground and conclude with the importance of applying the indigenous concept of *solesolevaki*.

HISTORY

The mission of the church began in 1814 at Oihi in the Bay of Islands well before the Three Tikanga Church came into being when Ruatara, a native of New Zealand, introduced his friend Samuel Marsden and the gospel to his people. Thus, the Anglican missionary church, Te Hāhi Mihinare, was born and soon became intertwined with the indigenous Māori culture. As Paterson notes "Anglican life in New Zealand was Māori, led by missionaries, some lay, some ordained with the language, hymns and prayers done in Māori."[3]

By 1857, the New Zealand settler church decided to put together a constitution for itself. The signing of the constitution was to define the settler church for the next 135 years with the development of seven Dioceses which were independent, each with their own episcopal leadership. This greatly impacted the missionary church as the Māori church was not asked to participate and struggled to be part of the seven Dioceses. As a result of the oppression and tensions relating to this, Frederick Augustus Bennett was appointed in 1928 as the first Māori suffragan Bishop and Te Pihopa o Aotearoa. As a suffragan Bishop, Bennett worked alongside the Bishop of Waiapu but was without a "seat as of right in the

---

[3] John Paterson, Sermon for Te Pouhere Sunday Evensong" (23rd June). My thanks to Bishop John Paterson who sent me a copy of his sermon on this Te Pouhere Sunday Evensong.

General Synod of the Church."[4] Gradually, the situation was addressed and eventually in 1978 Te Pihopatanga o Aotearoa was formed providing a new measure of independence to Te Hāhi Mihinare.[5]

The Diocese of Polynesia had its own story of ministry. When the Diocese of Melanesia was formed from New Zealand in 1849, Fiji, which was just close by, was not part of the script. However, missionary work was already in progress amongst the Fijian people and the "Comity of Missions"[6] clearly spelt out who the Catholics and Methodists were responsible for. Anglicans were prevented from entering Fiji and all ministrations of the church were carried out on board naval vessels. It was clear that whenever a naval ship would dock in Levuka, Fiji, the chaplain of the vessel would be eager to hold a communion service for the settlers.

After several attempts to get an Anglican priest to minister to the colonial administrators and plantation masters, William Floyd, from Melbourne responded in 1870. Floyd, a young curate, hearing that Fiji needed a chaplain, was released from his curacy at Holy Trinity, Northcote, Victoria and licensed by Charles Perry, the Bishop of Melbourne, who broke all the rules of licensing which should have been done by the Bishop of London. The Diocese of Polynesia was first established in 1908 with the consecration of Bishop Clayton Twitchell.[7] By 1925 the Diocese of Polynesia became an Associated Ministry Diocese and it flourished from a small settler church into a Diocese across Tonga, Samoa and Fiji, with indigenous clergy.[8] After

---

[4] "Canons," (NZ: Anglican Church in Aotearoa, New Zealand and Polynesia), 4. https://www.anglican.org.nz/Resources/Canons.
[5] Paterson, Sermon for Te Pouhere Sunday Evensong" (23rd June). John Paterson, Sermon for Te Pouhere Sunday Evensong" (23rd June).
[6] Charles William Whonsbon Aston, *Pacific Irishman* (Stanmore, Australia: Australian Board of Missions, 1970). http://anglicanhistory.org/oceania/whonsbon-aston1970.html.
[7] Diocese of Polynesia, *Celebrating 100 Years, 1908-2008* (Fiji: Anglican Church of Aotearoa, New Zealand and Polynesia, 2008), 5.
[8] Polynesia, *History of Polynesia*, 5.

becoming a Diocese with a Diocesan Bishop in residence, the Archbishops of Australia and New Zealand kept the Archbishop of Canterbury informed as to the state of Anglicans in the islands.

The Three Tikanga Church came into being in 1992 through the revised constitution which established three equal partners constituting the Anglican Church in New Zealand, the Anglican Church in Aotearoa and the Anglican Church in Polynesia, Pacific. Paterson clarifies that "each of these partners were given the right to govern themselves and define their mission in their own terms and to serve their people, their members within their cultural norms, within their cultural ways of behaving and believing."[9] Different as we are in relation to our Tikanga, the foundational doctrine is that the church is a body in which Christ is its head and all baptised persons are members believing that God is one, yet revealed as Father, Son and Holy Spirit. Tikanga basically means customary ways of doing things, 'tika' means correctness or right. Paterson added that "tikanga indicates the right way, the correct way to live and move and have our being as St Paul alludes to."[10]

The standing resolutions of bicultural partnership SRBP 5 states that, "

> In order for a body or event to be accepted as a three Tikanga or Common Life body or event each of the following criteria must be fulfilled. [The body or event must]:
> a....be established or organised by the three Tikanga, and the three Tikanga must be acting together.
> b....be controlled by people appointed by, or with the consent of, each Tikanga, acting through its normal processes.
> c....have clearly defined accountability to each Tikanga or to the General Synod / Te Hīnota Whānui or other

---

[9] Paterson, Sermon for Te Pouhere Sunday Evensong" (23rd June).
[10] Paterson, Sermon for Te Pouhere Sunday Evensong" (23rd June).

appropriate properly established three Tikanga body which is itself accountable to the General Synod / Te Hīnota Whānui.11

In the above standing resolution, the following words echo partnership "three Tikanga must be acting together," "body or event must have clearly defined accountability to each Tikanga or the General Synod or other appropriate properly established three Tikanga body." This takes into consideration a two Tikanga body or event as well. Cathy Ross alludes to the simple dictionary definition of a partner is "one who shares, takes part, is associated with another in action."[12] The Standing resolution speaks about acting together and being accountable to one another.

Paterson and Archbishop Emeritus, Sir David Moxon used metaphors to describe the partnership and journey of the Three Tikanga Church. Moxon uses the weaving of a kete or a woven flax bag which symbolises how "the most fundamental life forms are knit together, evolve and grow."[13] Moxon goes on to explain the spirituality of weaving, how the crossings of weaving one strand over another is about love, "love that goes forth," "love that comes back" and that "the dynamic of love given and received" brings about new life in its forms and shape.[14] Weaving a strand over another or the interweaving of the strands is so much more than just love, it is also about faith and hope. The faith of each strand to hold unto each other and supporting each other. Each Tikanga have faith in the other or would like to help the other no matter the circumstance. Faith is about believing that this supporting and holding onto the other will open doorways into mission and ministry in a Three Tikanga church.

---

[11] https://www.anglican.org.nz/Media/Files/SRBP-Bicultural-Partnership
[12] Ross, "The Theology of Partnership," 145.
[13] "The Woven Flax Cross - Te Ripeka Whiringa Harakeke," Anglican Church in Aotearoa, New Zealand and Polynesia, n.d., 2019, https://www.anglican.org.nz/About/The-Woven-Flax-Cross-Te-Ripeka-Whiringa-Harakeke.
[14] Moxon, "The Woven Flax Cross."

Hope is expecting each strand to hold unto each other to enable the kete to be used purposefully, to have the ability to hold food and other things which one can share with the other when going to community gatherings. As Moxon states, "the creation of the bag itself means that it becomes useful for carrying and sharing food and other treasures between a community of people."[15] Hope is when one Tikanga partner's expectations are taken into consideration and are supported, encouraged, loved by another Tikanga partner. This is the very nature of God, faith, hope and love.

Paterson describes the partnership as a "mooring post to which are tied three very different sea-going crafts." No matter how different one Tikanga is from another, the mooring post who is God means that everything should be centred on God. How they moor or are tied to the post depends on how intricately they are woven together internally. Where they are tied from or even if they drift a little bit but still tied to the post depends on what is happening on the inside. How the "sea-going craft" is tied, whether closely or loosely, depends on how well a Tikanga has gelled together. For an individual Tikanga to be able to be tied closely, the Tikanga should be working together, united, and have a uniformed front at all times. When there is unity within a Tikanga, they will be singing the same song. A Tikanga that is united will always find a way forward with the other Tikanga. Finding a way forward or through the most challenging times and supporting another Tikanga means working together for the betterment of the Three Tikanga Church.

SOLESOLEVAKI

Solesolevaki is a Fijian "concept of working together for the benefit of the group rather than its monetary or individual gain."[16]

---

[15] Moxon, "The Woven Flax Cross."
[16] Paul David Clark, "Social Capital and Vanua: Challenges to Governance Development in a Community-Based Natural Resource Management Project in Cuvu Tikina, Fiji" (University of Montana, 2008), 40, http://etd.lib.umt.edu/theses/available/etd-05202008-111818/.

Solesolevaki as the social capital of Fiji is important in the life of the three Tikanga Church. The word *sole* (pronounced solay) in some parts of Fiji means 'to give' and this is not implying individual giving but communal giving. Communal giving is simply giving your time and talent so that a lot of work done by many is completed with so little time. *'Vaki'* simply implies to 'make it happen.' To *solevaki* means to come together as one when building a house, cleaning the village, feeding people who come for funerals or weddings and other special occasions, people work together to ensure that everyone is taken care off and are happy with all that is happening. The coming together is not meant for only a few people because their house was being built or their father had passed away, but it is for the whole village. Being part of the village meant that the whole village will be there to support any individual who needs help of any kind. Social capital is a theory that relates to how communities connect, network and expand through interpersonal relationships. Bourdieu describes social capital as "the aggregate of the actual or potential resources which are linked to a durable network of more or less institutionalised relationships of mutual acquaintance and recognition." [17] Coleman added that social capital depends on connections and a number of things that bring about these connections and these are culture, finance, nature and human beings.[18] *Solesolevaki* as a social capital in a Three Tikanga Church is not only about working together but about building stronger bonds through communication networks, mission exchanges and information sharing (liturgy, courses, education). Stronger bonds would be seen through communication networks as it would enable the Three Tikanga church to understand and know that everyone is on a level playing field and that everyone understands the other well. Mission exchanges have been developed and done by young people

---

[17] P. Bourdieu, "Forms of Capital," in Handbook of Theory and Research for the Sociology of Education, ed. John G. Richardson (New York, N.Y.: Greenwood Press, 1986), 248.
[18] James S. Coleman, *Social Capital in the Creation of Human Capital* (Chicago: University of Chicago Press, 1988).

and women, but it needs to start from nurturing the children into understanding what Three Tikanga church means and taking them to children's ministry camps or even having a children's conference within the Three Tikanga Church. Thirdly, sharing information could range from a wide range of things such as sharing resource personnel or priest exchanges, liturgical exchanges to educational information exchange. This does not have to only happen at the top level but should start from one parish becoming a sister parish of another, right from the grassroots level. Connecting and coming together should start from the grassroots, from parish to parish within the Three Tikanga church.

The bonding needs to start from the grassroot level. *Solesolevaki* as a social capital, while communal and communitarian only happens through the collective and collaborative effort of the people. It is the bonds which people have with each other that shapes the coming together. In a Fijian village setting, it is the sound of the *davui* or conch shell which signals people to be still and listen to the village headman announcing the *"cakacaka vaka koro"* (work that is to be done by the whole village) and this can range from the building of a house, the cleaning of the village or cleaning of the grave site or any great task that demands the talent and time of the people to collaboratively work together for the betterment of the *koro* (village). The work is meant for the able-bodied men of the village and the older men and women in general know their roles and responsibilities. In any *koro* (village) scenery, while the able-bodied men are working, the older men would sit there to talk and offer advice, teaching what and how things should be done while the women would talk amongst themselves about morning tea and lunch preparations. Even those villagers who are in paid employment are part of the *cakacaka vaka koro* because they help to provide food for their fellow villagers who come together collaboratively to reciprocate, support and encourage one another in the development of social capital. In the *koro* (village) setting people have invested in each other, in their interpersonal relationships, in their pre-existing social structures and social connections to enable reciprocity and trustworthiness to take its place, thus allowing social capital to thrive. In any village activity through the act of *solesolevaki* certain vocabulary are expressed *'keda'*(we/us), *'meda'* (ours) and such plural pronouns are used rather than the personal pronoun of *'au'* (I).

WHY *SOLESOLEVAKI*?

Solesolevaki is an indigenous Fijian concept for the community coming together. It is more about each individual person offering what they have as a gift to the community. An individual's offering is also seen as a form of partnership and developing good non-linear and multi-level relationships. Understanding the dynamics of coming together helps to uncover interactions at the micro or family level which could also lead to complex implications at the macro or village level or vice-versa. *Solesolevaki* as a social capital focuses on social connections which emphasises an investment in inter-personal relationships. The Three Tikanga church is a symbol of the body of Christ. It is also about people collectively learning from each other and working collaboratively together for the betterment of the church. It is the people that make up the church and in exploring how well the Three Tikanga church work together throughout the different levels and committees it is time for more indigenous explanations on how the interpersonal relationship is significant. However, a lot of the time people's views or understanding of the Three Tikanga church depends on what their diocese or parishes do or their experiences in the different Three Tikanga committees. The different Three Tikanga committees which exist in the Anglican Church in Aotearoa, New Zealand and Polynesia have different representatives from the Three Tikanga, evident in the different levels and for example in the women's group and the youth. *Solesolevaki* is seen when women or young people from the Three Tikanga come together for a youth exchange, retreat or any other form of get together where they learn from each other culturally and socially. In any of the Three Tikanga church gatherings, it is more than just a gathering or business. Solesolevaki as a social capital is a theory that relates to how communities connect, network and expand through interpersonal relationships.

SOLESOLEVAKI AND PARTNERSHIP

Solesolevaki is a Fijian indigenous way of forming partnership, but it can happen in many facets of life. *Solesolevaki* in a Fijian sense can be anything which brings about working together collaboratively. In any family it starts from the time when a man and woman come together in holy matrimony. This sees two families from different clans, tribes, villages and family come together to work through things for the betterment of the couple. This partnership extends its horizons as its social, family and village network expands. Two different people come together and make a vow to be one, for better or for worse, in sickness and in health. This can also be said for our bicultural relationship and our Three Tikanga Church. This is the relationship or bond which means that our *veiwekani* (relationship) come with the appropriate behaviour. Within a Fijian culture and custom, the appropriate behaviour would be, *veidokai* (honouring the other), *veilomani* (loving the other first before self), *veinanumi* (thinking of the other first), *veikauwaitaki* (looking out for the other). In any relationship, respectful partnership is important because it forms a bond with every other individual person.

Ross speaks about the concept of partnership in three ways:

- The element of trust is foundational in relation to giving up control and sharing the responsibility.
- Partnership involves a ready acceptance of responsibility.
- There is also a readiness to pay the price of partnership.[19]

Ross speaks about partnership as what we seek in a good relationship with one of the ways being love. Our individual encounters come through love, "love is patient, love is kind, love does not envy, it does not boast, it is not proud, it does not dishonour others, it is not self-seeking, it is not easily angered, it keeps no record of wrongs, love never fails..." (1 Cor 13:4-8).

---

[19] Ross, "The Theology of Partnership," 146.

Solesolevaki is similar to Ross's concept of partnership in so many ways. *Solesolevaki* is about vulnerability, intentional listening, obedience, humility, availability and patience. When the village conch shell is sounded, villagers know that something is calling them to listen. In every household, if the radio or television is loud, a member of the family would tune it low or turn it off straight away so that they could hear what is being said through the village crier. After the village headman has announced the news of village work during the week, each family would organise itself. This calls for vulnerability, obedience, humility, availability and patience. Each family member takes responsibility in what the family has decided in accordance with what the village council wants to be done. In taking responsibility this means that every member of the family's trust is on the individual who will be part of the communal gathering during the week, whether it is building a house, cleaning the village or catering for visitors that come from the church or the government. Being sent by the family to be part of the work in the *koro* (village) means you represent the whole family.

The Three Tikanga church in all its ways of being together and working across tikanga forms the bi-cultural or inter-tikanga partnership which echoes love and trust. Paths are crossed numerous times, no matter how hard it may seem, love will always triumph. There are times when one tikanga may feel otherwise about another tikanga in relation to the sharing of resources, or whatever it may be, love will always shine through. *Solesolevaki* in relation to intentional listening, obedience, humility and patience will always come through. The *'wairua'* (spirit or soul) will always be felt in the *solesolevaki* because it will always be part of an individual person and when they give everything from their heart and perform everything to the best of their abilities people will always feel there is something missing when they do not see that individual present. Therefore, when one tikanga is missing, it is felt when it comes to decision making within the Three Tikanga church.

Solesolevaki then is when an individual is part of the *koro* (village), and in the Fijian sense being part of the *koro* means being there and doing everything to the best of your ability, to love being part of the work that is needed to be done amidst the laughter and jokes. The laughter and jokes are just a small part of what it means to keep everyone going and moving on with what is needed. It revitalises and enhances people's ability to go the extra mile and to perform everything to the best of their ability. In the midst of going the extra mile, the individual does all that it can for the whole. Therefore, in the Three Tikanga church *solesolevaki* comes through when one tikanga goes the extra mile for another tikanga. In a General Synod sitting of the Three Tikanga church, one tikanga gave up some funds to enable one tikanga to keep their school open. This is done out of love for the other tikanga and to also enable children to remain in school and come out with a high school qualification. Here is not only the element of love but of trust that the other partner would accept and know that each tikanga is responsible for the happiness of another tikanga "love is kind" (1 Cor 13). The concept of good relationship through partnership, through *solesolevaki* means knowing, understanding, respecting, trusting, honouring and responding to the needs of another tikanga whatever it may be.

Partnership is important in the art of *solesolevaki*. *Solesolevaki* as a form of partnership embodies the mission of the Three Tikanga church, the love and Tūrangawaewae it upholds. Tūrangawaewae, is translated as a 'place to stand.'"[20] It is

> grounded in a community's genealogical relationship from the divine to its ancestors to its living members; bounded by the natural landscape, such as mountains, ranges and rivers; metaphorically imagined as a *whare tapu* (sacred house). Thus, a community with God's mana; dedicated to God's purposes, holds responsibility

---

[20] Katene Eruera, "Turangawaewae - the Beginning," 2020, no. June 28 (2017). https://www.anglicansocialjustice.nz/resources/2017/8/21/a-theology-of-turangawaewae.

to share equitably in its resources for the well-being of all members of its community.[21]

It is about the shared human experiences through the community, the Three Tikanga lived experiences whether it be a home or church, an individual person's identity within one's own tikanga or inter-tikanga and belonging in a world. "Human communities embody *turangawaewae*, when they acknowledge and live out of God's blessing for humanity, in the flourishing of personal and communal well-being through creation."[22] The individual *whare tapu* within the Three Tikanga church is not only responsible for its individual members in every way but is also accountable to what is happening within the other two Tikanga. Therefore, the sharing of resources equitably is important for the well-being of the Three Tikanga church, if one is suffering it is the responsibility of the other two Tikanga to offer love and care. As Paul says "if one part suffers every part suffers with it. If one part is honoured every part shares with its joy" (1 Cor 12:26). This is significant in the life of the Three Tikanga church, it is about working collaboratively together and speaking in the public square about critical social issues.

THE THEOLOGY OF *SOLESOLEVAKI*

The theology of *solesolevaki* seeks to express an idea or a concept where it is ultimately about God. Firstly, *solesolevaki* is about the nature of God. Secondly, *solesolevaki* is about the trusting relationship between human beings. Thirdly, *solesolevaki* shows the relationship between God and human beings.

Grenz attributes the nature of God as a relational God in the Trinity. "The one, true God is the social Trinity – Father, Son and Spirit. The divine reality is eternally relational even apart from the world, in that the three trinitarian persons comprise the one God."[23]

---

[21] Eruera, "Turangawaewae - the Beginning."
[22] Eruera, "Turangawaewae - the Beginning."
[23] Stanley Grenz, *Theology for the Community of God* (Grand Rapids, Mich.: Eerdmans, 2000), 78.

However the relational focus for understanding the language and certain aspects of God in community is talking about the God that we have come to know. It is the God of relationships, Father, Son and Spirit beyond their eternal relations. Therefore, God in community speaks of the relationship within the Trinity till eternity. However, it is more about God's relationship to the world, to creation and having fellowship with us. God therefore is immanent in this world; God is present to creation. Paul speaks about this immanent God "he is not far from each one of us. For in him we live and move and have our being" (Acts 17:27-28). This shows that God is not far from us, he is present and active always in whatever is happening in and throughout the world. As Grenz suggests God is self-sufficient, beyond the universe that we "neither place him so far beyond the world that he cannot enter into relationship with his creatures nor collapse him so thoroughly into the world processes that he cannot stand over the creation which he made."[24]

Solesolevaki as a way of collaboratively working together in a Three Tikanga church speaks about the nature of God when people who are created by God work together by relating to one another, understanding and trusting each other. In moving together as a Three Tikanga church we are portraying the God of relationships, the trinitarian God working through the Three Tikanga church which have made them one. It also depicts that in working together, the Three Tikanga church not only want to have fellowship with God but also with each other. Relationships developed through prayers, celebrating each Dioceses success when there is a consecration of a bishop, being present in Diocesan synods when invited by the Diocesan Bishop, teaching, presiding in each other's Diocesan synods, developing curriculum together in a Three Tikanga College, working through the different committees within the Three Tikanga church. This is the way *solesolevaki* works and the very nature of God is to be

---

[24] Grenz, *Community of God*, 81.

in relationship. Relationship with each individual tikanga and the nature of God in themselves is to be in relationship with each other.

God is Spirit is another nature of God which affirms the life principle of an individual person. In our theological understanding of God as Spirit, we look to the Hebrew word *ru'ach,* and this means "breath" or "wind." "The Hebrews took this from breath as in life principle to acknowledging that God is the source of all life and "Spirit" is the divine power which creates and sustains life."[25] This maintains the biblical affirmation "God is Spirit" an acknowledgement of a significant element in the relationship of God to creation. Here is a declaration of God as the source of life, who gives life to each living being and most importantly on humans. God as spirit means to not only understand God as the Living One but to also "acknowledge that the vitality of the triune God overflows to creation."[26]

When the church as a community whether it be a Diocese or parish or the Three Tikanga church come together to meet, worship, pray, individuals become part of the community, and each come with their *'wairua'* spirit or soul. *Solesolevaki* happens when the community comes together, work done is successfully completed because each individual being created in the image of God seek to work in collaboration with another individual. Working in collaboration with each other cannot happen if there is no *wairua* and it is God who gives this *wairua*. The God of the Three Tikanga gives life to each tikanga, it gives life to the head of each tikanga so that the breath of God is felt through the nurturing of the relationships developed over the years. The relationship developed within each tikanga and across another tikanga declares or shows the God we worship, and this affirms the acceptance of God, "God is spirit. Those who worship him must worship him in spirit and in truth" (John 4:24). The *wairua* each tikanga bring into the Three Tikanga sustains

---

[25] Grenz, *Community of God*, 82.
[26] Grenz, *Community of God*, 83.

and holds them together. *Solesolevaki* as a metaphor is seen in the way each tikanga trusts, love, forgive, care and leaves the door open for the other to *talanoa*.

God's relationship with individuals and each individual persons with one another speaks volumes about the depths of God's existence, which is mysterious and beyond any human ability to comprehend. God as a person comes through the will and freedom of human beings. Grenz speaks of "God is person" which arises from our experience of God as "will and freedom."[27] God's will is beyond our control and our understanding. God as freedom is when other human beings act beyond our control and come under the control of another human being. *Solesolevaki* is seen as God's will when people come with their heart and soul to pitch in and work together. It is God's spirit that brings an individual to do an extraordinary act to bring something into fruition. The will to come and work together through love and care is important to enable the whole to be one. God as person through will and freedom is reflected when the Three Tikanga Church come together during the General Synod or during the different committee meetings. Being together as a Three Tikanga church to talanoa, korero, and share about what God is doing in each backyard or in each tikanga is very important.

God is Spirit and God is person is also seen when the Three Tikanga church celebrate what is common in their life as a church. An important part of the common life of the Three Tikanga church is worship. *Solesolevaki* through worship is also seen in understanding the triune or the trinitarian God. The concept of the Trinity sees relationship, connections, sacred spaces to be divine as each person relates to the other. This clearly comes through when we have our communion, with the Eucharist cup in the centre which is a sacramental sign of our communion with God and with each other. When God says "and now we will make human beings. They will be like us and resemble us" (Gen 1:26-28), this is saying that it was God

---

[27] Grenz, *Community of God*.

who brought us into communion with each other and with him. Our God is a communitarian God who wants to connect with us and wants us to connect and relate to each other. When we relate to each other through *solesolevaki*, by connecting, networking and expanding our interpersonal relationships with other human beings we are connecting to God because every human being is made in the image of God. In connecting, networking and expanding our relationships we are moving towards accepting our neighbours and there is no discrimination "in Christ there is neither Jew nor Gentile, neither slave nor free, nor is there male and female, for we are all one in Christ Jesus" (Gal 3:28).

Secondly, *solesolevaki* is about having trusting relationships and connections between human beings. When we connect to another human being it is important to see God in that person and allow that person to be part of the whole when you are connecting. Connecting is also about trusting everyone that is there in that moment, this brings about unity and diversity. Working in unity and diversity can only come through the work of the Holy Spirit. *Solesolevaki* is a way in which one can experience otherness - the otherness of God from humanity. Through engagement, connections and networking one would really learn to appreciate the other. When a faith community, let alone the Three Tikanga church, successfully comes and works together, it means that their spirit or *wairua* have come together as one. Therefore, there is not only a bond but a relationship which they share, and this has enabled them to successfully work together as one.

Thirdly, *solesolevaki* shows the relationship between God and human beings. The Three Tikanga church through *solesolevaki* shows no matter how diverse our cultural identities may seem; it is our God-given identities which allow us to be united in community. Acts)speaks about a community gathered on that first day of Pentecost as being transformed by the Spirit of God and they were able to understand each other in a diversity of language. No matter how different our languages are, God lives in the diversity of any language. God through *solesolevaki* wants us to not only have a relationship with him but also with other human beings no matter how diverse our culture is within the Three Tikanga church. *Solesolevaki* is about connecting, relationships, networking and through it, people show love, care, kindness, patience, forgiveness, humility, respect, and obedience.

SOLESOLEVAKI AND THE THREE TIKANGA CHURCH

The heart of the Three Tikanga church is the partnership which has been established since 1992. A partnership which has come a long way. A partnership that has been weaved together through love, love for God and love for each other. *Solesolevaki* or connecting, networking and relationships is seen through the different Three Tikanga committees that exist within the Anglican Church in Aotearoa, New Zealand and Polynesia, inclusive of this Three Tikanga College in Auckland, New Zealand. The Three Tikanga church has had its ups and downs. There have been honest conversations plus difficult ones which have challenged the church. Throughout the most challenging times, the church stood together and prayed. The church as the body of Christ through its Three Tikanga sought to understand each other and to stand together as one.

However, in order for *solesolevaki* to truly happen in a Three Tikanga church there are still things that needed to be thought through in relation to what we are, what we have and how it is within before looking outside. What would it look like if people within each Tikanga looked within and really have honest conversations and collaborated with each other? What are ways in which indigeneity could be celebrated within each Tikanga? Is it only through the languages? What are other ways? What of indigenous theologies, metaphors, methodologies, and pedagogies? I believe that the Three Tikanga Church are intricately woven together as a people of God, and we need to celebrate our indigeneity and our identity.

The Three Tikanga church has celebrated using indigenous ways of reconciliation. This was seen in Samoa in 2016 when the General Synod Standing Committee held its meeting there. This is when the Diocese of Polynesia through the Samoan *ifoga* sought forgiveness, sought to reconcile themselves to the two other Tikanga as a way of creating a space of unity through humility. What is the *ifoga*? Macpherson states that the "*ifoga* is a public act of self-humiliation – accompanied by the gift of '*ie toga*' or fine mats,[28] part of the presentation is a number of speeches, contrition and food, made as a form of apology by one group for the conduct of one of its members to another offended group."[29] Pratt defines the term '*ifoga*' from the root word '*ifo*' meaning "to bow down as do those conquered in war, in token of submission."[30] Milner added that the word *ifoga* means a "ceremonial request for forgiveness made by an offender and his kinsman to those injured" and among other specific usages "to make a formal apology."

In the Three Tikanga church, the need for the *ifoga* came to light when the question of the Three Tikanga resource sharing was brought up. In 2012 Tikanga Māori called for a bilateral discussion with Tikanga Pakeha on the resources of the church leaving Tikanga Polynesia out when the General Synod was hosted by Tikanga Polynesia in Nadi. However, this motion was retracted from the agenda. In 2014, Tikanga Polynesia was reminded about what happened in 2012 and went into the next General Synod, at Waitangi with a mind to seek forgiveness from Tikanga Māori for what had happened in Nadi in 2012 and this was accepted by Archbishop Brown Turei. In 2016, when the General Synod Standing Committee (GSSC) met in Samoa, Archbishop Emeritus Winston Halapua offered an *ifoga* to Tikanga Māori asking them to forgive all that has been done by his predecessors. Bishop Kito accepted the *ifoga* and replied that the matter was closed and that the Three Tikanga must work closely together.

It was important that the traditional way of seeking forgiveness or *ifoga* is done in a proper manner in Samoa because the

---

[28] Penelope Schoeffel, "Samoan Exchange and 'Fine Mats': An Historical Reconsideration," *Journal of the Polynesian Society* 108 (1999).
[29] Cluny Macpherson, "The Ifoga: The Exchange Value of Social Honour in Samoa," *Journal of the Polynesian Society* 114, no. 2 (2005): 109.
[30] George Pratt, *A Samoan Dictionary* (Whitefish, Mont.: Kessinger Publishing, 2010), 49.

GSSC which is a high governing body of the Church and represents all the Three Tikanga equally within the Anglican Church in Aotearoa, New Zealand and Polynesia was present. Secondly, having it done on that particular day, time and space is the way of the land, nothing moves forward until the way is clear. Though done in Waitangi, when it is done in the traditional way, the *'faka* Samoa' (Samoan Way), the space is different, more sombre and meaningful. Thirdly, as Solomona stated 'the *ifoga* is the highest form of apology that is performed for a very serious offence even killing someone. In saying this we explained to Archbishop Winston that the *ie toga* (fine mat) would mirror what the *'tabua'* (whale's tooth) would do in Fiji, but that it was a symbol of creating a sense of "healing" in that, here was a brother being angry with another and the other one not being confrontational but attempting to find peace and solace in the midst of what I saw as a threat from Polynesia. So, the *ie toga* was presented in a traditional setting after the kava ceremony to welcome GSSC to Samoa and Bishop Kito accepted it on behalf of Tikanga Māori. He responded to the presentation and was greatly humbled and at the same time also apologised on behalf of Tikanga Māori. Archbishop Philip responded on the provincial level and welcomed the sincerity of Polynesia and the act of forgiving one another. The *ie toga* on such occasions is always named to honour the event, it is called *"Le Tolu ua Tasi"* translated to mean 'The three that are now One.'

Using the *ifoga* as a methodology of reconciliation in our pedagogies and methodologies is a step towards a more intentional partnership as it signifies the culture of trust, acceptance, and openness. This is what God would want us to be and do as a community of believers. This encourages and enhances intercultural theology in partnership within the Three Tikanga church.

Solesolevaki is about togetherness, it is about trusting each other, it is about seeking ways of enabling the other, it is more than just a bond and relationships, it is about celebrating who we are in this part of the world. *Solesolevaki* as a social capital for the Three Tikanga church would enable each tikanga to seek out the best from another tikanga through learning, resourcing and enabling. This could be done by using the Three Tikanga College as a way and means of introducing indigenous methodologies, pedagogies, metaphors and ontology so that as a Three Tikanga one could get to know the other better.

Conclusion

I began with a brief historical context of the Three Tikanga Church and introduced the Fijian concept of working together for the benefit of the group known as *Solesolevaki*. The nature of *solesolevaki* often connects relationships in ways that promote trust and reciprocity. These connections are integral to developing partnership. I compared this with a theology of Tūrangawaewae and then explored *solesolevaki* as a theology for partnership in our Three Tikanga Church. In articulating partnership as a form of *solesolevaki*, I have applied an indigenous concept, language and practice from my homeland of Fiji to our theological discussion. It is a process that offers ways for indigenous people to encounter the God revealed in Jesus Christ in the language God gives us.

9

Te Puna Atuatanga/ The John Kinder Theological Library, a Journey in Partnership

JUDITH BRIGHT & COLENSO ERAMIHA

Te Puna Atuatanga

INTRODUCTION

THIS PAPER DESCRIBES the journey that the Kinder Library at St John's Theological College undertook to become the John Kinder Theological Library Te Puna Atuatanga,[1] following the principles of partnership and bicultural development. This journey has brought a significant Anglican resource from an essentially pre-constitution College Library to a centralised coordinated resource. It is rooted in a worldview that acknowledges the need to take into account the faith experiences of the past, and their culture and history, as a context in which to support the theological developments of the future.

This partnership journey has received wisdom from many, giving a wider perspective to what it is to offer library and archival resources in a unique part of the Anglican Communion and acknowledging a bicultural partnership as integral to the journey. Many years ago, some words of former Archbishop, Sir Paul Reeves resonated, and looking back, these reflect the direction that we have been trying to follow. Sir Paul's words:

> We talk about biculturalism and there's a Pakeha understanding, and then there's a Māori understanding. The Pakeha understanding of biculturalism is being sensitive to Māori issues, and Māori understanding of biculturalism is sharing power where the decisions are made.[2]

But before moving towards the partnership and bicultural journey story, some historical background will set the context.

BACKGROUND

In 1841, Bishop George Augustus Selwyn, newly appointed Bishop of the Diocese of New Zealand, persuaded his friends and

---

[1] See website for overview, http://www.kinderlibrary.ac.nz/about/
[2] http://anglican.webstation.net.nz/main/biculturalpolicy/ Accessed 29 June 2005, no longer available (also published in the New Zealand Herald, 7 February 1998.)

family to provide books for a library for his new Diocese (the Library) and its planned theological college, an integrated venture. Arriving in New Zealand, he unpacked the many crates of books donated into the second floor of the Church Missionary Society stone goods store at Kerikeri, in the Bay of Islands, and occasionally indulged in the ten mile walk to enjoy reading. In the Bishop's own words, "A delicious day in my library."[3] Although the Bishop's printing press produced a significant number of publications in Māori and then Melanesian languages, in the context of the missionary era, it is doubtful if any of these were seen as an integral part of a library focused on nineteenth century folios in Greek and Latin as well as English.

By 1845 the Library (and College) was moved to Auckland and found its home in various buildings in the Diocese and at St John's College. In 1910 a purpose-built library was built at St John's College and followed by a new library building in 1981. By now what had been known as the Kinder Library became more commonly known as the St John's College Library and although a few non-College borrowers found their way to the Library, there was a decidedly "hands-off" approach to non-College use.[4] Selwyn's vision of a close interrelationship of Diocese of New Zealand, the College and the Library, had gone.

By the 1970s, the St John's College Library was, as were most academic libraries at that time, a traditional western concept of a theological library. The leather-bound books had been relegated to the back room, and gradually being built to degree and then postgraduate standards. But New Zealand publications or anything that might support the concept of a Treaty Partnership, or any other cultural context was not a focus. The Library at this time was very

---

[3] Quoted in Nola Easdale, *Missionary and Maori: Kerikeri, 1819-1860* (Lincoln, N.Z.: Te Waihora Press, 1991), 136.
[4] The Kinder Library was named after the Reverend John Kinder, Master of the College 1871-1880, who donated his collection of 3000 books.

much an in-house College library but starting to think about how it might be more widely used.

General Synod Theological Education Commission

In 1994, with a revised Church Constitution/te Pouhere in place,[5] General Synod set up a Commission on Theological Education to look at how the principles of partnership and Three-Tikanga principles of the Constitution might be applied to St John's College and other theological education within the Church. Its terms of reference were very detailed, but the key direction was to define foundational issues of theological education and ministry training within the context of the new Constitutional framework. Included in its deliberations were a focus on theological education outside of the St John's College Campus, equitable resource allocation and the need to reflect the principles of partnership referred to in Te Pouhere.[6] The Kinder Library was included in the review and the Librarian had a number of discussions with the reviewers.

In 1996 the Commission made its final report with 10 key recommendations.[7] Recommendation Seven read:

> It is recommended that a report be prepared outlining an integrated development plan for the Library resources available within the three Tikanga over the next ten years giving particular attention to:
> The development of resources which serve and are accessible to each Tikanga
> Resources which serve the needs of regional and distance education students and in particular how

---

[5] https://www.anglican.org.nz/About/Constitution-te-Pouhere
[6] Graham Hingangaroa Smith, Philip Richardson, and John Bluck, *General Synod Report/Te Hinota Whanui Commission on Theological Education and Ministry Training* (Rotorua,NZ: The Anglican Church in Aotearoa, New Zealand and Polynesia, 1996), 5.
[7] Smith, Richardson, and Bluck, *Proceedings*, 29.

access of library resources to non-residential students might be enhanced,
Outlining detailed proposals for the appropriate development of on-line resources.

It sounded simple, but it wasn't. Suddenly the Library as a jewel in the crown of the church (as someone described it) was being fought for. The College was keen for the Library to remain under the three heads of College and even the idea of three separate tikanga-appointed librarians sharing the managerial role was suggested as a serious possibility. By this time, requests for assistance with archives and libraries from Dioceses and Hui Amorangi were being received but little could be done officially. There were many reports written about how the library should be governed and operated and many uncomfortable discussions in specially convened meetings, usually including some who had little knowledge of the Library. It wasn't until February 2004 that Te Kotahitanga was able to secure agreement to move forward with a new direction for the Kinder Library.[8] It had taken eight years.

The Kinder Library Oversight Committee starts its work

The motion as passed by Te Kotahitanga read

Recognising that ... The Kinder Library is a resource for the whole Church, Te Kotahitanga seeks to improve the capacity to support St John's College and regional resource centres and to ensure accessibility to information resources of this Church and beyond. Therefore, Te Kotahitanga acting as the Board of Governors establishes a Kinder Library Oversight Committee (a subcommittee of the Board of Governors)

---

[8] Te Kotahitanga was set up with a number of functions, one of which was to convene as the Board of Governors of St John's College.

responsible for ... Strategy, Policy, Employment, Service contracts, Budget development ...[9]

Te Kotahitanga was giving permission for the Kinder Library to support information resourcing for the whole Church and to be governed by a new body known as the Kinder Library Oversight Committee (or KLOC), which reported directly to Te Kotahitanga as did St John's College at that point in time. There was excitement but also nervousness. The Library had been the College's Library for 161 years and not everyone was pleased with the decision.

A meeting to establish The Kinder Library Oversight Committee was held in November 2004 with the Chair of Te Kotahitanga, Rev (now Archbishop) Philip Richardson, and an external facilitator leading the discussion. This committee was set up by Te Kotahitanga as a three tikanga body with delegated powers of oversight to the Kinder Library Oversight Committee. The vision for the library included the rationalisation and linking of resources of all tikanga, and notably that the bishops should be made aware of the value of making more use of the resources of the Library – the Minute noted resources not only as books but also people and the skills and training skills that the Library staff could bring to a wider resourcing for all tikanga and all regional theological training. Specifically mentioned in the minutes of that meeting was a "centralised portal" (i.e., website) as a key ingredient. It was clearly noted that in order to build up trust among the stakeholders, partnership in the decision making and development was key.

The first Chair was Rev Turi Hollis, appointed for six months, to bring some continuity and sense of purpose from Te Kotahitanga and the previous St John's College Board of Governors. A later change to the KLOC membership allowed for an additional Committee member so that a Chair could be appointed for those skills, not necessarily from within the other committee areas of expertise. This

---

[9] Kinder Library Oversight Committee Minutes of the Meeting of November 2004, unpublished.

Kinder Library Oversight Committee make-up was an interesting departure from the model of each tikanga having an appointment to each role on a Committee. From the start, the Committee was agreed to be expertise based, with appointments to reflect library expertise, the stakeholders of St John's College, regional theological delivery and from the oversight body Te Kotahitanga. Within that mix, all Tikanga needed to be represented. Further non-specific appointments were later added to give room for "seats" to be shared around between tikanga.[10]

Hui

At that set-up meeting it was agreed that KLOC needed to hear from the Church as to its expectations, aspirations and dreams for the Library in widening its support for theological education. In 2006 there was a Hui of representatives from each Tikanga, who had some knowledge of what might work for their Tikanga in library support for theological education. This included Ministry Educators, members of KLOC and representatives from regional resource centres. The Hui met for two days in April 2005. After an overview of presentation of cutting-edge possibilities in the library world of the 21st century, each Tikanga group spent the rest of the day in caucus, dreamed and planned, then shared their work with the other Tikanga, giving a basis to spark further ideas.

These many ideas were sorted into themes and then key goals for the next five-year period. These were considered, prioritised and agreed to by all present. Each Tikanga had been generous in suggesting ways forward for other Tikanga. This was a significant partnership moment as no Tikanga saw their needs as necessarily ahead of anyone else's. It was humbling to be in the room and see the support for one another. Given the long journey to this moment, it was totally unexpected.

---

[10] See Title E of Education in Canons, https://www.anglican.org.nz/Resources/Canons

Strategic goals for 2005-2008

The goals that were agreed on, and in priority order were

- A theological library and ongoing purchasing for the Diocese of Polynesia and its St John the Baptist Theological College[11]
- A shared library catalogue and access to online resources for Hui Amorangi and Diocesan Libraries and associated church bodies
- A clearing house to enable redistribution of many resources throughout the libraries
- The refurbishment of the John Kinder Theological Library to reflect its three tikanga purpose.[12]

RANDALL JIMERSON – LIBRARIES ARCHIVES AND SOCIAL JUSTICE

Even before the Hui, the Librarian of the Kinder Library had been looking for ways forward, looking for threads, a philosophy, that could perhaps offer context to ensure partnership decision making for KLOC and the Library. Sir Paul Reeves, as previously quoted, spoke of sharing power where the decisions are made. Once decision making has happened, the implementation of the decisions has to offer not only information resource support for all of our Tikanga partners, but also a new way of looking at what it is that we are collecting.

As alluded to at the beginning of this paper, the context of the Library collections is to enable the past to be remembered, as well as offering opportunities to look forward. The words of Randall Jimerson, Professor of History and Director of Archives at Western Washington University offer a direction for action. Jimerson sees archives (and by extension books) as a call for justice. He said that remembering through archives (and for that matter, books) can be

---

[11] Suva, Fiji Islands, https://www.anglican.org.nz/Directory/Diocese-of-Polynesia/Diocese-of-Polynesia

[12] Outcomes from the Hui, as recorded in the minutes of the KLOC meeting of April 20, unpublished.

seen as a "thoroughly religious act of world-making." It can be a way to define the past and strengthen attachments to a sense of place.[13] Stephen Bevans also helpfully connects social location to a context for faith and the need to value and appreciate whether one is at the centre or the margins of power.[14] To quote Jimerson:

In looking at the history of archives since ancient times and how they have been used to bolster the prestige and influence of the powerful elites in societies, I contend that archivists have a moral professional responsibility to balance that support given to the status quo by giving equal voice to those groups that too often have been marginalised and silenced. We can see many precedents for this professional imperative. Examples of the use of records and archives to redress social wrongs and support the causes of justice and community consciousness among marginalised groups are growing more numerous. Archivists can become active agents for change, in accordance with their existing professional principles, by taking active steps to counter the biases of previous archival practices.[15]

Jimerson spoke of a partnership theme in archives (and it is possible to extend this to a library context) – and the need for the librarian or archivist to ensure that all voices are represented in our library and archives, not just the dominant one, which is the easy option. He reflected on the Librarian or Archivist's power to shape the collective memory because there is never neutrality. It is the same when shaping a library collection. Whoever selects the books and other resources does so from a context that is themselves, even

---

[13] Randall Jimerson, *Paper delivered at the ARANZ Conference Auckland,* August 2010, see http://aranzconference.blogspot.com/2010/08/randall-jimerson-archive-is-politics.html
[14] Stephen B. Bevans, *Models of Contextual Theology* (Maryknoll, New York: Orbis Books, 2002), 6.
[15] Randall C. Jimerson, "Archives for All: Professional Responsibility and Social Justice," *The American Archivist* 70, no. 2 (2007),
https://meridian.allenpress.com/american-archivist/article/70/2/252/24093/Archives-for-All-Professional-Responsibility-and.

if working to taught papers or research topics. Accepting records or papers for an archive, again it is too easy for an archive to be shaped only by those who are grounded in a western tradition of records keeping.

In a bicultural partnership context, the Librarian must acknowledge all partners who have a stake in the library and ensure that all voices can be heard in the pages of the collection, in both purchases and donations. Jimerson says that the archivist or librarian cannot just be passive and wait for the books or archival records to come: the unseen silent part needs to be sought out and recorded. It is very easy to have only the voice of the powerful recorded, especially when two of our Tikanga have an oral tradition.

Many years ago, I was organising some of the archives of the Diocese of Polynesia in Suva, and I remember being impressed by the number of paper records that had survived. But then I looked again – they were all European voices, no Fijian, no Tongan, no Samoan. There was a part explanation as I was later told, and that was in the agreed early membership of the Anglican Church in that area of the Pacific Diocese of Polynesia. But that still unsettled me, even as I knew that paper records were a western construct anyway, it still spoke of a dominant voice. Thus, the Kinder Library has a very important role for this Church in ensuring that all voices can be heard as collections of books and archives are developed. This is not necessarily easy.

IMPLEMENTING THE DECISIONS

There were three very key developments that have brought the Library to where we are today: the repurposing of the space and refurbishment of the Library building; the development of an access hub to resources of all partners; and the appointment of a Kaiwhakamana. Somewhere in the mix was the re-naming to The John Kinder Theological Library, which while a mouthful, moved neatly from being the Kinder Library at St John's College to a new body without losing a link with the past name. A total renaming would have been nice, but it was felt that there was still too much good in the brand to start again from scratch.

Refurbishing the library

There had been a lot of feedback about how the physical Kinder Library was viewed as unwelcoming. The St John's College Trustees after a lengthy consultation process of several years agreed to the refurbishing of the current space to better reflect who we served. This was done in full consultation with the KLOC, the governance group, and another consultation group from our bicultural partners, especially around naming of spaces and the library itself.

Archbishop Brown Turei offered us the name *Te Puna Atuatanga* (Wellspring of Divine Wisdom). The subtle weaving of partnership symbolism together in layouts, floors, shelf-ends and more was a very creative solution coordinated by our architect, who entered the project new to concepts of bicultural and library. The Library is now a space furnished to weave the Tikanga together, allow conversation areas, and group working spaces. A dawn reopening service led by Archbishop Brown Turei cemented the partnership that had led to this moment.

Access Hub: Coordination of Resources

Following through from the visioning in that set-up meeting for KLOC, a shared library catalogue for most of the regional libraries of all tikanga was a given. *Anglicat* was achieved by the central cataloguing of thousands of books. At its peak there were ten libraries involved. This was an exercise in partnership: staff worked closely and respectfully with each diocese or regional College to catalogue their book collections; to encourage a certain amount of judicious weeding; and to acknowledge the creative tension of some books as taonga because of past ownership while not stifling a current book collection. Donations of quality recent books supported local teaching needs. The process led to conversations and better understanding around a common goal, but possibly also some misunderstandings on both sides.

The development of a library for the St John the Baptist College in the Diocese of Polynesia was requested by all present at the Hui as the first development urgently needed. Working in partnership, a good small library of around 2000 volumes was established and made accessible by the library catalogue, *Anglicat*, and is kept current by book ordering and visits. Any library of printed books in English does not sit well in the Pacific for many reasons, both practical and intellectual. There have been opportunities for dialogue with decision makers in the Diocese and we have had many conversations around the concept of a library and how else resourcing might be offered in a creative and Pacific way.

Archbishop Winston Halapua in his development of Moana theology, speaks of "giving grace and space to others to tell their stories."[16] There are wonderful possibilities, if together, we can re-vision and rework the concept of library. *Does a library need books? If so, how might one choose and arrange to provide appropriate access to the content? Is it just a Pakeha perception that we need to do anything differently anyway? How do we ensure equality of access to resources, what are the other ways forward?*

This is all to some extent hampered by accreditation requirements, a very limited offering of print material from more marginal voices and all the technical issues of trying to develop and preserve an oral and pictorial record. More accessible information formats – audio and visual are fleeting and almost impossible to keep beyond the present. They can't just be put on a shelf and left, and if your internet allocation runs out before the end of the month, any online access is gone. There is the practical challenge of trying to maintain a paper record in a Pacific climate, as well as how one enables development and then hands over, rather than being seen to be a necessary part of the ongoing picture.

The graciousness of Māori and Pasefika as we developed understandings was greatly appreciated. For example, my suggestion that one way to begin a library of works in local languages was to print some student essays and make them available, got a very gentle

---

[16] Winston Halapua, *Waves of God's Embrace: Sacred Perspectives from the Ocean* (London: Canterbury Press, 2008), 11.

"no" from a former Archbishop, and I learned that this suggestion was inappropriate. Being the only Pakeha on an Academic Board for the Whare Wananga ki Te Pihopatanga o Aotearoa with its three Taapapa degree delivery sites was a significant learning experience, as was being asked to Chair the final two meetings of that Board.[17] It has been possible to provide the people resources and skills named again in that first set up meeting of KLOC: by travelling to work alongside others as invited, by developing a significant archival resource to safeguard the Churches' records, and developing access points for researchers and inhouse Church needs.

Kaiwhakamana Appointment

Significant in the journey was the appointment of a Kaiwhakamana. Experience in the library when providing for library users from a variety of cultural backgrounds is that the cultural background of a library staff member plays a significant role, one which no amount of learned cultural intelligence can provide. In the case of our bicultural commitment, it is much wider than that. We are committed to a Kaiwhakamana or enabler on the Library staff as key to our bicultural commitment. That position is currently held by Colenso Eramiha, and he now describes that role.

COLENSO ERAMIHA[18]

The role of Kaiwhakamana is to break down barriers of misunderstanding, misinformation and apprehension that Māori often feel when entering a library. However, I see the role as more than just an enabler or go-between for Māori patrons. It is a role tasked with helping in the welcoming of all people, the building of relationships, being accessible to all, and helping to develop a sense of community and belonging. The Kaiwhakamana has a

---

[17] Te Pihopatanga o Aotearoa ministry training and education programs for church leaders, ministers and members of the wider community.

[18] Colenso Eramiha, Kaiwhakamana, John Kinder Theological Library.

responsibility to both stakeholders and patrons alike to maintain the integrity or mana of both the patrons and library staff throughout all our dealings and a tikanga Māori based values system is applied to help achieve these aims.

Tikanga Māori helps to make people feel safe and happy to engage with us. The role of Kaiwhakamana also applies to my work colleagues. If I can't build relationships within my own workspace, I cannot build them with others. The role is not based on the 'me' but it is based on the 'we.' We here at the John Kinder Theological Library have adopted this mindset, that 'we', with all our different skill sets will work together - mahi ngatahi - by using the tikanga Māori values of manaakitanga, rangatiratanga and aroha as our puna or wellspring, as the tuapapa or foundation for all our dealings with all users of the library. What the role of Kaiwhakamana has brought to the library working environment is biculturalism at work, that is, an awareness of self and others, an appreciation of self and others and the desire to work together. We recognise and celebrate our differences and our similarities.

CONCLUSION: CHALLENGES AND SUMMARY

The greatest challenge surprisingly, has been moving the Church's perception of the Library from that of being the Kinder Library of St John's College to what is now a Tikanga partnership stand-alone John Kinder Theological Library resource for all Anglicans in the first instance, and as an outreach to members of other churches, other faiths and members of the general public. Keeping this availability of the Library in front of the Church is an ongoing challenge. So, despite having completed the work set out in the goals, has the Library succeeded in a library-based partnership model?

The goals were very much about doing, about practical things such as refurbishing a space, enabling the development of regional libraries, appointing a Kaiwhakamana, and contributing another voice to several tikanga committees. As Sir Paul Reeves states, "it is not so much about the doing, but about the thinking and understanding as to what it means to be in a partnership." While significant thought took place regarding what it meant to be in partnership, it was necessary for us to have an outward visible expression of that thinking by doing. A former Archbishop's gentle rebuke of the suggestion that his students' voices could be a good starting point to build resources illustrated different cultural values and communication styles. There were many such cultural learnings and understandings on the part of the Library staff, together with hands on work, as well as much dialogue to ensure that we really did understand what the needs were and how others would see these expressed.

At the end of the Strategic Plan period, all goals had been achieved. But it was of course not as simple as that. There had been much talking and visiting – with ministry committees, bishops, educators and in fact anyone who would listen – the same message that the Library was there and available to all, and that we had the expertise to develop and support local collections to enhance and underpin theological education in all its regional forms.

Had we done enough thinking and understanding together? Probably not. There is a need to find new ways to continue the dialogue so that it is not our story and our journey but one belonging to partners. Just as with the journey to inclusive language in worship, some that fought that battle, find it surprising and challenging that a new generation is not necessarily aware of what it took for inclusive language to become the norm or that it was ever an issue, yet in some of our parishes, it has been recently noted that the inclusive language conversation needs to happen again. It is the same with operating the John Kinder Theological Library in a partnership model.

New generations come into the space, the story has not always been handed on and we are once again conscious that we need to rebuild, and make space for the conversations to be regenerated, to initiate further opportunities to sit and reflect and listen, for new ways forward, but this time hopefully starting from several steps further on.

Glossary of Māori Terms

This glossary focuses on Māori language terms used within the chapters in this book. Since Māori words appear in a broad spectrum of chapters and often without explanation this glossary aids reading those papers.

Aotearoa	New Zealand (translated as land of the 'long white cloud')
Ahorangi	A teacher of the highest standing
Aroha	Compassion, sympathy, empathy, love
Atua	God
Awa	River
Hāhi / Haahi	Church, religion
Haka	Māori dance, traditionally performed by men
Hapu /hapū	Sub-tribe
He iwi tahi tatou	We are one people
He Karakia Mihinare o Aotearoa	The New Zealand Prayer Book
Hīmene	Māori language hymns
Hui	Gathering, meeting
Hui Amorangi	Tikanga Māori Diocese(s)
Iwi	Tribe
Kaiwhakamana	Leader, or someone who holds authority in an area/field
Karakia	Prayer, worship
Kaupapa	Topic, issue or matter at hand
Kāwanatanga	Government
Kingitanga	The Māori King movement, with Turangawaewae being the national marae of the Kingitanga
Ko te mea nui, ko te aroha	The main thing is love (c.f. 1 Corinthians 13:13)
Koha	Gift
Kōhanga reo	Māori language pre-schools
Korowai	Cloak

Glossary of Māori Terms

Maha	Numerous, many, abundant
Mahi ngatahi	Working together
Mahinga kai	Garden or cultivation
Mana	Prestige, authority, power, influence
Manaaki / manaakitanga	Hospitality, care and support
Marae	Meeting house and complex
Marae kawa	Protocol and ceremonies associated with a Marae
Mātauranga	Knowledge
Mīhinare	Missionary, Anglican
Minita	Minister, priest
Minita-a-Iwi	Non-ordained and non-stipended Māori lay person working within community
Minita-a-Whānau	Non-ordained and non-stipended Māori lay person working with whanau A whānau member tasked with leading karakia (worship) in the absence of the priest.
Ngā Ra Waho/ Ngā Rāwaho	The outsiders
Ngāi Tahu	South Island tribe
Noho marae	Live-in learning on the marae
Pākehā	Non Māori – frequently used to refer to New Zealanders of European descent, the word has a broader reference to all non-indigenous people.
Pasefika	Pacifica, Polynesia
Pīhopatanga	Diocese / Bishopric
Pono	True, truth
Puna	Wellspring
Rangatiratanga	Political autonomy /self-determination, principality
Rangimārie	State of peace and tranquility
Raupatu	Confiscated Māori land
Rerenga	Flowing, variation
Rongopai (Te Rongopai)	The good news, the gospel
Runanga Whaiti	Standing Committee of Te Pīhopatanga o Aotearoa/ the Bishopric of Aotearoa

Runanganui	Tikanga Māori Synod
Taapapa	Seed Bed (Lit). The name of the former tertiary provider established by Tikanga Māori to provide theological education and ministry training to the various Amorangi (Bishoprics) within Te Pīhopatanga o Aotearoa.
Tangata	People
Tangata Tiriti	Treaty Partner / People of the Treaty
Tangata whenua	Indigenous / First people of the land
Taonga	Treasure, things highly prized
Tapu	Holy, sacred, sacredness
Tauiwi	Non-indigenous people
Te Hāhi Mihinare	Missionary church, Māori Anglican Church
Te Hīnota Whānui	General Synod
Te Hui Amorangi o te Manawa o te Wheke	The Diocese / Bishopric of the greater Waikato/Coromandel/Hauraki/Taupo/Rotorua/Northern King Country area (Bombay Hills to Taumarunui)
Te Paipera Tapu	Māori language Holy Bible
Te Pihopatanga o Aotearoa	The Bishopric of Aotearoa (see Te Pouhere / The Constitution of the Anglican Church in Aotearoa, New Zealand and Polynesia)
Te Pouhere	The Constitution of the Anglican Church of Aotearoa, New Zealand and Polynesia.
Te Rāwiri	The Māori language version of the 1662 Book of Common Prayer
Te reo / te reo Māori	The Māori language
Te Rūnanganui o Te Pīhopatanga o Aotearoa	The Synod of the Bishopric of Aotearoa
Te Taitokerau / Te Tai Tokerau	North Auckland or Northland region
Te Tiriti o Waitangi	The Treaty of Waitangi
Te Wai Pounamu	The South Island of NZ

Glossary of Māori Terms

Te whānau o te Atua	The family of God
Tena koutou katoa	Greetings to you all
Tika	Correct, right
Tikanga	Custom, habit, manner, convention, principle; The name given to the governance structures established in Te Pouhere / The Constitution of the Anglican Church to enable the principles of partnership and bicultural development for ministry and mission in its Māori, Pasefika and Pākehā expressions. (In this volume when spelled with a capital, Tikanga refers to the church structure – without the capital, tikanga refers to "custom" etc.)
Tikanga karakia	Liturgy, or an authorised order of service
Tikanga Māori	The name describing the ecclesial arrangements for Anglicanism in its Māori expression (see Tikanga).
Tikanga Māori	Māori customary values and practices
Tikanga Pākehā	The name describing the ecclesial arrangements for Anglicanism in its Pākehā expression (see Tikanga).
Tikanga Pasefika	The name given to describe the ecclesial arrangements for Anglicanism in its Pacific expressions (see Tikanga).
Tino rangatiratanga	Sovereignty, self determination
Tuapapa	Foundation
Tūrangawaewae	Standing place (Lit); where one belongs, especially an ancestral marae
Tūrangawaewae Marae	The national marae of the Kingitanga, the Māori King movement; formal home to the Māori King.
Wahi tapu	Sacred place(s)
Waikato	The greater Hamilton region, including the districts of Waikato, Waipa, Matamata-Piako, Hauraki, Coromandel Peninsula, Northern King Country, Taupo & parts of Rotorua.

Waka	Canoe, vessel
Whakamaa	Embarrassed, feeling shamed
Whakapapa	History, genealogy
Whānau	Family, extended / clan
Whanaungatanga	Kinship
Whare Wānanga	Tertiary education institute / College
Whenua	Land

References

"Rabbis without Borders." n.d., accessed 19 June, 2021, https://rabbiswithoutborders.org/ruth-abusch-magder/.

Adare, Sierra. *Mohawk*. New York, N.Y.: Gareth Stevens, 2003.

Adeney, Bernard T. *Strange Virtues: Ethics in a Multicultural World*. Downers Grove, Ill.: InterVarsity Press, 1995. http://catalog.hathitrust.org/api/volumes/oclc/32132816.html.

Aldred, Ray. "An Indigenous Reinterpretation of Repentance." In *Race and Racism: North Park Symposium on Theological Interpretation of Scipture, 2015*, edited by Klyne Snodgrass. Eugene, Oregon Pickwick Publications, an imprint of Wipf and Stock Publishers, 2016.

———. "A Shared Narrative." Chap. 12 In *Strangers in This World*, edited by Allen G. Jorgenson, Hussam S. Timani and Alexander Y. Hwang, 193-206. Minneapolis: Fortress Press, 2015.

———. (Raymond Clifford). "An Alternative Starting Place for an Indigenous Theology." ThD, University of Toronto, 2020.

Alexander, T. D., and B. S. Rosner. *New Dictionary of Biblical Theology*. La Vergne, U.S.A.: IVP, 2020. http://ebookcentral.proquest.com/lib/stjohns/detail.action?docID=6201852.

Allard, Pierre. "Restorative Justice: Lost Treasure." Regina, Saskatchewan: Canadian Theological Seminary, March, 11, 1999. Lecture.

Allen, Danielle S. *Talking to Strangers: Anxieties of Citizenship since Brown V. Board of Education*. Chicago: The University of Chicago Press, 2004.

Andrew, M. E. *Treaty Land Covenant*. Dunedin: M. Andrew, 1990.

Anglican Church. *New Zealand Prayer Book: He Karakia Mihinare O Aotearoa.* Auckland: Collins, 1989. https://anglicanprayerbook.nz/404.html.

Aston, Charles William Whonsbon. *Pacific Irishman.* Stanmore, Australia: Australian Board of Missions, 1970. http://anglicanhistory.org/oceania/whonsbon-aston1970.html.

Athanasius. *On the Incarnation of the Word.* Translated by unknown. Christian Classics Ethereal Library. Grand Rapids, MI: Calvin College, c296-373. https://ccel.org/ccel/athanasius/incarnation/incarnation?queryID=10351578&resultID=2038.

Barr, James. *The Semantics of Biblical Language.* London: Oxford University Press, 1961.

Bauckham, Richard. "Introduction." In *Jürgen Moltmann: Collected Readings*, edited by Margaret Kohl, 1-6. Minneapolis: Fortress Press, 2014.

Bell, Shirley. "'Cultural Vandalism' and Pakeha Politics of Guilt and Responsibility." In *Tangata Tangata: The Changing Ethnic Contours of New Zealand*, edited by Paul Spoonley, David G. Pearson and Cluny Macpherson. Melbourne: Thomson Dunmore Press, 2004.

Belmessous, S. *Empire by Treaty: Negotiating European Expansion, 1600-1900.* New York: OUP, 2015.

Bevans, Stephen B. *Models of Contextual Theology.* Maryknoll, New York: Orbis Books, 2002.

Bhabha, Homi K. *The Location of Culture.* Routledge Ltd, 2012. https://www.dawsonera.com:443/abstract/9780203820551.

Bi-cultural Commission. *Te Rīpoata a Te Kōmihana Mo Te Kaupapa Tikanga Rua Mo Te Tiriti O Waitangi = the Report of the Bi-Cultural Commission of the Anglican Church on the Treaty of Waitangi.* (Christchurch, N.Z. : Provincial Secretary of the Church of the Province of New Zealand, 1986).

REFERENCES

Black Elk, and Joseph Epes Brown. *The Gift of the Sacred Pipe: Based on Black Elk's Account of the Seven Rites of the Oglala Sioux.* Norman: University of Oklahoma Press, 1982.

Bluck, J. "Stunned Mullets, Untested Vehicles and Other Things Anglican." In *Te Awa Rerenga Maha: Braided River*, edited by D. Moffat. Three Tikanga Church Colloquium, 1-20. Auckland: Anglican Church in Aotearoa, New Zealand and Polynesia, 2018.

———. *Wai Karekare Turbulent Waters: The Anglican Bicultural Journey 1814–2014.* Auckland: Anglican Church in Aotearoa, New Zealand and Polynesia, 2012.

Bluck, J., P. Carrell, J. Dawson, A. Fletcher, P. Harvey, C. Holmes, R. Kereopa, et al. *Te Awa Rerenga Maha: Braided River.* Three Tikanga Church Colloquium. Edited by D. Moffat. Auckland: Anglican Church in Aotearoa, New Zealand and Polynesia, 2018.

Boulding, M. Cecily. *The Church Makes the Eucharist and the Eucharist Makes the Church.* St. Mary's College, University of Durham, 1993, an "occasional" printed lecture.

Bourdieu, P. "Forms of Capital." In *Handbook of Theory and Research for the Sociology of Education*, edited by John G. Richardson. New York, N.Y.: Greenwood Press, 1986.

Bouteneff, Peter C., and Alan D. Falconer. *Episkopé and Episcopacy and the Quest for Visible Unity: Two Consultations.* Geneva: WCC Publications, 1999.

Brandt, Agnes. *Among Friends? On the Dynamics of Māori-Pakeha Relationships in Aotearoa New Zealand.* Göttingen: V&R Unipress, 2013.

Branson, Mark Lau. *Memories, Hopes, and Conversations: Appreciative Inquiry and Congregational Change.* 2nd ed. Lanham: Alban Institute, 2016.

Brown, Jennifer S.H. "Rupert's Land, Nituskeenan, Our Land," in *New Histories for Old: Changing Perspectives on Canada's Native*

Pasts, edited by Theodore Binnema and Susan Neylan. Vancouver, B.C.: UBC Press, 2007

Brown, Juanita, and David Isaacs. *The World Café: Shaping Our Futures through Conversations That Matter.* San Francisco, CA: Berrett-Koehler Publishers, 2005.

Browning, Don S. *Equality and the Family: A Fundamental, Practical Theology of Children, Mothers, and Fathers in Modern Societies.* Grand Rapids: Eerdmans, 2007.

———. *A Fundamental Practical Theology.* Minneapolis: Fortress, 1996.

Browning, Don S., Bonnie J. Miller-McLemore, Pamela D. Couture, K. Brynolf Lyon, and Robert M. Franklin. *From Culture Wars to Common Ground: Religion and the American Family Debate.* 2nd ed. Louisville: Westminster John Knox, 2000.

Brueggemann, John, and Walter Brueggemann. *Rebuilding the Foundations: Social Relationships in Ancient Scripture and Contemporary Culture.* Louisville: Westminster John Knox, 2017.

Bussidor, Ila, and Üstün Bilgen-Reinart. *Night Spirits: The Story of the Relocation of the Sayisi Dene.* Manitoba Studies in Native History. Winnipeg: University of Manitoba Press, 1997.

Callaghan, Moeawa. "Look to the Past to See the Future." *First Peoples Theology Journal* 4, no. 1 (2006): 104-109.

Callister, P. "Ethnic Measurement as a Policy Making Tool." In *Public Policy and Ethnicity: The Politics of Ethnic Boundary Making* 142-155: Palgrave Macmillan, 2007.

Campbell, J. Y. *Three New Testament Studies.* Leiden: Brill, 1965.

Carleton, Hugh. *The Life of Henry Williams.* Wellington, N.Z.: A.H. & A.W. Reed, 1948.

Carrell, P. "The End of the Three Tikanga Church? Ephesians on the Unity of the Church.". In *Te Awa Rerenga Maha: Braided River*, edited by D. Moffat. Three Tikanga Church Colloquium, 40-56.

References

Auckland: Anglican Church in Aotearoa, New Zealand and Polynesia, 2018.

Chittister, Joan, and Rowan Williams. *Uncommon Gratitude: Alleluia for All That Is.* Collegeville, Minn.: Liturgical Press, 2010.

Clark, Paul David. "Social Capital and Vanua: Challenges to Governance Development in a Community-Based Natural Resource Management Project in Cuvu Tikina, Fiji." University of Montana, 2008. http://etd.lib.umt.edu/theses/available/etd-05202008-111818/.

Clark, Yvonne. "What's in a Name? Lateral Violence within the Aboriginal Community in Adelaide, South Australia." *The Australian Community Psychologist* 27, no. 2. (2015): 19-34. Accessed 2021. https://doi.org/Network (Australian Psychological Society. College of Community Psychologists) 1320-7741. https://www.psychology.org.au/for-members/publications/journals/Australian-Community-Psychologist/ACP-Issues.

Clarke, John, and et al. *He Hīnātore Ki Te Ao Māori: A Glimpse into the Māori World.* Wellington, NZ, 2001.

Cockell, Jeanie, and Joan McArthur-Blair. *Appreciative Inquiry in Higher Education: A Transformative Force.* San Francisco: Jossey-Bass, 2012.

Coleman, James S. *Social Capital in the Creation of Human Capital.* Chicago: University of Chicago Press, 1988.

Consedine, Robert, and Joanna Consedine. *Healing Our History: The Challenge of the Treaty of Waitangi.* Auckland, NZ: Penguin, 2012, 2005.

Craigie, Peter C. *The Book of Deuteronomy.* Grand Rapids: Eerdmans, 1976.

Cuthand, Doug. *Askiwina: A Cree World.* Regina: Coteau Books, 2007.

Davis, Brian. *The Way Ahead: Anglican Change & Prospect in New Zealand.* Christchurch: Caxton, 1995.

Davis, Lynne, and Heather Yanique Shpuniarsky. "The Spirit of Relationships: What We Have Learned About Indigenous / Non-Indigenous Alliances and Coalitions." Chap. 20 In *Alliances: Re/Envisioning Indigenous-Non-Indigenous Relationships*, edited by Lynne Davis, 334–348. Toronto: University of Toronto Press, 2010.

Deane, R. "Globalisation and Constitutional Development." In *Building the Constitution*, edited by Colin James, 112-117. Wellington, N.Z.: Institute of Policy Studies, Victoria University of Wellington, 2000.

Deloria, Vine, and James Treat. *For This Land: Writings on Religion in America.* New York, N.Y.: Routledge, 1999.

The Dictionary of Classical Hebrew. Edited by David J. A. Clines. Vol. III, Sheffield: Sheffield Academic Press, 1996.

Diocese of Polynesia. *Celebrating 100 Years,1908-2008.* Fiji: Anglican Church of Aotearoa, New Zealand and Polynesia, 2008.

A Disciple's Prayer Book Canada, Reprint from 1992. https://www.anglican.ca/wp-content/uploads/A-Disciples-Prayer-Book.pdf.

Durie, E. "The Treaty in the Constitution." In *Building the Constitution*, edited by Colin James, 201-204. Wellington, N.Z.: Institute of Policy Studies, Victoria University of Wellington, 2000.

Durie, Mason. *Ngā Kāhui Pou Launching Māori Futures.* Wellington, Aotearoa N.Z.: Huia Publishers, 2003.

———. "Nga Tai Matatu: Tides of Maori Endurance." *OUP Catalogue* (2005).

———. *Whaiora: Maōri Health Development.* Australia and N.Z.: Oxford University Press, 1998.

Easdale, Nola. *Missionary and Maori: Kerikeri, 1819-1860.* Lincoln, N.Z.: Te Waihora Press, 1991.

REFERENCES

Eilers, Kent. "New Monastic Social Imagination: Theological Retrieval for Ecclesial Renewal." *American Theological Inquiry: A Biannual Journal of Theology, Culture & History* 6, no. 2 (2013): 45–58.

Ellithorpe, Anne-Marie. "Towards a Practical Theology of Friendship." PhD, University of Queensland, 2018.

———. *Towards Friendship-Shaped Communities: A Practical Theology of Friendship.* Wiley, Forthcoming.

Fletcher, A. "Finding Identity in the Body of Christ." In *Te Awa Rerenga Maha: Braided River*, edited by D. Moffat. Three Tikanga Church Colloquium, 188–201. Auckland: Anglican Church in Aotearoa, New Zealand and Polynesia, 2018.

Ford, David. *Christian Wisdom: Desiring God and Learning in Love.* Cambridge; New York: Cambridge University Press, 2007.

Fox, D. "Black Days." *Mana* (2009).

France, R. T. *The Gospel of Matthew.* Grand Rapids, Mich.: William B. Eerdmans, 2007.

Gadd, Bernard "The Teachings of Te Whiti O Rongomai, 1831-1907." *The Journal of the Polynesian Society* 75, 4 (1966): 445–457 http://www.jps.auckland.ac.nz/document//Volume_75_1966/Volume_75,_No._4/The_teachings_of_Te_Whiti_O_Rongomai,_1831-1907,_by___Bernard_Gadd,_p_445_-_457/p1.

Glanville, Mark R. *Adopting the Stranger as Kindred in Deuteronomy.* Atlanta: SBL Press, 2018.

New Interpreter's Dictionary of the Bible. Nashville, Tennessee: Abingdon Press, 2006-2009.

Goldingay, John. *Israel's Faith.* Old Testament Theology. Vol. 2, Downers Grove, Ill.: IVP, 2006.

———. *Israel's Gospel.* Old Testament Theology. Vol. 1, Downers Grove, Ill.: IVP, 2003.

Grant, R. M. *Irenaeus of Lyons, against the Heresies.* The Early Church Fathers. New York, N.Y.: Routledge, 1997.

Grenz, Stanley. *Theology for the Community of God.* Grand Rapids, Mich.: Eerdmans, 2000.

Halapua, Winston. *Waves of God's Embrace: Sacred Perspectives from the Ocean.* London: Canterbury Press, 2008.

Hancock, Frances, David Epston, and Wally McKenzie. "Forging Treaty Hope: The Application and Relevance of Narrative Ideas and Practices in Developing Treaty-Based Policy and Practice." *Community Development Journal* 41, no. 4 (2006): 453-466.

Haran, M. "The Běrît 'Covenant': Its Nature and Ceremonial Background." In *Tehillah Le-Moshe: Biblical and Judaic Studies in Honour of Moshe Greenberg*, edited by M. Coogan, N.L. Eichler and J.H. Tigay. Winona Lake: Eisenbrauns, 1997.

Havea, J. "Welcome to Talanoa." In *Talanoa Ripples: Across Borders, Cultures, Disciplines...* edited by J. Havea, 11-22. Auckland: Masilamea Press, 2010.

Hayward, Janine. "'Flowing from the Treaty's Words': The Principles of the Treaty of Waitangi." In *The Waitangi Tribunal: Te Roopu Whakamana I Te Tiriti O Waitangi* edited by Janine Hayward and Nicola Wheen, 29-40. Wellington, N.Z.: Bridget Williams Books, 2004.

Heitink, Gerben. *Practical Theology: History, Theory, Action Domains.* Translated by Reinder Bruinsma. Grand Rapids: Eerdmans, 1999.

Hoekema, Anthony A. *Created in God's Image.* Grand Rapids: Eerdmans, 1986.

Humpage, Louise. "'Liabilities and Assets': The Maori Affairs Balance Sheet." In *Tangata Tangata: The Changing Ethnic Contours of New Zealand* edited by Paul Spoonley, David G. Pearson and Cluny Macpherson, 25-42. Melbourne: Thomson Dunmore Press, 2004.

Inge, John. *A Christian Theology of Place.* Aldershot, England: Ashgate, 2003.

References

James, Colin. *Building the Constitution.* Wellington: Institute of Policy Studies, Victoria University of Wellington, 2000.

Jennings, Willie James. *The Christian Imagination: Theology and the Origins of Race.* New Haven: Yale University Press, 2010.

———. "New Winds." *Pneuma* 36, no. 3 (2014): 447–455. https://doi.org/https://doi.org/10.1163/15700747-03603047. https://brill.com/view/journals/pneu/36/3/article-p447_9.xml.

Jimerson, Randall C. "Archives for All: Professional Responsibility and Social Justice." *The American Archivist* 70, no. 2 (2007): 252-281. https://meridian.allenpress.com/american-archivist/article/70/2/252/24093/Archives-for-All-Professional-Responsibility-and.

Kawharu, Hugh. "Foreword." In *Waitangi Revisited: Perspectives on the Treaty of Waitangi*, edited by Michael Belgrave, Merata Kawharu, David Vernon Williams. Melbourne: Oxford University Press, 2005.

Kawharu, Merata. "Rangatiratanga and Social Policy." In *Waitangi Revisited: Perspectives on the Treaty of Waitangi*, edited by Michael Belgrave, Merata Kawharu, David Vernon Williams, 105-122. Melbourne: Oxford University Press, 2005.

Kelsey, Jane. "Maori, Te Tiriti, and Globalisation: The Invisible Hand of the Colonial State." In *Waitangi Revisited: Perspectives on the Treaty of Waitangi*, edited by Michael Belgrave, Merata Kawharu, David Vernon Williams, 81-102. Melbourne: Oxford University Press, 2005.

Kereopa, R. "Equal Partnership Enabling New Expressions of Indigenous Mission in a Three Tikanga Church." In *Te Awa Rerenga Maha: Braided River*, edited by D. Moffat. Three Tikanga Church Colloquium, 21-39. Auckland: Anglican Church in Aotearoa, New Zealand and Polynesia, 2018.

Kidwell, Clara Sue, Homer Noley, and George E. Tinker. *A Native American Theology.* Maryknoll, N.Y.: Orbis Books, 2001.

Koenig, John. *New Testament Hospitality: Partnership with Strangers as Promise and Mission.* Philadelphia: Fortress Press, 1985.

Köhler, L. , and W. Baumgartner. *Hebrew & Aramaic Lexicon of the Old Testament.* Vol. 1, Leiden: E.J. Brill, 1994.

Kutsch, E. *Theological Lexicon of the Old Testament.* Translated by Mark E. Biddle. Edited by E. Jenni and C. Westermann. Vol. 1, Peabody, MA: Hendrickson, 1997.

Laliberte, R., P. Settee, Waldram J.B., R. Innes, B Macdougall, L. McBain, and F.L. Barron. *Expressions in Canadian Native Studies.* Saskatoon, Saskatchewan: University of Saskatchewan Extension Press, 2013.

Lethbridge, Christopher. *The Wounded Lion: Octavius Hadfield, 1814-1904, Pioneer Missionary, Friend of the Maori & Primate of New Zealand.* Christchurch: Caxton Press, 1993.

Levenson, Jon Douglas. *The Love of God, Divine Gift, Human Gratitude, and Mutual Faithfulness in Judaism.* Princeton: Princeton University Press, 2016.

Levine, H. B. "Moving Beyond Cultural Essentialism." In *New Zealand Identities: Departures and Destinations*, edited by J. H. Liu, T. McCreanor, T. McIntosh and T. Teaiwa, 104-117. Wellington, N.Z.: Victoria University of Wellington. Centre for Applied Cross-Cultural Research, 2005.

Liava'a, L. F. C. "*Felupe* Theology: A Theological Reflection on the Three Tikanga Church and Ministry." In *Te Awa Rerenga Maha: Braided River*, edited by D. Moffat. Three Tikanga Church Colloquium, 217–232. Auckland: Anglican Church in Aotearoa, New Zealand and Polynesia, 2018.

Lincoln, Andrew. "Communion: Some Pauline Foundations." *Ecclesiology* 5, no. 2 (2009): 135-160.

Lindbeck, George A. *The Nature of Doctrine: Religion and Theology in a Post-Liberal Age.* Philadelphia: Westminster Press, 1984.

Liu, J.H. "History and Identity: A System of Checks and Balances for Aotearoa/New Zealand." In *New Zealand Identities:*

REFERENCES

Departures and Destinations, edited by James H Liu, T. McCreanor, T. McIntosh and T. Teaiwa, 69-87. Wellington, N.Z.: Victoria University of Wellington. Centre for Applied Cross-Cultural Research, 2005.

Luz, Ulrich, and Helmut Koester. *Matthew 21-28*. Hermeneia - a Critical and Historical Commentary on the Bible. Philadelphia, Pa.: Fortress, 2005.

Maaka, Roger, and Augie Fleras. *The Politics of Indigeneity: Challenging the State in Canada and Aotearoa New Zealand.* Otago University Press, 2005.

Macpherson, Cluny. "The Ifoga: The Exchange Value of Social Honour in Samoa." *Journal of the Polynesian Society* 114, no. 2 (2005): 109-133.

Malina, Bruce J. *The Social Gospel of Jesus: The Kingdom of God in Mediterranean Perspective.* Minneapolis, Minn.: Fortress Press, 2001.

Martin, Ralph P. *The Family and the Fellowship: New Testament Images of the Church.* Exeter Paternoster Press, 1997.

Mason, Bruce. "The Principle of 'Partnership' and the Treaty of Waitangi: Implications for the Public Conservation Estate." *Dunedin, NZ: Public Access New Zealand, Monograph Series*, no. 6. (1993). Accessed 28/01/2003. http://www.publicaccessnewzealand.org/files/partnership_abstract.html.

McCall, Sophie. *First Person Plural: Aboriginal Storytelling and the Ethics of Collaborative Authorship.* University of British Columbia Press, 2012.

New International Dictionary of Old Testament Theology and Exegesis. Grand Rapids, MI: Zondervan, 1997.

McDermott, John M. *The Biblical Doctrine of Koinōnia* Vol. N.F.19, 1975.

McLeod, Neal. *Cree Narrative Memory: From Treaties to Contemporary Times.* Saskatoon, Sask.: Purich Pub., 2007.

Mead, Sidney M., and Neil Grove. *Ngā Pēpeha a Ngā Tipuna: The Sayings of the Ancestors*. Wellington, NZ: Victoria University Press, 2003.

Metge, Joan. *In and out of Touch: Whakamaa in Cross Cultural Context*. Wellington, N.Z.: Victoria University Press, 1986.

Mikaere, Ani. "The Treaty of Waitangi and Recognition of Tikanga Maori." In *Waitangi Revisited: Perspectives on the Treaty of Waitangi*, edited by Michael Belgrave, Merata Kawharu, David Vernon Williams, 330-348. Melbourne: Oxford University Press, 2005.

Miller-McLemore, Bonnie J. *Christian Theology in Practice: Discovering a Discipline*. Grand Rapids: Eerdmans, 2012.

———. "Introduction: The Contributions of Practical Theology." In *The Wiley Blackwell Companion to Practical Theology*, edited by Bonnie J. Miller-McLemore, 1–20. Malden: Wiley-Blackwell, 2012.

Miller, J. R. *Compact, Contract, Covenant: Aboriginal Treaty-Making in Canada*. Toronto: University of Toronto Press, 2009.

———. "Compact, Contract, Covenant: The Evolution of Indian Treaty-Making." Chap. 4 In *New Histories for Old: Changing Perspectives on Canada's Native Pasts*, edited by Theodore Binnema and Susan Neylan. Vancouver, B.C.: UBC Press, 2007.

Moffat, D. "Ezra and Separate Development." In *Te Awa Rerenga Maha: Braided River*, edited by D. Moffat. Three Tikanga Church Colloquium, 57-72. Auckland: Anglican Church in Aotearoa, New Zealand and Polynesia, 2018.

———. "Introduction." In *Te Awa Rerenga Maha: Braided River*, edited by D. Moffat. Three Tikanga Church Colloquium, v–x. Auckland: Anglican Church in Aotearoa, New Zealand and Polynesia, 2018.

Moltmann, Jürgen. *God in Creation: A New Theology of Creation and the Spirit of God*. Minneapolis: Fortress, 1993.

REFERENCES

Monture, Patricia A. *Journeying Forward: Dreaming First Nations' Independence.* Halifax, N.S.: Fernwood, 1999.

Morris, Alexander. *The Treaties of Canada with the Indians of Manitoba and the North-West Territories: Including the Negotiations on Which They Were Based, and Other Information Relating Thereto.* Toronto: Belfords, Clarke, 1880; repr., 2014.

Morris, Grant. "James Prendergast and the Treaty of Waitangi: Judicial Attitudes to the Treaty During the Latter Half of the Nineteenth Century." *Victoria University of Wellington Law Review* (2004).

Movono, Apisalome, and Susanne Becken. "Solesolevaki as Social Capital: A Tale of a Village, Two Tribes, and a Resort in Fiji." *Asia Pacific Journal of Tourism Research* 23, no. 2 (2018): 146-157.

New International Dictionary of Old Testament Theology and Exegesis. Grand Rapids, MI: Zondervan, 1997.

Nicholson, E. W. *God and His People: Covenant and Theology in the Old Testament.* Oxford: Clarendon Press, 1986.

Nicholson, R. "'Ko Te Mea Nui, Ko Te Aroha': Theological Perspectives on Māori Language and Cultural Regenesis Policy and Practice of the Anglican Church." PhD., University of Auckland, 2009.

———. "The Theological Implications of Three Tikanga Church." In *Doing Theology in Oceania: Partners in Conversation (Proceedings of Theology in Oceania Conference, Dunedin, 1996).* Dunedin, NZ: Centre for Contextual Theology, School of Ministry, Knox College, 2000.

———. "Theological Perspectives on the Bicultural Partnership and Missional Standing Resolutions of the Three Tikanga Church." In *Te Awa Rerenga Maha: Braided River*, edited by D. Moffat. Three Tikanga Church Colloquium, 160-187 Auckland: Anglican Church in Aotearoa New Zealand and Polynesia, 2018.

Nouwen, Henri J. M. *Life of the Beloved: Spiritual Living in a Secular World.* New York, N.Y.: Crossroad, 1992.

O'Malley, Vincent. *The Great War for New Zealand: Waikato 1800–2000.* Wellington: Bridget Williams Books, 2016.

Office of the Treaty Commissioner. *Treaty Essential Learnings: We Are All Treaty People.* (Saskatoon, Saskatchewan: 2008). https://www.horizonsd.ca/Services/SafeandCaring/Documents/TELS.pdf.

Ogereau, Julien M. "The Jerusalem Collection as Κοινωνία: Paul's Global Politics of Socio-Economic Equality and Solidarity." *New Testament Studies* 58 (2012).

———. *Paul's Koinonia with the Philippians: A Socio-Historical Investigation of a Pauline Economic Partnership.* Vol. 377: Mohr Siebeck, 2014.

Ogletree, Thomas W. *The Use of the Bible in Christian Ethics.* Philadelphia: Fortress Press, 1983.

Orange, Claudia. *The Treaty of Waitangi.* Wellington: Allen & Unwin, 1987.

Panikulam, George. *Koinonia in the New Testament a Dynamic Expression of Christian Life.* Rome: Biblical Institute Press, 1979. Analecta Biblica 85.

Paterson, John. Sermon for Te Pouhere Sunday Evensong" (23rd June).

Pearson, D. "Rethinking Citizenship in Aotearoa/New Zealand." In *Tangata Tangata: The Changing Ethnic Contours of New Zealand*, edited by Paul Spoonley, David G. Pearson and Cluny Macpherson, 291-314. Melbourne: Thomson Dunmore Press, 2004.

Percy, Martyn. *Clergy: The Origin of Species.* London; New York: Continuum, 2006.

Poata-Smith, E. S. "Ka Tika a Muri, Ka Tika a Mua? Maori Protest Politics and the Treaty of Waitangi Settlement Process." In

REFERENCES

Tangata Tangata: The Changing Ethnic Contours of New Zealand, edited by Paul Spoonley, David G. Pearson and Cluny Macpherson, 59-88. Melbourne: Thomson Dunmore Press, 2004.

Pratt, George. *A Samoan Dictionary.* Whitefish, Mont.: Kessinger Publishing, 2010.

Prebble, E. "Incarnational Theology and the Constitution." In *Te Awa Rerenga Maha: Braided River*, edited by D. Moffat. Three Tikanga Church Colloquium, 85–102. Auckland: Anglican Church in Aotearoa, New Zealand and Polynesia, 2018.

Preston, Richard J. *Cree Narrative: Expressing the Personal Meanings of Events.* Carleton Library Series. 2nd ed. Montreal: McGill-Queen's Univ. Press, 2002.

Rata, Elizabeth. "Rethinking Biculturalism." *Anthropological Theory* 5, no. 3 (2005): 267-284.

Ray, Arthur J. *The Canadian Fur Trade in the Industrial Age.* Toronto: University of Toronto Press, 1990.

Reumann, John "Koinonia in Scripture: Survey of Biblical Texts." In *On the Way to Fuller Koinonia: Official Report of the Fifth World Conference on Faith and Order [Santiago De Compostela]*, edited by Thomas F. Best and Günther Gassmann. Geneva: WCC Publications, 1993.

Ricœur, Paul. *Political and Social Essays.* Athens: Ohio University Press, 1975.

Rienecker, Fritz, and Cleon L. Rogers. *A Linguistic Key to the Greek New Testament.* Grand Rapids, Michigan: Zondervan Publishing House, 1976.

Rogers, Lawrence M. *Te Wiremu: A Biography of Henry Williams.* Christchurch, N.Z.: Pegasus, 1973.

Ross, Cathy. "The Theology of Partnership." *International Bulletin of Missionary Research* 34, no. 3 (2010): 145-148.

Sampley, J. Paul. *Pauline Partnership in Christ: Christian Community and Commitment in Light of Roman Law.* Philadelphia Fortress Press, 1980.

Schaer, Cathrin. "She's Right, Mate (on Falconer & Watson's Cultural Detective)." *New Zealand Herald* (Auckland), 2006, Canvas. https://natlib.govt.nz/records/20605173.

Schmeman, Alexander. *For the Life of the World: Sacraments and Orthodoxy.* 2nd ed. Crestwood, N.Y.: St. Vladimir's Seminary Press, 1973.

Schoeffel, Penelope. "Samoan Exchange and 'Fine Mats': An Historical Reconsideration." *Journal of the Polynesian Society* 108 (1999): 117-148.

Schreiter, Robert J. *The New Catholicity: Theology between the Global and the Local.* Faith and Cultures Series. Maryknoll, N.Y.: Orbis Books, 1997.

Schmeman, Alexander. *For the Life of the World: Sacraments and Orthodoxy,* 2nd ed. Crestwood, N.Y.: St. Vladimir's Seminary Press, 1973.

Schwarzenbach, Sibyl A. "Fraternity, Solidarity, and Civic Friendship." *AMITY* 3, no. 1 (2015): 3–18.

———. *On Civic Friendship: Including Women in the State.* New York: Columbia University Press, 2009.

Sharp, A. "The Treaty in the Real Life of the Constitution." In *Waitangi Revisited: Perspectives on the Treaty of Waitangi,* edited by Michael Belgrave, Merata Kawharu, David Vernon Williams, 308-329. Melbourne: Oxford University Press, 2005.

Slack, D. *Bullshit, Backlash & Bleeding Hearts: A Confused Person's Guide to the Great Race Row.* Auckland: Penguin, 2004.

Smith, F. "Relational Hermeneutics in the Three Tikanga Context as the Anglican Church in Aotearoa, New Zealand and Polynesia." In *Te Awa Rerenga Maha: Braided River,* edited by D. Moffat. Three Tikanga Church Colloquium, 103-119. Auckland:

REFERENCES

Anglican Church in Aotearoa, New Zealand and Polynesia, 2018.

Smith, L. T. *Decolonizing Methodologies: Research and Indigenous Peoples.* Dunedin: University of Otago Press, 1999.

Snedden, P. The Treaty of Waitangi: Source of Disunity or Template for Cultural Inclusion. 2004. Auckland

Sullivan, A. "The Treaty of Waitangi and Social Well-Being: Justice, Representation and Participation." In *Waitangi Revisited: Perspectives on the Treaty of Waitangi*, edited by Michael Belgrave, Merata Kawharu, David Vernon Williams, 123-135). Melbourne: Oxford University Press, 2005.

Sullivan, Francis A. *From Apostles to Bishops: The Development of the Episcopacy in the Early Church.* Mahwah, New York: The Newman Press, 2001.

Tate, H. A. "Towards Some Foundations of a Systematic Māori Theology." PhD, Melbourne College of Divinity, 2010.

Taylor, Charles. *A Secular Age.* Cambridge: Harvard University Press, 2007.

Taylor, K. D. "Dwelling with Honour: Perspectives on Honour, Shame and Human Dignity Today, from Luke 7: 36-50." MTheol., University of Otago, 2015. http://hdl.handle.net/10523/5598.

"To Say My Fate Is Not Tied to Your Fate Is Like Saying, 'Your End of the Boat Is Sinking': A Heartfelt Critique of the Three Tikanga Church." Progressive Christianity Aotearoa, 2014, https://progressivechristianityaotearoa.com/2014/03/24/critique-three-tikanga/.

Tigay, Jeffrey H. *Deuteronomy: The Traditional Hebrew Text with the New JPS Translation.* Philadelphia: Jewish Publication Society, 1996.

Travis, Stephen. *Christ and the Judgement of God: The Limits of Divine Retribution in New Testament Thought.* Milton Keynes, U.K.: Paternoster Hendrickson Publishers, 2009.

Tremewan, C. "Re-Politicising Race: The Anglican Church in New Zealand." In *Public Policy and Ethnicity: The Politics of Ethnic Boundary Making* 95-112: Palgrave Macmillan, 2006.

Trompenaars, Alfons. *Riding the Waves of Culture: Understanding Cultural Diversity in Business.* 2nd ed.. ed. London: Nicholas Brealey Pub. , c2000, c1993.

Turner, Stephen. "'Inclusive Exclusion': Managing Identity for the Nation's Sake in Aotearoa/New Zealand." *Arena Journal*, no. 28 (2007): 87-106.

Tuuta, E. "Feast or Famine: Customary Fisheries Management in a Contemporary Tribal Society." In *Waitangi Revisited: Perspectives on the Treaty of Waitangi*, edited by Michael Belgrave, Merata Kawharu, David Vernon Williams. Melbourne: Oxford University Press, 2005.

Vercoe, Whakahuihui. "By the Rivers of Babylon." In *Te Ao Mārama. Regaining Aotearoa: Māori Writers Speak Out. He Whakaatanga O Te Ao: The Reality* edited by Witi Ihimaera. Auckland: Reed Books, 1993.

Waitangi Tribunal. "He Whakaputanga Me Te Tiriti the Declaration and the Treaty: The Report on Stage 1 of the Te Paparahi O Te Raki Inquiry." *Lower Hutt, New Zealand: Legislation Direct* (2014).

———. *The Taranaki Report: Kaupapa Tuatahi.* Wellington: GP Publications, 1996.

Walker, R. *Ka Whawhai Tonu Matou: Struggle without End.* Auckland: Penguin, 1990.

Walton, John H. *Ancient Near Eastern Thought and the Old Testament: Introducing the Conceptual World of the Hebrew Bible.* Grand Rapids: Baker, 2006.

Ward, C., and E-Y. Lin. "Immigration, Acculturation and National Identity." In *New Zealand Identities: Departures and Destinations*, edited by J. H. Liu, T. McCreanor, T. McIntosh and

References

T. Teaiwa, 155-173. Wellington, N.Z.: Victoria University of Wellington. Centre for Applied Cross-Cultural Research, 2005.

Wellhausen, Julius. *Prolegomena to the History of Ancient Israel.* Edinburgh: Adam and Charles Black, 1885.

Wepa, D. "Chapter 5: Cultural and Ethnicity." In *Cultural Safety in Aotearoa New Zealand*, edited by D. Wepa, 65-78. Melbourne, VIC, Australia: Cambridge University Press, 2015.

Wesley, Andrew. "Traditional Aboriginal Spirituality." Paper presented at the Consultation on First Nations Theological Education, Thornloe University, Sudbury, Ontario, May 21 2009.

Williams, C. Peter. *The Ideal of the Self-Governing Church: A Study in Victorian Missionary Strategy.* Leiden: E.J. Brill, 1990.

Williams, J. "The Treaty of Waitangi and Western Democracy in Practice." Paper presented at the Proceedings of Treaty Conference 2000, Auckland, 2000.

Winiata, W. "The Reconciliation of Kawanatanga and Tino Rangatiratanga." In *Rua Rautau Lecture, Rangiatea Church, Otaki*, 51'18". Aotearoa New Zealand Radio NZ, 6 February 2005. https://www.rnz.co.nz/national/programmes/waitangiruarautaulectures/audio/2508851/2005-professor-whatarangi-winiata.

Zerwick, M., and M. Grosvenor. *A Grammatical Analysis of the Greek New Testament.* 4th revised ed. Rome: Editrice Pontificio Istituto Biblico, 1993.

Index of Authors

Abusch-Magder, R. 120-121
Adare, S. 7
Adeney, B. 117, 124
Aldred, R. 4, 6, 11
Alexander & Rosner............ 118
Allard, P. 15
Allen, D. 161
Andrew, M. 75, 83, 87
Aston, C. 171
Athanasius 19-20
Barr, J. 82
Bauckham, R. 157
Bell, S. 47
Belmessous, S. 77
Bevans, S. 200
Bhabha, H. 128
Black Elk & Brown.....................5
Bluck, J. .... 30, 139, 146 - 151, 161, 162
Boulding, M. 97, 99
Bourdieu, P. 175
Bouteneff & Falconer 64
Brandt, A. 142, 143, 151
Branson, M. 115, 125-126
Brown, J.S.H. 13
Brown & Isaacs ..114, 125-126
Browning, D. 144, 155, 156, 160
Brueggemann & Brueggemann 159
Bussidor & Bilgen-Reinart 12, 14
Callaghan, M. 51
Callister, P. 49
Campbell, J. 93, 101
Carleton, H. 77
Carrell, P. 66

Chittister & Williams.......... 124
Clark, P. 174
Clark, Y. 25
Clarke, J. 153
Clines, D. 84
Cockell & McArthur-Blair. 125
Coleman, J. 175
Consedine & Consedine. ....38 - 49
Craigie, P. 152
Cuthand, D. 5, 14, 16
Davis & Shpuniarsky. 151, 162, 164
Davis, B. 149
Deane, R. 38
Deloria & Treat 24
Durie, E. 37
Durie, M. 36, 43, 46
Easdale, N. 194
Eilers, K. 162
Ellithorpe, A. 140, 141, 156, 161
Eruera, K. 180, 181
Fletcher, A. 30, 67, 95, 114 163
Ford, D. 119
Fox, D. 43
Gadd, B. 148
Glanville, M. 152, 153
Goldingay, J. ....84 - 86
Grant, R. 18, 19, 22
Grenz, S. 181- 184
Halapua, W. 187, 203
Hancock, Epston & McKenzie.. 49
Haran, M. 76
Havea, J. 126

Index of Authors

Hayward, J. 34-36
Heitink, G. 143
Hoekema, A. 157
Humpage, L. 46
Inge, J. 123
James, C. 45, 48
Jennings, W. 140, 158-159
Jimerson, R. 199-201
Kawharu, H. 37
Kawharu, M. 40
Kelsey, J. 39, 40, 44
Kereopa, R. 53, 151
Kidwell, Noley & Tinker 14
Koenig, J. 108
Kutsch, E. 83, 84
Laliberte, Settee, Waldram, Innes, Macdougall, McBain & Barron 7
Lethbridge, C. 147
Levenson, J. 121
Levine, H. 47
Liava'a, L. 150, 164
Lincoln, A. 96
Lindbeck, G. 15
Liu, J. 46
Luz & Koester 122
Maaka & Fleras 39, 44-48
Macpherson, C. 187
Malina, B. 117-118
Martin, R. 106-107
Mason, B. 38
McCall, S. 13
McDermott, J. 93, 101
McLeod, N. 5, 11
Mead & Grove 143
Menary, C. 162
Metge, J. 117
Mikaere, A. 39

Miller, J. 6-13, 158-159
Miller-McLemore, B. 143
Moffat, D. 113, 117, 125, 139, 145, 163
Moltmann, J. 157, 158
Monture, P. 12, 13
Morris, A. 10, 18, 20
Morris, G. 147
Movono & Becken 169
Nicholson, E. 80-83
Nicholson, R. 32, 49, 51, 52, 162-164
Nouwen, H. 22-23
Office of the Treaty Commissioner 16
Ogereau, J. 93, 102-105, 108
Ogletree, T. 87
O'Malley, V. 100
Orange, C. 77-79, 145
Panikulam, G. 107, 109
Pearson, D. 37
Percy, M. 61
Poata-Smith, E. S. 39
Pratt, G. 187
Prebble, E. 146, 149, 150
Preston, R. 4
Rata, E. 47-48
Ray, A. 8
Reumann, J. 109
Ricœur, P. 24
Rienecker & Rogers 109
Rogers, L. 77
Ross, C. 169, 173, 178-79
Sampley, J. 103
Schaer, C. 132
Schmemann, A. 19
Schoeffel, P. 187
Schreiter, R. 13

Index of Authors

Schwarzenbach, S. ... 141, 142, 154
Sharp, A. 41, 48
Slack, D. 39, 40
Smith, F. 114
Smith, L. 50
Snedden, P. 48
Sullivan, A. 43
Sullivan, F. 61
Tate, H. 136, 154-158
Taylor, C. 140, 141
Taylor, K. 125
Tigay, J. 76, 152, 153
Travis, S. 118
Tremewan, C. 38, 40
Trompenaars, A. 116
Turner, S. 132
Tuuta, E. 42
Vercoe, W. 79
Walker, R. 48
Walton, J. 157
Ward & Lin 48
Wellhausen, J. .... 80 - 82
Wepa, D. 116
Wesley, A. 5
Williams, C. 67
Williams, J. 47
Winiata, W. 42
Zerwick & Grosvenor 94

Index of Scripture References

Genesis 78, 157
   1.26-28 184
   1-2 127
   6-8 122
   15, 17.1, 7-8, 14 85
   17.7-8 86
Exodus 78, 81
   6.7 86
   12.38 89
   20.3 86
Deuteronomy 81, 152, 153, 155
   10 .... 152, 154
Joshua 50
   9 87
1 Samuel
   18-20 86
   20.14 84
   20.8 .... 76, 84
   23.18 76
2 Samuel
   5.3 76
   21 86
Psalms
   89.39, 132.12 85
Jeremiah
   5.21 123
   29.1-9 121
Ezekiel
   34.24, 36.28 86
Amos
   8.8 159
Matthew
   13.13 123
   24.36-25.46 115
   24.36-41 115
   24.39 122
John
   3.16 19
   4.24 183
   15.12 55
   17.20-23 65
Acts 185
   2.42 108
   4.32-37 108
   16.1-3 97
   17.27-28 182
Romans
   1.14 99
   11.17 96
   12.20 100
   14.1-4 97
   15.25-31, 26, 27 107
1 Corinthians 97
   1 68
   1.9 94
   8 97
   9 95
   10.16-17 95
   12.12-26 95
   12.26 181
   13 180
   13.13 207
   13.4-8 178
   16.1-4 107
2 Corinthians
   8.1-5, 8.4, 8-9, 9.13 107
   8.13-14 108
   13.14 95

Index of Scripture References

Galatians
- 2.9 93
- 2.10 107
- 3.28 185
- 3.28-29 89
- 5.2-12, 5.6, 6.15 97

Ephesians
- 2.11-22 .... 89, 98
- 2.19 96

Philippians
- 1.5 .... 94, 103, 105
- 1.5-7 103
- 1.27 96
- 1.29, 30 100
- 2.1, 6-11 99
- 2.25 105
- 3.10 99
- 3.20 .... 96, 109
- 4.10-20-22 103
- 4.14 100
- 4.3, 16, 18 105

Colossians
- 3.11 .... 89, 99

Philemon
- 12.20 101

Hebrews
- 11.7 122

1 John
- 1.1-7 109

www.ingramcontent.com/pod-product-compliance
Lightning Source LLC
Chambersburg PA
CBHW051424290426
44109CB00016B/1426